PRAISE

I0458941

"This book serves as a beacon of light for anyone navigating life's turbulent waters! Joe's insightful and educational autobiography offers a guiding hand for those facing struggles, whether at the campsite or within their own mind. I found solace in Joe's content during a low point in my own life. He inspires everyone to embrace the outdoors, confront their own demons, and be open to learning!"

- ADAM PEDERSEN
Filmmaker & Director of "Nerves"
www.adampedersen.ca

"In this gripping tell-all, Joe takes readers on a profound and emotional journey through the Canadian wilderness and the depths of their own struggles. The honesty and vulnerability displayed throughout the book make it a compelling and relatable read for anyone facing their own battles."

- BRIAN ASPINALL
Founder: Code Breaker Inc.
www.codebreakeredu.com

"We first met Joe during the early days of AGAWA, and his adventurous spirit has been a continuous source of inspiration ever since. His willingness to openly share both the triumphs and struggles of his backcountry adventures and life has invited numerous people to join him on his journey. Joe's creativity, passion, and authenticity serve as a powerful reminder of why wilderness stories and experiences hold such profound significance."

- GRAHAM BECK & BRAD ROTHWELL
Co-owners: Agawa Gear
www.agawagear.com

PRAISE

"We have been delighted to support Joe on his numerous Wabakimi adventures. Joe has a deep passion for the wilderness, with a special fondness for Wabakimi. He enjoys sharing this love with his fans and subscribers. Joe demonstrates physical toughness while also showing gentle care for the boreal forest!"

- BRUCE HYER
Founder: Wabakimi Outfitters
www.wabakimi.com

"Joe is one of the most authentic and raw voices in the backcountry and bushcrafting scene. This book is a deeply personal story of how Joe's immersion in the Canadian wilderness allows him to navigate his personal wilderness within."

- DAN DURSTON
President & Product Architect: Durston Gear
www.durstongear.com

"Joe Robinet's journey through unimaginable hardship is a testament to his resilience, honesty, and strength. He's not only a Canadian icon and generational talent, but also a personal inspiration to both of us!"

- JASON MACHADO AND BRETON KENNEDY
Owners: Hamilton Adventure Expo
www.hamiltonadventureexpo.com

"Joe is an inspiration to us all! His true love for the outdoors, for a life that embraces hardships, and his loyalty to his family are a model worth emulating."

- BRICE HOSKIN
Founder: Ganesha Cookstove Project
www.ganeshastove.com

CODE BREAKER INC.

SURVIVING JOE

MY LIFE IN THE BACKCOUNTRY: OVERCOMING DEMONS, DRUGS AND DEATH

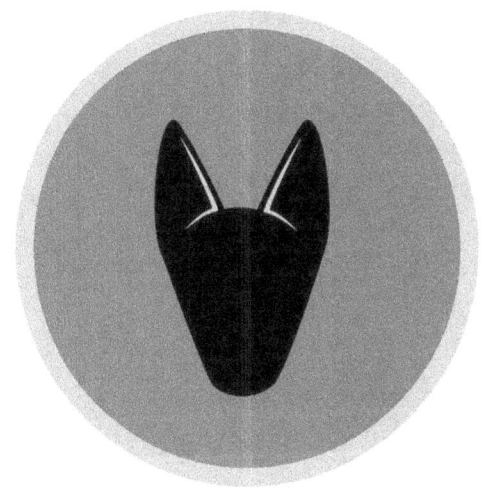

JOE ROBINET

Code
BREAKER

SURVIVING JOE
MY LIFE IN THE BACKCOUNTRY: OVERCOMING DEMONS, DRUGS AND DEATH

Book design & editing by Brian Aspinall
www.mraspinall.com

Chapter 10 by Wilhemina Robinet

Code Breaker Inc.
Next-gen publishing for the most influential talent in the world.

www.codebreakeredu.com

TO MY WIFE AND CHILDREN:

You are the heartbeats of my life and the inspiration behind every word written in these pages. Your unwavering love, patience, and support have been my guiding light throughout this creative journey and so many other adventures. In the moments of doubt and solitude, your presence has been my solace and strength. I am forever grateful.

- Love Joe (Dad)

PREFACE

HEY FOLKS, HOW ARE YOU? Ol' Joe here! We are about to embark on a rather unorthodox journey together, a voyage that will take us through uncharted territories of the heart and mind. Some parts of this journey may feel like déjà vu, resonating with your own experiences, while others will be entirely new and unexpected. This adventure is a tapestry woven with threads of love, laughter, tears, and yes, even a sprinkle of colourful language. So put on your life jacket, hold on tight, and get ready to explore the depths of human emotion and the boundless possibilities of the human spirit!

Welcome to an immersive experience within the pages of this book, where I extend a heartfelt invitation for you to accompany me on a transformative journey through the untamed wilderness. Together, we will delve into the awe-inspiring beauty of nature, witnessing its wonders unfold in real-time as we navigate through rugged terrain and embrace the elements. Along this expedition, we will confront the formidable challenges of survival, testing our courage and resilience in the face of adversity. As the words flowed from my pen, I meticulously captured my adventures, journaling the trials and tribulations of solo survival with honesty and introspection. Through the lens of my experiences, you will not only witness the raw essence of wilderness exploration but also embark on a personal odyssey of self-discovery and growth. Join me as we traverse the untamed landscapes, forging a deeper connection with nature, ourselves, and the profound journey of life itself.

PREFACE

Within the pages of this book, you will discover my life story thus far intertwined with real-time journal entries from my longest solo journey yet. You'll notice changes in font throughout this book as well as three campfire symbols, which indicate a transition from story to journal, or journal to story.

🔥🔥🔥

This font face embodies the essence of the journal portion of my book, capturing the raw authenticity of my thoughts as I penned these pages. Each word reflects the real-time journaling experience that helped shape this memoir. During my 19 solitary days, I meticulously added the final touches, infusing my work with passion and dedication to create something I am very proud of. Thank you for reading this!

🔥🔥🔥

I extend a warm invitation for you to embark on this thrilling adventure with me, not only through the captivating pages of this book but also by immersing yourself in the visual journey captured on film. As you read along and delve into my experiences, you will have the unique opportunity to witness the unfolding of my wilderness escapades in vivid detail, from the challenges faced to the moments of triumph and everything in between. By following along on YouTube, you can further engage with the sights and sounds of my expeditions, allowing you to feel as though you are right there beside me, exploring the wonders of nature firsthand.

So grab your gear, pack your curiosity, and let's embark on an unforgettable expedition together - a 19 day solo canoe expedition in the Canadian wilderness!

INTRODUCTION

LAKE SUPERIOR IS A place of tranquility and connection with nature. The waters are calm and reflective, mirroring the sky above. The shoreline is rocky and lined with tall trees, their leaves rustling in the gentle breeze. The sound of waves lapping against the shore creates a soothing melody, while the fresh scent of pine fills the air. Indigenous Peoples are present, adding a sense of cultural richness and history to the serene, Canadian landscape. It is a place where time seems to stand still, allowing for moments of introspection and wonder at the beauty of the natural world. Campfires exude a mesmerizing beauty, with dancing flames casting a warm glow that illuminates the darkness, creating a cozy and enchanting atmosphere that brings people together in shared moments of storytelling and camaraderie.

In the distance I can hear my brother, only I am uncertain if he is behind the trees or in the hallway outside my hospital room. His laughter fills my mind, ears and heart and reminds me of the beauty this world has to offer. I'm glad he is winning the battle against his demons. I've had my own fair share of fights.

At 35 years of age, I find myself deeply in love with life, especially when I'm out camping. The crisp scent of pine, the crackling of the campfire, and the symphony of nature's nighttime chorus all come together to create a sense of peace and contentment within me. As I sit under the starlit sky, surrounded by towering trees and the gentle rustling of leaves, I feel a profound connection to the natural world around me. Camping allows me to escape the commotion of everyday life, offering a chance to slow down, breathe in the fresh air, and appreciate the simple joys of existence. Whether it's frying fish over the fire, hiking through scenic trails, or simply unwinding in the great outdoors, each moment spent camping fills me with a sense of gratitude and wonder for the beauty that surrounds me.

In this unexpected moment, the reality of my surroundings comes crashing down on me. The peaceful illusion of camping and the comforting familiarity of being 35 are shattered, replaced by the harsh truth of my current situation. I'm 40 and I almost died. My brother Isaac has passed too. The emptiness left in his absence echoes through the stillness of the night, a painful reminder of the irreplaceable loss I continue to carry with me. The flickering flames of the imaginary campfire offer no solace, only a stark contrast to the darkness that now envelops me, both in the wilderness and in my heart.

Wolfie's howl echoes in my ears as I try to make sense of this world. The natural beauty I have become accustomed to continues to float in and out like driftwood moving downstream. In one instance, I find myself fully immersed in the art of building fires, the rough texture of the flint in my hand - a familiar comfort. The sparks fly as I strike the flint against the steel, each movement deliberate and precise. But then, in a sudden and unexpected turn of events, my flint slips from my grasp, disappearing into the darkness as if swallowed by the night. Panic sets in as I realize that not only is my trusty flint gone, but the use of my hands seems to have vanished as well, leaving me feeling helpless and vulnerable in the wilderness. The crackling flames before me now seem like a distant memory, replaced by a sense of uncertainty and unease as I wrestle with this newfound challenge.

As I grapple with the weight of the thoughts swirling in my mind, that has just become coherent for the first time in three weeks, the idea of leaving my family behind fills me with a profound sense of emptiness. The name "Joe" echoes in my consciousness, a reminder of my own identity that feels both familiar and distant after emerging from a three-week coma. The world around me seems to blur and shift as I try to make sense of the fragments of memory and reality that dance at the edges of my awareness.

SURVIVING JOE

Despite enduring a harrowing accident and a three-week coma, I have emerged stronger. As I celebrate my 40th birthday, I proudly embrace my roles as a devoted father, a loving husband, a caring son, a loyal friend, and a trusted ally.

The journey ahead feels daunting and uncertain, a path that I must navigate with newfound clarity and purpose, even as the shadows of the past linger in the corners of my mind. The weight of my name, my family, and the legacy of my brother's memory converge in this moment of awakening, shaping the road that lies ahead with both challenge and possibility.

My name is Joe Robinet and this is my story.

1

DAY 1 OF 19 — JUNE 26, 2025 — 10:00PM

Where do I even begin? It's 9:30pm on Thursday, June 26, 2025. Here I am, sitting alone at the base of a lively rapid, nestled in a picturesque campsite just outside Wabakimi Provincial Park, just as the sun sets. The orangey-pink sky radiates a glow across the rushing water and surrounding backdrop. Just hours ago, I was dropped off by a train in the heart of the wilderness. What was meant to be a leisurely day turned into a challenging journey, pushing myself to the limit to reach this peaceful spot. Today, on the very first day of a three week journey, I found myself inexplicably reaching for a mickey of whiskey after a late lunch. It was a regrettable decision, one that left me feeling awful and struggling to paddle swiftly to find solace on solid ground. Thankfully, that moment has passed, and I recognize the need to address my relationship with alcohol. Perhaps there are underlying emotions I've been avoiding, ones that I must confront and overcome now as I put the pen to paper. I'm just grateful to be able to write again, with my hands. As I gaze up, I'm captivated by the sight of dragonflies gracefully darting about, a reminder of the beauty and resilience of nature that surrounds me. I could learn a thing or two from them. Sometimes I'm the victim of my own circumstance.

Alright, here we go. What's about to come out of me that I've suppressed for decades? As my publisher said, "You just start."

Every male role model who I have ever loved, or would have loved to know has left me, abandoned me in life in some capacity. Some are not to blame; others definitely are. I grew up without a dad, that, to this day still affects me in many different aspects. My mom married Ron, my "dad" when I was six. He left as well, abandoning not only me but also my brother, my sister, and my mom. It was something I never wanted for them. Discovering a photo of my brother Isaac nestled in Ron's embrace, beaming with a joy I had almost forgotten he possessed, brought a flood of conflicting emotions. In that moment captured in the picture, everything seemed right. Everything seemed calm. Everyone was at peace. Yet, the bitterness of his departure still lingers, fuelling my resentment towards him for leaving my family behind. For a decade, he was the father figure I called "Dad" in haste, fulfilling a childhood wish for a father, brother, and sister. That image of Isaac and Ron stirs up a mix of anger and regret within me, prompting thoughts of the missed opportunities not just for Isaac, but also for my sister Abby and my mom. I swore I'd be a much better father.

The news of Tony's passing, the best man at my wedding, hit me hard while I was camping in Ohio. It took me a couple of days after reaching home to truly process and mourn his loss. This heartbreaking experience left me deeply shaken and instilled a fear of venturing far from home to camp again, as I never wanted to receive such devastating news while away from the comfort of home. Scout, my beloved companion and the furry friend who played a pivotal role in the creation of my YouTube channel, holds a special place in my heart. Tragically, he succumbed to lymphoma shortly after our family relocated north, his place of origin. His passing left a profound void, as he was not just a pet but a cherished member of our family.

But the pain I endured from past traumas paled in comparison to the devastating loss I would later face. My dear little brother, Isaac, passed away. I had a hand in raising him, and we shared a unique bond as friends. He confided in me with things he kept hidden from everyone else. The weight of responsibility weighs heavily on me still. I was well aware of the battles he fought within his own mind — dealing with psychosis, schizophrenia, depression, and addiction. He turned to drugs and alcohol in an attempt to silence the tormenting voices in his head.

Leaving Windsor to provide my family with a fresh start up north meant leaving behind my mother, brother, and sister. Reflecting on my decision, I realize I missed an opportunity to invite my brother to live with me, out of concern for his lifestyle and its impact on my daughters.

In hindsight, I see my actions as selfish, as I should have trusted him and considered offering him a chance for a better life with us. While I can't be certain if he would have accepted the invitation, I can't help but feel that I should have at least made the effort to persuade him to join us. Hindsight is a powerful lens that often reveals the missed opportunities and lessons hidden in the past. I feel like I'm about to uncover more on this journey. Thank you for joining me on it.

In my youth, I shared an unbreakable bond with a best friend, our companionship so strong that we were inseparable for a long time. However, as time went on, he gradually distanced himself from me, leaving me feeling abandoned. Moreover, the individuals I befriended through YouTube, whom I had trusted and considered friends, revealed their true colours as deceitful and untrustworthy, at least to me.

The recurring pattern of men in my life letting me down, turning their backs on me, and departing without warning has inflicted deep emotional wounds that continue to cause me pain. I don't write this for pity, I write it for empathy and understanding. I write it to give and to understand perspective.

Throughout my life, my relationship with God has been inconsistent, swinging like a pendulum that never stops, often leaning towards being distant. Raised in a devout born-again Christian family, where church attendance was a thrice-weekly ritual and speaking in tongues was commonplace, my mother's unwavering faith has always been a cornerstone. I am beginning to recognize that I have had a "father figure" watching over me all along. Despite the challenges, I have been fortunate to lead a fulfilling life, surrounded by a family that loves me unconditionally and blessed with a successful career. I have defied medical odds and survived when doctors predicted otherwise. Reflecting on these blessings, I am filled with gratitude and a growing realization of the presence of divine guidance in my life.

It seems like the perfect time to call it a night. The clock strikes 10:00pm, accompanied by the gentle rumble of distant thunder, and I am feeling completely exhausted. Today took a lot out of me, but I'm glad I looked within myself and took the first step to begin writing. This book seems like a ridiculously daunting task, but I am committed to finishing it. Off to bed I go! Good night!

DAY 2 OF 19 — JUNE 27, 2025 — 1:50PM

It's currently 1:50pm on Friday, June 27. I woke up this morning feeling under the weather. Surprisingly, I had a restful night's sleep until 4:00am, then managed to doze off again until 7:00, which is the latest I've slept in a very long time. It was a much needed rest. However, I had to rush to the woods with diarrhea due to an upset stomach! I suspect that the spicy fish crisp I ate may not have agreed with me! Welcome to Day 2!

This morning started off a bit sluggish for me. It took some time after having oatmeal and getting all my gear packed before I finally set out on the water around 9:00am. As I paddled, I spotted my first portage directly across from my campsite. Despite the need to unload and carry my gear, I decided to delay that task and tried my luck at fishing first, unfortunately with no success. I then proceeded to the next 30 metre portage, followed by a series of quick, but very short ports. Travelling upstream against the current, I realized running any of the rapids was out of the question. Instead, I waded through the water, getting thoroughly soaked in the process. Despite the drenching, it was a worthwhile trade-off to avoid the hassle of portaging. While at a rapid, I decided to try my hand at jigging. To my delight, I managed to reel in a small pike on my first attempt. Encouraged by this success, I gave it another shot, and suddenly, there it was — a massive blue walleye!

In a moment of emotional release, I found myself calling out Isaac's name while crying, my voice echoing across the water. As if in response, a fish suddenly broke the surface, creating a splash just behind my boat. Acting on instinct, I swiftly reached for my fishing rod and cast my jig towards the spot where the fish had surfaced. There was a sense of certainty within me that I was about to catch something. Allowing the jig to sink to the bottom, I felt a strong bite almost immediately. I had a gut feeling that a nice walleye was on the other end of the line, and indeed, I successfully reeled in a large, strikingly blue walleye. I felt Isaac's presence with me at that moment.

Feeling compelled to keep it, I respectfully dispatched the stunning fish. In that moment, a sense of companionship enveloped me, reassuring me that I was not alone. Grateful for my growing proficiency in jigging, I continued on my journey. After navigating a few more brief portages, I stumbled upon a picturesque island campsite. The lush grass, level ground, and blooming flowers all around made it a truly enchanting spot. After savouring a satisfying meal of freshly caught fish, I made the spontaneous decision to call it a day and set up camp on the tranquil island. Today's journey, spanning less than four hours, felt just right to me. I'll be back soon to finally dig in!

My earliest memories revolve around my mom, who, along with my nan, formed my first family. We moved frequently, residing in various apartments and also spending time living with my nan at her place. Unfortunately, I had no contact with my biological father, Jerry. I do remember being very young and while my mom was at work one day, my nan showed me some toys, a "dancebot" on a remote with a cord and a toy gun that shot discs. I was stoked! She told me they were from my dad and I could play with them for a bit while my mom was at work. I remember being very confused. If I had a dad, where was he? Why don't I know him? Why doesn't he live with us? I could be wrong, but I don't remember getting answers to those questions. I don't know why my mom didn't explain it. I don't know why I didn't inquire more. It always felt like a sore spot. So I never asked.

My mom is a saint. I love her dearly. She gave me a good life. The best she could have. She was always very loving and there for me. She is also a born again Christian, which made things difficult for me because our differing beliefs sometimes caused tension and misunderstandings in our interactions. I know she didn't intend to hurt me or make it more challenging by not having a dad. She and my nan were my parents. My mom took me camping a couple of times; she really made an effort. The burden of feeling abandoned by my dad has always lingered with me. It prompts me to contemplate my role in my own children's lives, particularly when I am away for extended periods.

I attended Maranatha Christian Academy (MCA), a Christian public school on the southwest side of Windsor in Ontario, Canada. My mom worked as a bus driver. We were still residing with Nan when, at around six years old, my mom returned home one day and inquired about my thoughts on having a dad. I was ecstatic! For a while, I had been praying for a dad, a brother, and a sister. My mom always encouraged me to pray whenever I needed something or faced a problem. And finally, my prayers were answered! It turned out that she had met a man named Ron at church, and they had been dating without my knowledge. I suppose she wanted to be sure before introducing him to me. I was thrilled and filled with excitement at the thought of having a dad. I stood by their side at the wedding, along with my best friend of many years, Nikki.

The wedding took place at Windsor Christian Fellowship, our church in Windsor. Soon after, Ron moved in with me, my mom, and Nan. Ron worked as a bricklayer. He was a quiet, kind man, but I didn't feel like he was a dad to me, even though I started calling him dad right away. His family lived in Tilbury, a town outside of Windsor, about a 45 minute drive away. My new "grandparents" were kind, especially Grandma, while Grandpa was a bit reserved. I now had many cousins, some of whom were my age, which was a new experience for me because on my mom's side there were none. They were very Catholic and very French, with a large extended family of aunts and uncles. During this time, my mom had my sister, Abby.

When I was eight, we moved into a rental house as there were too many people for my nan's place. I switched schools to attend the private Christian school at WCFA, Windsor Christian Fellowship Academy, where uniforms were mandatory. The school had a unique setup where we sat in cubicles and didn't need to raise our hands for the teacher since there wasn't a traditional teacher-student interaction. The school utilized the P.A.C.E. method, where students worked at their own pace using workbooks. The P.A.C.E. method, developed by Dr. Dan Hughes, is a therapeutic approach focused on building strong, trusting relationships with children and young people, particularly those who have experienced trauma. The acronym P.A.C.E. stands for Playfulness, Acceptance, Curiosity, and Empathy. It's a way of thinking, feeling, communicating, and behaving that aims to create a safe and secure environment for children, helping them feel understood and accepted.

All students were in one room, with cubicles lining the walls of the vast, hospital-like space. There were two holes in the cubicles: one for a "monitor" flag, coloured blue, and one for a "supervisor" flag, coloured red. Each student worked independently at their own level or grade. When we needed assistance, such as to use the bathroom, we would raise the supervisor flag. A supervisor would then approach the cubicle, whispering, "What do you need?" and either provide assistance or not, depending on the situation.

When we completed a workbook, we would raise the monitor flag to receive our next book. The quality of our work determined the length of our breaks and lunchtime. This routine continued day after day, until Saturday, when I finally had a break from this environment. However, the respite was short-lived as I had to wake up early on Sunday morning to attend church at the same location, surrounded by the same people. Church services were held twice on Sundays, once in the morning and once in the evening, each lasting two and a half hours. Additionally, there was another service on Wednesday, not to mention the youth group gathering on Friday nights. Some people outside the community viewed our church involvement as cult-like. For real!

I had a close-knit group of friends who had been attending church with me for most of my life, including Keith, David, Matthew, and Philip, among others. My friend Nikki and her mom were also part of our church community. I recall a moment when Matthew teased me for spending time with the "cool" kids, highlighting the dynamics within our social circle. In a playful moment, I jokingly hit Matthew with my soft lunch box, unaware that there was a hard plastic cup inside, which accidentally cracked his tooth. Feeling remorseful, I faced the consequences as the teacher intervened and attempted to discipline me with a paddle. Refusing to comply, I stood my ground until they had to call home. This incident marked my first memory of extreme defiance, which surprisingly worked in my favour. Despite Matthew being fine, I couldn't help but wonder what he thought of me after that incident.

In 1994, my brother Isaac was born when I was ten years old, fulfilling my longing for a brother to accompany my sister. Our family moved to Devonshire Heights, a geared-to-income housing block with duplexes, where I found a sense of community. I made new friends outside of school and church, with my best friend Chris living down the street from me on Labour Crescent. At Chris's place, I experienced my first horror movie and discovered new music before we moved again shortly after. Transitioning to John A. McWilliam, a public school near Devonshire Heights, I began Grade 7. Moving from the self-paced learning environment to a full Grade 7 curriculum, I felt lost and overwhelmed by the sudden change!

In Math, having only been at a Grade 5 level equivalent at WCFA, I found myself struggling with the Grade 7 curriculum at John A. McWilliam. I had never taken a French class before and was suddenly thrust into unfamiliar territory. I distinctly recall encountering a French-speaking alien in the textbook, adding to my confusion with phrases like "Bonjour" that felt like a foreign language to me, because it was. Amid meeting new friends, I took on the responsibility of babysitting my younger brother and sister frequently while Mom and Ron were at work. As the kids grew older, I recall a distressing incident when Isaac accidentally grabbed a hot coffee cup handle on the dining room table, causing scalding coffee to spill over his head, face, and body. We were all deeply concerned, and Mom turned to prayer for comfort. Thankfully, Isaac did not sustain any lasting physical harm or scarring from the incident.

Isaac's tendency to drool a lot earned him the endearing nickname "Goober," which later evolved into "Mr. Goo," a moniker we affectionately used for him for a long time. Even after he outgrew the drooling phase, he would entertain us with songs about "the chickens in the back-ey-odd." As the youngest in the family, he was truly my mom's baby. Reflecting on his passing at such a young age, I can't help but feel immense sadness for my mom. The thought of her loss is truly heartbreaking, and as a father myself, I can't imagine anything more devastating. I'm so sorry, Mom. So sorry.

At the age of 12 in 1996, after befriending Chris, I learned that his mom had been diagnosed with cancer. Tragically, she passed away when he was 11, and I was 12. Chris had to move to Quispamsis, New Brunswick, to live with his dad, leaving us both devastated. I struggled with the loss of my best friend but tried to remain strong for him. I vividly recall giving him my new Nike hat, purchased with my saved money, as a token of our friendship before he left. As he departed with his dad, I feared our friendship was over. However, we managed to stay in touch, and I was fortunate enough to visit him in New Brunswick later that year. My mom's tears at the airport triggered my own, as I've always been a crier, a momma's boy, and a softie at heart. I even kept the napkin I received on the plane as a cherished souvenir, which I still have to this day.

Despite our financial struggles, I managed to escape on a plane for a whole week, a memory I hold dear. During that time, I had a great experience. Meanwhile, Chris was going through a tough phase, understandably so. With a new step-mom he disliked, an unsupportive father, new siblings, and a new environment, his anger was palpable. His dad treated us to a three-day boat trip in the Atlantic Ocean. We reached a camp on an island, using a dinghy to travel from the boat to the island. It was an incredibly cool experience! My nan had entrusted me with her camera, and I eagerly snapped numerous pictures of dorsal fins. I relished the challenge of capturing the perfect shot for her, a passion that continues to this day on Instagram. Chris and I stayed connected through phone calls for some time following that memorable adventure.

While in Grade 7 at John A., I encountered a host of new faces, including a wonderful teacher, Mr. Miller. One midday during class, the school secretary appeared at Mr. Miller's door with a new student in tow. This boy, Jeremy, sported a buzz cut and a wide, Jim Carrey-esque smile, particularly in his teeth. He was seated near my desk, and although the exact details escape me, we seemed to hit it off almost instantly. Prior to meeting Jeremy, and after Chris had been absent for a few years, I didn't have many close friends apart from Nikki, a girl who was like a sister to me. Our families were tightly knit, always in each other's company. Nikki, a year older than me, was a steadfast companion who, as we navigated puberty, played the role of a trusted confidante and occasionally, "Doctor." She was someone I could learn and grow with, a constant presence in my life for an extended period. Besides Nikki, I didn't have many close friends, so I often spent time playing with my brother and sister.

When Jeremy entered the picture, everything shifted. From the moment he arrived in that first week until well into our high school years, we were practically joined at the hip. Dubbed "Skater 1" and "Skater 2" by our peers, I must admit I was more of a poser. We spent countless nights at each other's homes, dated the same girls, delved into experimenting with weed and alcohol, and eagerly followed the Stone Cold era of WWE (back when it was still WWF) together. Shortly after introducing Nikki to Jeremy, they hit it off and dated for a while. Following their breakup, Nikki and I drifted apart in terms of hanging out, although we still crossed paths frequently. Jeremy had become my closest friend, and it was evident to everyone around us.

One day, not long after meeting Jeremy, I was walking home from his house to mine, maybe a 30 minute walk, when a black corvette passed me then stopped in front on the same side of the road. Hearing my mom's warnings, I started to cross the road to avoid the car. A lady opened the passenger door, looked at me and said "Joey, come here, we will drive you." It turned out to be Jeremy's mom and her boyfriend, a wealthy man who owned the Million Dollar Saloon in Windsor. Grateful for the ride, I accepted their offer. Since their Corvette was a two-seater, Jeremy's mom suggested I sit on her lap. I complied, and they drove me home. Upon arriving, I hopped out in the driveway, feeling content about the ride. I bid them farewell and headed inside, where my mom was waiting for me. She inquired angrily about who had dropped me off, and I shared the details with her.

Upon my return home, my mom questioned how I managed to fit in a two-seater car with three people, to which I explained where I sat. She then informed me that I was no longer permitted to stay over at Jeremy's house or spend time with him due to his mom's boyfriend occasionally staying there, a decision she didn't approve of. That same evening, Nikki revealed her intention to break up with Jeremy. The following day at school, I faced the difficult task of informing Jeremy about his girlfriend's decision and the unfortunate news that I could no longer continue our friendship. Jeremy tried to brush off the news, but I could sense that he was deeply hurt. Despite the restrictions, we managed to spend time together at school. It took considerable effort to persuade my mom to allow me to resume hanging out with him. Our families even sat together at the Grade 8 graduation ceremony. I recall feeling anxious that my mom might say a prayer before dinner, so I asked her not to.

Looking back, I can't quite pinpoint why I felt so embarrassed about it. Anticipating Jeremy's teasing, I braced myself. However, I felt a wave of relief when Matt, the same person I accidentally hit in the tooth with my lunch pail back in private school, now attending John A. as well, volunteered to say grace for the entire group. His gesture put me at ease, and looking back, I realize I was unnecessarily embarrassed by the situation.

Our entire friend group from John A. was transitioning to Honourable W.C. Kennedy Collegiate for Grade 9. Among us were Jeremy, Shannon and Amanda. We remained a tight-knit group. Kennedy High School had a striking resemblance to an old castle and was rumoured to have tunnels beneath it, situated near Jackson Park on Tecumseh Road in Windsor. The park itself featured old planes showcased on cement podiums and a sizeable, murky pond where the "frosh week bullies" would play pranks by tossing Grade 9 students in. It was a relief that I managed to steer clear of such antics. During that time, I embraced the skater punk aesthetic, sporting wide-legged jeans where the legs matched the width of the waist.

I even went as far as dyeing my hair blonde with leopard print, a style I eventually abandoned once it grew out and I opted for a haircut.

My music taste leaned towards bands like Korn, Limp Bizkit, Slipknot, and others known for their high-energy shows and intense, aggressive music. I eventually gave up skateboarding because, let's face it, I was terrible at it. I couldn't even nail the basic ollie!

I soon switched gears and took up inline aggressive skating, rocking those K2 Fatty's with a metal grind plate – talk about a sweet setup! A K2 Fatty is a type of aggressive inline skate known for its durability and performance in skate parks and street skating. It typically features a sturdy boot design, durable frames, and grind plates for executing tricks and grinds. The K2 Fatty line has been popular among inline skaters for its versatility and ability to handle the rigours of aggressive skating. I snagged them second-hand from a guy in need of quick cash, which worked out perfectly since my family and I were struggling financially. Those K2s were a real score for me and my street cred!

On one of the initial days of high school, during an outdoor class walk, I spotted a kid sporting the same wide-legged jeans and a haircut reminiscent of the Hanson's lookalike band, "The Moffats." He hopped onto a picnic table seat as if he were grinding with his rollerblades. Glancing at Jeremy, who had also witnessed the scene, I had a feeling we would hit it off and become friends. The Moffat boy turned out to be Kyle, who happened to be best friends with another skateboarder named Tim. Tim and Kyle were my height, which was a rarity since most other boys towered over me. This fact made me like them even more. We started hanging out at school and eventually after school as well. Tim and Kyle resided in Remington Park, a neighbourhood close to Devonshire Heights, roughly a half-hour rollerblade ride from my house.

Growing up, I had never witnessed my mom drink, let alone use drugs. One day after school, while still in Grade 9, I was at Kyle's place, just skating and hanging out. We ventured into his garage, where he retrieved a large bag of what I later learned was low-quality outdoor weed – complete with seeds, stems, and all the trimmings. I was beyond excited. It was a moment of firsts for me as I watched him roll a joint, taking in the entire experience for the very first time. I watched him "baptize" the joint, feeling a bit grossed out by the idea of putting my lips on his saliva-coated roll.

"Baptizing a joint" is a term used to describe the act of wetting the end of a joint with saliva before lighting it. This is believed by some to help the joint burn more evenly or smoothly. It's a common practice among some smokers, though not everyone chooses to do it.

Despite my reservations, we smoked it, but I didn't feel much of an effect. Kyle then suggested that eating the roach would enhance the high. I tried it, but it didn't do the trick. We hung out for a while until Tim arrived with three joints from his older brother. We headed to Beckers, marched out back, and had a smoke session. Three guys, three good joints, smoked quickly. That's when I got absolutely stoned. Afterward, we ventured into the corner store. I felt like I was in a movie, experiencing an out-of-body sensation. I absolutely loved it. We laughed and had a great night. I rollerbladed home, indulged in some late-night snacks, and slept like a baby. I even remember having a weed hangover, if that's even a thing. That night marked the beginning of my relationship with weed - pot, bud, chronic, flower - although it wasn't legal here yet.

I was rebellious, not wanting to babysit, and fighting with Mom and Ron all the time. I moved in with Nan again when I was 16. Nan lived closer to Jeremy, and I had had enough of life at home with Mom, Ron, Abby, and Isaac. I felt I needed more freedom, which is what I got at Nan's. She was a great person, Depression-era cooking, raised kids on her own after her husband, my mom's dad, died when she was still young. But she was old now, and I did what I wanted. Spending my free time either at home, at Jeremy's house or vice versa, rollerblading, smoking weed, making bongs, listening to Ludacris and Nirvana on my tiny TV using my PS1. I had a room upstairs in an old wartime house from the 1940s, no air conditioning in Windsor. I would often fall asleep at Jeremy's place, in the cozy living room they had set up in the basement of their duplex on Daytona Street, just behind Huron Church Road. Jeremy's dad had passed away when he was young, leaving his mom to raise him with very few rules. I found a connection with Jeremy over our shared experience of being fatherless and appreciated the freedom of living by "no rules."

We were inseparable for many years. Jeremy didn't really get into smoking weed as much as I did. I would hang out with Tim, Kyle, and a bunch of other stoner, skater bums. I did poorly in high school, treating it like a big party. Shannon's cousin, Amanda, came to Kennedy a couple of months after we did. We started dating, and I finally lost my v-card in Grade 9. I was proud of myself, but we didn't date long. I then dated a girl named Shalayna, someone completely unlike me or anyone I'd ever hung out with. She introduced me to rap music. Unfortunately, she ended up sleeping with my good buddy.

After that, I dated a girl named Sarah. I was aware that she was more open with her affections and I was lacking a father figure to guide me on how to be a gentleman and show respect and love towards a woman. Coupled with my own naivety as a teenage boy, I found comfort in dating her for a while. However, I eventually decided to end the relationship. Tragically, her father passed away the very next day. I remember feeling relieved that I didn't have to deal with the funeral arrangements. Looking back, I realize I was acting like an asshole. It's like I had the mind of a narcissist, only caring about what I could gain. For a long time, that's how it was. The weight of my actions and the impact of my behaviour slowly revealed the hidden scars of trauma that I had been carrying all along, and still do to this day.

One day, I returned home to find a bedsheet draped over our large box TV in the living room. A note was taped to it, reading "40 day TV fast." It was clear that my mom and dad had picked up on this idea from church and decided that I would have to join them in their 40 day fast. I wasn't happy. No cell phones, no computers in the house, no internet!!! No second TV, no laptop, no playstation, no Nintendo, no Atari. I had books. Lots and lots of books. Mainly Christian preteen books but some others that my nan got me like "Danny, Champion of the World," "When the Lights Go On Again," "Uncle Tom's Cabin," tons and tons of "Archie" comics. I have always had a deep love for reading. As a child, I would immerse myself in the pages of the "Children's Picture Bible," reading it repeatedly. Surprisingly, I found it incredibly captivating. It was a reflection of the sheltered life I led and the people I was surrounded by.

TRANSITIONING TO ALMOST LIVING on my own at my nan's house was a liberating experience. She was old and didn't intervene much in my decisions. Jeremy and I ventured out together to get our first tattoos, opting for flash designs off the wall like excited kids. I chose a Taurus bull head outline on my shoulder blade, while Jeremy went for a blue sun on his bicep. Though the tattoos were far from perfect, we were thrilled to show them off to everyone we knew.

It was in Grade 10 that Jeremy began dating Amanda. We used to spend a lot of time together, hosting parties and occasionally staying out all night. Amanda and I, being neighbours, often walked home together. I always felt a strong connection with her, believing she felt the same, even though she was flirtatious with everyone. I had hoped to pursue a relationship with her since we had already shared some intimate moments. Interestingly, we shared the same birthday.

I began forming new friendships at school and delved into experimenting with various drugs on campus. I vividly recall a day when I consumed acid, mushrooms, and ecstasy all within the school premises. Walking into Science class after lunch, I playfully showed my buddy a hit of acid by sticking out my tongue, only for him to respond by revealing two hits on his tongue. I wasn't fond of drinking and had limited experience with it.

One day during lunch, I had a can of Coke with just about two ounces left in it. While hanging out in the alley where we smoked joints, someone had a 26 ounce bottle of Jack Daniels. I jokingly said, "If you fill the rest of this can up with JD, I'll chug it all." Everyone laughed and doubted I would do it. I confidently replied, "Just watch." As the can was filled up, I had no clue what to expect. Nevertheless, I chugged it almost empty. As the bell was about to ring, signalling the end of lunch, we all headed back to school. I had Math class after lunch, but feeling exhausted, I rested my head on the desk and passed out. When I woke up some time later, disoriented, I quickly grabbed my backpack and left the classroom without saying a word to anyone, not even the teacher. Feeling unwell, I puked in the hallway, then stumbled out of the door and made my way to the restaurant next to Kennedy.

SPYS, short for Subs, Pizza, Yogurt, Salad, had an interesting logo featuring the "Spy vs. Spy" characters (though I had my doubts about its legality). Eventually, I found myself at a picnic table outside SPYS, a popular spot where students from Kennedy and the neighbouring Catholic Central school gathered to relax and smoke after classes. I regained consciousness around 5:30pm, a time when both schools had dismissed, and students had come, noticed me, hung out for a while around me as I slept, and then left. Finding myself alone when I woke, I felt so fucking hungover. I began the long walk home from school, which took about an hour.

As I was rounding the big bend on Tecumseh road, Ron pulled up next to me and asked, "What are you doing?" Thinking on my feet, I replied, "I tried a cigarette after school and felt nauseous, so I couldn't take the bus. That's why I'm walking." Ron did something incredibly kind for me that day. He covered for me with my mom, and somehow managed to call the school to inform them that I had left due to feeling unwell. I was truly surprised by his actions. Ron was typically "by the book," much like my mom. After that incident, I refrained from drinking for a long time. Instead, I delved into using various drugs, particularly weed. Weed became a driving force behind most of my actions. Whenever I had money, it went towards buying weed. I even enjoyed building bongs as a hobby.

I began spending time with a classmate, Rob, who sat in front of me in Math class. Rob was generally quiet, but he had a great sense of humour and was a genuinely nice guy once you got to know him. I used to ride my bike to his place near Remington Park, where Tim and Kyle also lived. We would often smoke weed in his room, go for bike rides around the area, and venture out to buy more weed. This was during my Grade 11 year. Rob was in a relationship with a girl named Sherry, who lived in Remington Park, also known as "The Park." One day, Rob mentioned that Sherry could help us get weed from a guy named Ken who lived nearby. We decided to ride our bikes to "The Park" and locate the house as instructed. Upon arrival, Sherry and another blonde girl greeted us at the door. We entered, obtained our weed, and lingered awkwardly for about five minutes before Rob and I decided to leave. We found ourselves returning to that place a few more times, and before long, the blonde girl, whose name was Will (short for Wilhemina, a German name), began striking up conversations with me. I later learned from Rob and Sherry that Will had developed a liking for me and wanted to spend time together. So, we all decided to hang out. One evening, Rob and I visited Sherry's house while her parents were away. That night, we all indulged in a bit of drinking, and Will led me into the bedroom where things escalated between us. She took charge and even had a condom ready. While I found the experience exciting at the time, I must admit that I was still quite self-centred and didn't attach much significance to it beyond just having a good time. I was just as asshole.

Trauma can deeply impact how we behave and feel. It can lead to defensive or self-protective actions that may be misunderstood as self-centred or insensitive. I was both.

It turned out that Kyle, Tim, and the other residents of Remington Park were familiar with Will - she was Ken, the weed man's daughter. Will was a year older than me, one grade above, but she didn't attend my school. I had never met or known her before meeting her through Rob. We continued to spend time together, often gathering at Will's place. Her room was located in the basement of her parents' house. An enduring fixture of Remington Park, Will's grandparents had operated a corner store in front of the house for many years. Over time, the store had been transformed into a spacious living room with a high ceiling, serving as the main entrance to the house. Will's father, Ken, a man with a tough exterior and demeanour (reminiscent of a blend between Charles Manson and Tommy Chong, in my opinion), took over the space to sell weed to the neighbourhood. It was common for Ken to sell weed to anyone who asked, even if he didn't recognize them. This house became my go-to hangout spot for years. I would ride my bike or rollerblade from my nan's house on Rankin on the west side to Will's house in Remington Park, almost 10 kilometres away.

Shortly after meeting Will, I mentioned to my nan that I was planning to get my tongue pierced. She warned me that if I went through with it, I would have to move out. Despite her warning, I decided to get the piercing anyway, only to find out that she wasn't bluffing. The next day, I ended up moving back in with my mom and Ron. They had recently moved to the west side too, closer to Jeremy. I was relieved to move in with my mom. However, their frequent arguments took a toll, and one day, Ron disappeared without a word, leaving us with no goodbyes or explanations.

My worst fear became a reality. The thought of my brother and sister facing the same fate as me, growing up without a father, enraged me. I stormed into his workroom in the basement and unleashed my anger. I destroyed everything in sight, swinging a bat, cutting off bench legs, and smashing the shit out of everything. How could a so-called "man" abandon his family like that? I was in disbelief and couldn't comprehend his actions. I believed that even if a breakup was inevitable, he should have at least made an effort to see his kids and be a part of their lives. While I didn't understand the reasons behind his departure, I was deeply upset by his absence. This experience reinforced my unwavering conviction that if I were to have children in the future, I would never abandon them under any circumstances. I vowed to always be open and honest with my kids, sharing everything with them and never keeping secrets.

Ron returned a few days later without offering any explanation for his sudden departure. When he inquired about the state of his room, I proudly admitted to causing the damage. His silence spoke volumes. I can't recall how long he stayed this time, perhaps just a couple of weeks, before vanishing once more. This time, it was for good.

Despite our lack of closeness, his absence left me feeling abandoned once again, and I couldn't help but feel sorry for my mom, brother, and sister who were also affected by his departure. I have a vivid memory of Will and I driving down Tecumseh road a few years later when we spotted him walking down the street. I urgently asked her to pull over, got out of the car and approached him. Tears streamed down my face as I cried out, "Where have you been, Dad?" Even after everything that had happened, I still referred to him as "Dad" and felt a sense of relief seeing him. However, he only exchanged a few words, declined a ride, and that marked the end of our interaction for years.

I recall sobbing in the car afterward, with Will comforting me as she always did. While Will and I weren't officially dating, we were intimate frequently, yet I didn't feel a sense of commitment. She was fun, kind to me, attractive, and up for almost anything. This dynamic continued for quite some time, during which I distanced myself from spending time with Jeremy for the most part. One day, early on in my interactions with Will, we were intimate at Kyle's house. When we emerged from the bedroom, she insisted on wearing my shirt. As we entered the living room, we found a mix of familiar faces and some of Kyle's tougher acquaintances. One particular individual, a guy named "Bud," seemed upset by the sight, perhaps wanting Will for himself. He took me aside and asserted that it was acceptable for me to be with her but warned me not to mess around. Despite feeling angry, I was too meek to speak up, so I simply replied, "Ok." It's amusing to reflect on that moment from many years ago, knowing now that Will is the love of my life, the mother of my children, and my closest confidante. As for "Bud," well, karma has a way of working things out, even for tough guys like him.

One day, I received news that Jeremy and Amanda had split up. She called me, expressing her desire to come over. I was thrilled at the prospect, especially since my parents were not at home. We ended up being intimate, and it felt like something that had been building up for a while. I was happy in that moment. While I didn't feel like I had betrayed Will or owed her anything, I was certain that I didn't want her to find out. I didn't want to jeopardize what we had. A few days went by without any word from Amanda, leaving me wondering. Then, about a week later, Kyle's sister Randy casually mentioned to Will that Amanda and I had been intimate. Will was understandably devastated and furious.

CHAPTER 2

Later that day, I went to see her, unaware of what had transpired. We ended up in a heated argument, during which I began to grasp the extent of the pain I had caused her and the depth of her feelings for me. It was a moment of realization for me, as the foolish, immature boy I was had been oblivious to the impact of my actions and too selfish to see anyone else's perspective. That night, Will and I engaged in a lengthy argument that culminated in me offering my apologies and pledging not to communicate with Amanda anymore. It's worth noting that Amanda and I had been close friends since around Grade 7, and I believe I was supposed to be in Grade 12 at that time (though the exact timeline is unclear). It must have been a significant decision for me to agree not to communicate with Amanda anymore, especially when I believed it might have been our best opportunity to pursue a relationship. This commitment underscored the seriousness of my connection with Will. I stayed true to my word and refrained from contacting Amanda until after Isaac's passing in 2023. When we did reconnect, our interactions remained strictly platonic, just as I had promised.

I eventually moved in with Will, her mom, dad, brother, and sister. Meanwhile, my own brother and sister were growing up, both now in the later part of elementary school. My mom was working and had a place behind our old geared-to-income spot on Labour Crescent. The house on Conservation was reminiscent of the duplex we lived in years prior. I resided in Remington Park, while my mom lived in Devonshire Heights, just a quick bike ride away.

DAY 4 OF 19 — JUNE 29, 2025 — 7:30PM

It's the end of the day out here. I've been writing my story every single day, though I may have skipped journaling a bit. In my Durston X Mid Pro 2+ tent, thunder was booming for most of the afternoon. It's now 7:30pm, and I've been at this campsite marked as "good" on the map since roughly 3:00pm. I have just completed the most challenging portage I have ever encountered in Wabakimi, technically in Crown land outside of the park. I plan to stay here until

36

tomorrow or the next day, when I will cross the train tracks to head back north into the Flindt River.

I found the portage trail easily, marked by a blaze on a tree in the most expected spot to start the trail. However, during my first carry with my heavy pack and loose items, which was a long trek of at least 800 metres, I got lost right away. The trail simply disappeared, which was a first for me.

Despite being familiar with the trails in this area after six years of exploring and covering countless metres of portage, I had never encountered a trail that just vanished like this.

Despite finding the marked start on the map, the trail led me through challenging terrain — muskeg, dense alder thickets, moss-covered fallen trees, and a tangle of trees resembling a Jenga stack. I had to rely on my GPS to navigate, setting waypoints and anticipating the difficulty of bringing the canoe and food bag later. After a prolonged struggle, I finally caught sight of blue water ahead. I made a beeline for what turned out to be more of a swampy pond than a lake.

Emerging from the dense alder jungle, I was drenched in sweat and morning dew. I used my BeFree filter to gather some water, quenching my thirst before scanning the area for the actual portage entry point by the water's edge. To my relief, I spotted a blaze on a tree right where one would expect the portage to begin.

Excited, I anticipated an easier carry on the proper trail. However, my hopes were dashed as I noticed flagging tape on some trees leading away from the water and into the woods, indicating a different path. After following the trail for less than 100 metres, it abruptly ended with no clear path in any direction and no more flagging tape to guide the way. I turned around, scanning the surroundings eagerly in search of the real trail, unencumbered by my pack. Despite my efforts, I couldn't spot any remnants of a trail — no cut logs, no tree blazes, and no signs of foot traffic on the ground.

I relied on my GPS to guide me back to where I left my canoe and food bag. Exhausted, I finally made it back to the beginning of the portage. I picked up my heavy food bag, hoisted my canoe over my head, and began following the only actual part of the trail. However, after just about 30 metres, the trail faded away. Navigating with a heavy bag, canoe, and GPS in hand proved to be quite challenging. Realizing the difficulty of navigating with the canoe obstructing my view while trying to follow the GPS, I made a swift decision to drop my canoe and bag. I carefully marked the canoe's location on my Avenza Maps GPS app and proceeded to the next waypoint with my heavy bag in tow.

I finally reached the end of the portage after a journey filled with swearing, sweating, and even some bleeding. I had a mishap while crossing a high log, tripping and using my hand to break the fall, only to end up with a deep cut on my palm from a sharp, broken spruce branch.

Despite more trips and falls, along with a swarm of bugs — an overwhelming number of them (surprisingly, I only got bitten a few times) — I persevered through it all. As I caught sight of the blue water, I navigated my way out and found myself near where I had left my heavy bag. After hydrating and retracing my steps back to where I left the canoe, I realized I had made three or four waypoints shuttling between my gear and the canoe. It was a relief to finally be done. I then searched for the "good campsite" that was marked on the map, eager to rest after such an adventure.

I stumbled upon a slanted rock that offered a place for swimming, a fire pit, and a spot to dry clothes, but it lacked space for setting up a tent or being truly comfortable. After venturing back into the woods, I discovered a spot that was just about big enough for my two-person tent. Exhausted, hot, sweaty, bug-bitten, and hungry, I decided not to travel any further. With the sky darkening, I was more than ready to rest and recuperate.

As thunder rumbled in the distance, I weighed my options and decided that the next campsite was too far away. Concerned that if this current site was considered "good," the next one might not be as favourable. Given that the portages were barely used and the campsite was small and seldom visited, I didn't want to take any chances. I began setting up camp to ensure I had a safe and comfortable place to weather the approaching storm. After setting up my tent in a cozy mossy spot, I decided to take a refreshing swim not once, but twice — it was truly invigorating.

I took advantage of the blazing sun to dry all my clothes. Just as I finished, dark clouds rolled in once more, signalling the impending storm. I quickly gathered all my belongings and sought shelter in my tent. As I continued to write, the thunderstorm intensified with high winds and heavy rain. Suddenly, the realization hit me — I had left my canoe halfway down the portage, right-side up. Unable to shake off the worry, I changed into dry clothes and trudged back through the storm to retrieve my canoe. It sucked.

As I braved the huge raindrops soaking me to the bone, I reached the canoe only to find it filled with water. Despite being drenched, my priority was ensuring the safety of the canoe — the most essential item out here. Relieved to see it intact and undamaged, I reflected on the lesson learned: Don't put off until tomorrow what you can do today. Just as I returned to my tent, the rain ceased. I couldn't help but think, "Another lesson in good juxtaposition" — a reminder to have patience. If only I had waited, I would have stayed much drier. Today has been a cycle of sun, dark clouds, rain, and wind. I'm calling it a day. Tomorrow brings a big paddle, followed by a challenging slog the day after. I need to conserve battery, so I'll go easy on filming.

While living at Will's house, I gained valuable insights into the "real" world - learning about human behaviour, social hierarchy, and how to read people. Coming from a background of poverty, I had long been in a "get mine however" mindset, shaped by a life of scarcity. Many teenagers around me shared a similar outlook, believing in taking advantage whenever possible. It wasn't until I met Eric a few years later that I realized not everyone operated in the same way.

Eric, a kind and generous individual, came from a wealthy background, which was uncommon among my friends. Before Eric, during my time at Will's, I met Brett. Brett, who used to date Will and resided in Remington Park, was well-loved by Will's family. Brett and I got along well, often attracting a crowd who would come to buy, smoke, and then leave. When I was alone at Will's place, Brett would still hang out. Our friendship grew stronger, and then Brett's lifelong best friend, Tony D., made an appearance one day. We instantly clicked, feeling like old friends reunited. Our activities also included doing drugs, having a few drinks (although I still wasn't fully into it), smoking weed, playing video games, and riding bikes - all before Brett got his little green truck. The Mazda version of the Ford Ranger, with its fold-down two seats in the back, became a significant part of my life for a long time. I worked at Dollarama, Canadian Tire, and

Tim Horton's, sold chocolate bars door-to-door, engaged in selling weed, and hustled as much as I could.

DAY 5 OF 19 — JUNE 30, 2025 — 6:15PM

Today was a particularly uneventful day of canoe tripping. I began around 9:00am. My clothes were all soaked from the previous night's rainy expedition to retrieve my canoe from the heart of the bush. To dry out my boots, socks, and pants, I wore my lighter camp clothes and shoes in the canoe, laying the damp items on top of my gear. With a good breeze and strong sun, I had a few kilometres without any portages, so I took the opportunity to dry out my clothes. They were about 80% dry by the time I reached the first portage. As I paddled, the sky darkened, thick clouds gathered, thunder rumbled, and light rain began. However, by the time I reached the portage, the rain had stopped, the sky cleared up, and the sun was shining once more. Nature's unpredictability certainly kept things interesting!

My bags were starting to feel heavier, which was the opposite of what I expected. I managed to catch a pretty decent-sized pike, but as usual, it swallowed the hook. Feeling hungry during lunchtime, I was looking forward to a meal when the black clouds returned, signalling an approaching storm. I made the choice to pause at a campsite, where I quickly set up a tarp and prepared a delicious lunch with the freshly caught pike. It had been a while since I last enjoyed fish, and the pike certainly hit the spot. As I continued my journey, I encountered some stormy weather, prompting me to don my rain jacket towards the day's end. Now, I'm situated on a peninsula, an unmarked site with a wonderfully flat area for pitching my tent. The tranquility of this spot is a welcome respite after a day of adventure.

I have the option of seeking shade and setting up a fire near the water by a large rock. Today, I decided not to film to conserve battery power for essentials. It has been a good day overall, and I look forward to either gaining strength or lightening my load in the days ahead. Tomorrow, I will cross the tracks and begin my journey back into Wabakimi. Exciting adventures lie ahead as I continue to explore the Canadian wilderness.

Will and I used to enjoy ecstasy together. I also experimented with acid and mushrooms. Later, after meeting Eric, I developed a liking for cocaine. We would often indulge in it together. It proved to be a waste of many years. As I lived there, I began to grow weary of the lifestyle. Throughout my life, I felt a deep longing. I wasn't quite sure what it was for - perhaps a father figure, a new hobby, or something I could truly enjoy aside from smoking weed.

The city I grew up in, Windsor, was not the best. The typical job options were working at Chrysler, in tool and die, or other factory jobs. I once tried a factory job, but after just one day, I walked out. It wasn't that I looked down on it; it simply wasn't for me. I never really had a strong hobby. I played baseball on a local team for two years with my friend Chris, but when it came to playing at a higher level with a travel team, I wasn't given the opportunity. I often had to skip baseball for church on Sundays. I had a fondness for baseball, but that chapter had long closed. My attempts at skateboarding and rollerblading were lacklustre; I was merely pretending. Hockey wasn't my thing, and I lacked skill in any musical pursuit. One cherished memory I hold is of my mom taking me car camping on Pelee Island when I was young. Pelee Island is a charming island located in Lake Erie, Ontario, Canada. It is the southernmost inhabited point in Canada and is known for its tranquil atmosphere, beautiful landscapes, and rich biodiversity.

I always loved watching "Grizzly Adams," "Little House on the Prairie," and "Fred Penner" with his secret tree. Coupled with those outdoor adventure books, I loved it. I should have clued in earlier, but living in Windsor might as well have been inner city Detroit, with no nature at all. Growing up, I had no one to share outdoor knowledge with - no dad, no grandpa. The idea of having a career in camping never crossed my mind. I believed that working in the wilderness meant being a park warden, and I couldn't envision any other options. I found myself without clear goals, stuck in dead-end jobs, living paycheque to paycheque in Will's parents' house. It was a tough time, with struggles involving drugs. It was shit.

One day, while Will was at work, I was flipping through channels in the era when people still watched cable TV. I landed on channel 56 and saw a guy building a fort or something. An hour later, I had finished my first episode of "Survivorman." The show had me captivated the entire time; this guy was amazing! From that moment on, I made sure to catch it whenever it was on. It's incredible how a single TV show can spark a newfound interest and passion.

During the early days of the internet, I eagerly searched for any information I could find about Les Stroud and his camping show. This marked the beginning of a journey that I am still living today, as I write this. The realization that you could actually make a career out of something like that was mind-blowing! I discovered Ray Mears shortly after and then Mors Kochanski. Around the same time, I also met Brian, who happened to be the brother of Will's friend Christine. It's amazing how a simple curiosity can lead to life-changing discoveries and connections.

Brian and I first crossed paths through a shared interest in coke. Will and Christine were friends, and our group of friends would often gather, indulge, and have a good time together. Brian and I hit it off, bonding over our mutual enjoyment of watching shows like "Survivorman" and similar outdoor adventures. He was the only person I knew who shared my budding interest in the great outdoors. It's fascinating how unexpected connections and shared interests can lead to meaningful friendships and shared experiences. Our shared passion for the outdoors blossomed, leading me to shift my focus away from drugs and towards learning about nature. I began seeking out green spaces in Windsor to practice my outdoor skills. Despite this newfound dedication, we still enjoyed smoking weed together, often indulging in it. One of my prized possessions was a book called "Northern Bushcraft" by Mors Kochanski, a renowned Canadian bushcraft expert. It's amazing how a shift in focus and a newfound passion can transform one's perspective and lifestyle.

In the book "Northern Bushcraft," Mors Kochanski detailed various skills, including how to assemble a bow drill fire kit. He explained the types of wood to use for each component and the specific shape the end of the spindle should have. Inspired by Les Stroud's demonstration on his show, I was captivated by the idea and felt compelled to give it a try. To me, mastering the bow drill fire kit seemed like the epitome of cool and manly outdoor skills.

It's truly remarkable how dedication and perseverance can lead to mastery. After more than a year of trial and error, experimenting with different wood combinations, refining techniques, and building muscle memory through countless attempts, I finally achieved success. It happened in Will's room at her parents' house. Although I didn't quite manage to blow it into flames, I did produce a burning ember. The room may have been smoky, but that was nothing new.

I scoured the neighbourhood, carefully selecting branches from parks and neighbours' trees that appeared suitable for the bow drill. I searched diligently for wood that met Mors Kochanski's criteria. As he suggested, if you can easily dent or scratch the wood with your fingernail, it's a promising candidate for the bow drill. This hands-on approach to gathering materials and following expert guidance has been instrumental in my journey to master bushcraft skills. To create a successful bow drill fire, you need a hearth board/base board, a spindle, a bearing block, a bow with a paracord string (preferably), and a tinder bundle to blow your ember into actual flames. There are several steps involved in using these components. The process involves trial, error, pain, misery, wonder, understanding, joy, and exuberance. I figured it out on my own, with only a hard copy book, no videos on YouTube, and no instructor. I felt great, like never before!

I thought of myself as a bushman. When I showed Brian, he found it cool, though perhaps not as cool as I did. Inspired, Brian and I began constructing a lean-to shelter in a small wooded area on Walker road, nestled between Glidden Paints and Ground FX Car Detailing. The spot bordered a train track, and the woods were no larger than a football field. Brian was familiar with the area, having grown up nearby, but there was always a sense that we weren't meant to be there. In Windsor, any forested areas seemed to belong to a company or factory, adding to the allure and secrecy of our little wilderness retreat.

I used to ride my bike from Will's house to meet Brian and his dog, Scrappy, a yellow lab mix. Scrappy would effortlessly run alongside Brian's bike without a leash, even on the bustling Walker road. I was always amazed by their bond and Scrappy's obedience. I had never owned a dog myself, except for a brief period with Sam, whom I received as a birthday present while still at WCFA. He was already over a year old when he was surrendered to the Humane Society, not known for his good behaviour. Despite this, my mom chose him and surprised me with the gift. I was ecstatic - every boy dreams of having a dog! However, Sam turned out to be quite a handful. He had accidents in the house and even behaved inappropriately towards my little sister, which was unacceptable. That incident led to my mom making the difficult decision to rehome him while I was at school one day. It was a tough lesson in responsibility and the realities of pet ownership.

During my time at Will's place, they had several dogs come and go. One time, they had a standard poodle named Hershey. I adored him, but I had little knowledge about raising, training, or caring for a dog. Hershey was originally meant for Will, but he ended up bonding with me instead. I played a crucial role in saving his life when he contracted parvovirus. Unfortunately, they never got him his shots – that was just their way of doing things.

Despite the challenges, my bond with Hershey grew stronger, and he became a cherished companion during my time at Will's. When Hershey contracted parvovirus from the dog park, the thought of losing him was unbearable. The vet's grim prognosis was to leave him in their care until he passed away. That was not an option for me – I couldn't give up without a fight. Determined to save him, I turned to the internet for solutions. After researching, I discovered a homemade remedy involving a mix of garlic and Pedialyte. With hope and determination, I administered the mixture to Hershey, refusing to accept defeat without trying everything in my power to help him recover.

In the following days, Hershey's condition was touch-and-go, but there were signs of improvement. A breakthrough came when he showed interest in a burger I was cooking. After over a week of not eating, he finally took a small bite. It was a moment of immense relief and joy - I was moved to tears. Hershey was not just a dog; he was a beloved companion to both me and Will. Despite his challenging behaviour due to past neglect, our love for him never wavered. I felt powerless at times, as I had no authority in the house or over Hershey, but my care and dedication to his well-being never faltered. I never rode my bike with Hershey; he pulled like crazy on a walk. The one time I brought him to meet Brian and Scrappy at the woods, he fought with Scrappy. I loved the fact that Brian's dog just hung out. It was the first time I had seen a dog that simply wanted to be around us.

Brian and I continued to enhance the lean-to, eventually dubbing it "The Hut," a name that encompassed not just the shelter but the entire wooded area. It became a familiar meeting spot, with phrases like "Going to meet Brian at the Hut, Will" becoming part of our routine. Those woods were where I honed my skills. I delved into the art of using an axe effectively, particularly with the hard fruit wood like crabapple that was abundant in Windsor. We would gather the dead wood for our hut construction, and it also served as excellent firewood. The tough, seasoned wood of Windsor presented a challenge, but I found joy in the process of working with it. I'd bring leftover pork chops or whatever we had the night before. We built an indoor fire pit. The Hut was large enough for four or five people to sit or stand comfortably. I'd rewarm the food, read, write, watch birds or raccoons, wait for Brian to show up, smoke weed, and hang out all day. This went on for a couple of years.

THE PROJECTS AT THE HUT were never-ending. I would borrow outdoor VHS tapes from the library and ask for outdoor books for my birthday and Christmas. I was absolutely enamoured with shows like "National Geographic," "Crocodile Hunter," "Departures," "Ed's Up," "Survivorman," and "Ray Mears." It became an obsession. I strongly believe it was a classic case of "you want what you don't have." Living in Windsor, I felt so removed from the outdoor experiences I craved. Despite the distance, I immersed myself in these shows and books, soaking up every bit of knowledge and adventure they offered.

At some point, Ron reached out to my mom, and we reconnected. He was living up north in a small town with his parents, Grandma and Grandpa, whom I hadn't seen in ages. They resided in a town called Foymount, the highest elevated populated town in Ontario. Foymount, situated in the Madawaska Valley, was once an old army base. He noticed my passion for the outdoors and extended an invitation for me to visit. Excited about the opportunity, I asked Brian to join me for a week in the bush, and he eagerly agreed.

We embarked on a Greyhound bus journey to the "north." In our youthful and inexperienced minds, we had spent a month and a significant amount of money outfitting ourselves with an excessive amount of cheap, bulky, and heavy gear. Carrying a whopping 70 lbs on my back, we set out with grand plans we had meticulously crafted over the month, only to have them fall apart. After just about an hour of hiking, which included frequent breaks, we found ourselves unable to continue. Inexperienced and naive, we ended up setting up camp in the middle of a vast opening with no shade, right in the midst of the height of black fly season in the scorching heat of the second week of May that year. We were devoured by bugs, scorched by the sun, and had a rough time that culminated in a fight. Despite the challenging experience, Brian and I managed to find humour in it later on. In fact, we joked about it over the phone as I was driving up for this trip. Despite the rough patch, Brian and I remain very good friends to this day.

Back in Windsor, I made the decision to stop smoking weed for the first time since I started. I felt a strong need for change in my life. Brian introduced me to a couple of courses that caught my interest at Sault College in Sault Ste. Marie, and I was immediately drawn to the idea. Meanwhile, Will had been accepted to the same college for an aesthetician course and was determined to go. She encouraged me to join her, but financial constraints held me back at the time. I also felt the need for a change and attempted to apply to Sault College. However, I soon discovered that a high school diploma, GED, or equivalent was required for admission. In my school, the system awarded nine credits per year if all classes were passed. Unfortunately, I had only earned eight credits in three and a half years, with seven of those credits coming from Grade 9. School had been more of a social experience for me, party after party, and I hadn't prioritized obtaining a GED in the limited time I had.

I decided to buckle down and cram for the high school equivalency test, and to my delight, I aced it! I was overjoyed with the news. With my success, I was approved for OSAP funding (Ontario Student Assistance Program), and both Will and I were all set to embark on our own independent journeys for the first time ever. The prospect of being on my own with Will and starting a new chapter in life with her filled me with excitement. While the love between Will and I didn't happen at first sight for me, it was a different story for her. She saw me that first day and was immediately drawn to me; I can still vividly recall her standing there, looking at me. When I looked her way, she quickly looked away. She knew I was the one right away.

I grew to deeply love Will. Her kind demeanour, unwavering affection for me, passion for animals, unconditional support, and willingness to tackle any challenge I presented her with all contributed to my admiration for her. And, of course, she wasn't bad to look at either. She also formed strong bonds with and cared for my nan, mom, brother, and sister, which further endeared her to me. She was also the eldest of three in her family, like I was. She is the most responsible person in her family; she grew up with her grandma as her best friend, just like me.

Our arguments were intense and filled with passion. There was one occasion when I ended things with her because during a visit to Foymount to see my grandma and grandpa, I met a girl who expressed interest in me. Feeling constrained and unable to explore relationships with other girls, I made the decision to break up. I moved back in with my mom and began a long-distance relationship with the new girl, using calling cards for those lengthy phone calls. I never cheated on Will with her, but I knew that when I came home from meeting her, I was going to break up with Will.

I "dated" the girl from up north for a few months. I visited her once, and she came down to visit me once. I had the audacity to bring her to Will's place, where I still hung out with all my friends. At the time, I didn't think much of it. Will was obviously devastated when I broke up with her, but several months had passed since then.

Eventually, Will started dating a guy named Gordy, who was a friend of Ken's. Seeing them together was tough for me, knowing I was the one who caused the initial hurt. After the girl from up north left, I found myself at Will's house, seeking comfort and ended up sleeping in her bed with her. We embraced each other and ended up being intimate, marking the first time since our breakup months earlier. It was then that I realized my feelings for the other girl had faded. I made the difficult decision to end things with her over the phone, acknowledging it was not the best way to handle it. This experience solidified my belief that I belonged with Will. She welcomed me back, let go of Gordo, and from that point on, we have remained together without any interference.

CHAPTER 3

When Will's dad discovered that I was planning to go with her to Sault Ste. Marie, he completely lost his temper. He yelled, "She used to be strong before you!" and "You're taking my daughter away to live." In reality, she had already made plans to go before I even considered it. Reflecting on it now, I understand his reaction. I was essentially a freeloader living in his house for years without paying rent, being fed, and not doing a great job at dating his daughter. He probably thought, "Finally, she'll go out on her own, be rid of this dummy, and meet a college boy." I can understand his perspective, although his way of expressing it was not the best. I had already been feeling some animosity towards him, but after that incident, I truly despised him. I was looking forward to moving away with his daughter, and I think I may have even yelled that at him. Despite the tension, we were preparing to start this new chapter together.

My mom began dating a man named Joe. Over time, he moved in with her, Isaac, and Abby. Joe made an effort to step into the role of a father figure, and he did a great job. He took Isaac to drum lessons, engaged in father-daughter activities with Abby (as much as she wanted), and even took us on a family vacation to African Lion Safari. He's a genuinely good guy. I'm happy to say that he and my mom are still together, growing old and building a life together. I didn't feel guilty about moving away. My mom had support from Joe, and my siblings were older now. However, we were still unsure about our transportation to Sault Ste. Marie and how we would navigate once we arrived. The idea of taking a bus up and relying on public transportation for school or work was our tentative plan. Unfortunately, OSAP didn't provide sufficient funds for a vehicle, and our financial situation left us broke, as usual.

About a year before making the decision to move north for school, Will and I embarked on our first canoe camping adventure. It wasn't just a canoe trip but a full canoe camping experience. Excited but inexperienced, we drove eight hours to Algonquin Park. We were as green as they come, like a new Canadian trying to camp for the first time. Opting for what I now recognize as a tourist hotspot, we headed to Highway 60 in search of adventure.

We settled on Rock Lake because it offered the convenience of parking, paddling in, and selecting a campsite all on the same lake. At that time, I don't think I even knew what a portage was. We rented a 17-foot-long kevlar canoe, which was relatively light, and the rental staff kindly strapped it to our car for us. After that, we took the short drive to the put-in point. We loaded the canoe with our gear, and the gunwales were barely above the waterline, indicating we had packed quite a bit. Realizing we had brought an excessive amount of stuff, we decided to make two trips to transport everything to our campsite.

Our packing choices were quite comical, including a bag of sugar for Kool-Aid, a case of bottled water, and even a whole loaf of bread. The list of unnecessary items went on, with many more silly things in tow. Not to mention, we didn't have an axe but instead relied on a tiny Canadian Tire folding Sierra saw.

We got into the canoe, both of us inexperienced paddlers. With no clue on where to sit to steer or which side to paddle on, we were in for a comical start. Should we paddle on the same side as the other person? The confusion led to some yelling as we finally set off from the put-in point.

Our paddling coordination was far from smooth, and any small wave caused us to panic. I lost count of how many times I grabbed the gunwales like a novice and Will did the same. It was definitely a learning experience!

Finally, we spotted an unoccupied spot, and that was all the invitation we needed. We beached the boat and headed up to explore the campsite. It was a beautiful site, spacious, open, and flat like many in Algonquin Park. Later, we discovered that this particular site was the former homestead of a railroad and logging baron, known as the "Barclay Estate."

We had a fantastic time, especially enjoying some fishing from the shore. I had no idea how amazing it was, nor did I even know the fish species we caught - I think they were smalleye (small walleye) or huge perch. We paddled out every day, left our canoe on shore, and drove to explore every hiking trail available in the park. It was a fantastic experience! Our canoeing skills slightly improved, and we ended up staying for the full week. I was absolutely hooked. I am so grateful that my first real camping trip was with my love.

The uncertainty about transportation for moving north for school was a major concern for me. One day, my mom surprised me by showing up at

Will's house a few weeks before our planned move. When I answered the door, she looked like she was about to faint from excitement. She then shared the incredible news with me, "I just won the accumulator at bingo!" She had won $39,000! Forty grand! She handed me an envelope containing five thousand dollars - five grand! I was in disbelief. I was determined to make the most of the money and decided to invest it in buying my first vehicle. I delved into researching used cars, with a specific focus on finding an SUV with around 100,000 km mileage and 4WD capability.

After thorough research, I settled on purchasing a 1994 Jeep Grand Cherokee LTD, the white one with the gold trim. This model boasted all-time 4WD and a powerful V8 engine. I purchased the Jeep for $3,500, which I thought was a pretty good deal. It had 120,000 km on it, which I was comfortable with. I absolutely loved that Jeep.

Will and I headed north shortly after, opting to avoid crossing the United States / Canada border to prevent any potential issues with being detained and searched. We were towing a double-axle U-Haul trailer. Around that time, I had started smoking a bit of weed and had some on me along with some paraphernalia. I resumed smoking right after getting the Jeep.

Just prior, Brian and I went camping, and I smoked a purple kush joint, which I thoroughly enjoyed. That night was a blast - swimming, playing gunwale wars, and spending time with my good buddy. However, I found that I could never just smoke occasionally; once I started again, it slowly escalated back to full pot head stage before long. It seems to happen every time. Anyway, Will and I embarked on a full 12-hour drive through Canada, and I drove the entire way, marking my first time pulling a trailer.

We drove through the night for what seemed like a silly reason - I thought I could avoid any Toronto traffic. I was concerned about handling the trailer as a relatively new driver. We set off at 9:00pm and continued driving through the night until I was on the verge of passing out. We stopped at a gas station, where I bought a Monster energy drink - my first time trying an energy drink. It made me feel like I was on drugs. We arrived in Sault Ste. Marie in the late morning after unloading our belongings from the U-Haul and Jeep. Will, myself, and Hershey - our beloved poodle who was 4 or 5 years old - were all together. Hershey was an essential part of the little family we were building! After unloading, we dropped off the trailer at U-Haul. The staff member asked me to back it into a spot, something I had managed to avoid throughout the entire trip. I completed the paperwork inside and ended up leaving the trailer in the middle of the parking lot. There was just no way I could have backed it into a spot without risking hitting another U-Haul. It was quite a funny situation! Sorry!

Three days before college started, we found ourselves in a whirlwind of emotions - overwhelmed by the new city, being on our own, and returning to school after a hiatus for both of us. We embarked on the task of furnishing our little one-bedroom apartment, mostly sourcing items from the dollar store and a budget-friendly second-hand furniture store. Despite the challenges, we took Hershey for walks, explored the new area, and gradually fell in love with our surroundings. It was a stark contrast to Windsor, with outdoor spaces aplenty and friendly people all around. In 2007, things were different, but Sault Ste. Marie remained a great place. As we started to settle in, we began to feel more positive about the move, despite the mix of excitement and nerves about starting school. On that first morning, I took charge, driving both of us to school. I shared a sweet moment with Will, kissing her goodbye and wishing her a good day with an "I love you" before heading off. It was a wonderful feeling to embark on something new, even if it was a bit later than expected, knowing that it could shape our future. The morning went well, with engaging professors and like-minded individuals, setting a promising tone for the journey ahead.

I received a phone call from our landlord, Angelique, around 1:00pm. I was puzzled as to why she would be calling, so I stepped out to answer it. She informed me that I needed to come home immediately as Hershey had been crying and howling all day. They were unsure if he was hurt or what was wrong. I hurried back to the apartment, and as I approached, I could hear him from outside - we lived on the first floor. I already had a hunch that Hershey was fine; he had never been left alone before. Back at Will's parents' place, with 8 or 9 other people around, someone was always there. In this new environment, being left alone for hours was a new experience for him, and I suspected he was just acting out. As expected, he stopped his howling as soon as I entered the apartment. I vividly recall attempting to leave for school, but the moment I shut the door, he resumed his vocal protests with even more enthusiasm. I was frustrated - it was the first day of school, and I needed to be there.

Despite my best efforts, my lack of knowledge about dogs, coupled with his previous living situation at Will's parents' place, made it challenging. I couldn't bear to leave him alone, so I ended up bringing him along to pick up Will from school. Upon our return, we were met by Angelique, who expressed concerns: "You can't have him here if he is going to do that." I didn't even argue; I felt awful about potentially disturbing our new neighbours. The situation with the new neighbours and Hershey's barking and howling, being a standard full-size poodle with a voice to match, was undoubtedly challenging. Later on, I discovered that Angelique couldn't actually force us to get rid of him since we had already signed a lease. It was surprising to learn that such a demand couldn't be legally enforced. However, her ultimatum was clear - if we didn't part ways with Hershey, we would have to find a new place to live. At that moment, I took her words at face value and fully believed that we were left with no choice but to comply. The following day, we made the decision to drive all the way back to Windsor to bring Hershey back to Will's house.

We were both deeply saddened by the situation. It was a painful experience, and I couldn't shake the feeling that we were abandoning Hershey. However, knowing that he was going back to Will's house and that we had a plan in place for his care helped soften the blow. We found some comfort in the fact that our courses were only one full year each, and Will's parents had already agreed to take him back.

The drive back and forth to Windsor was tough and emotionally draining for both of us. Upon our return from Windsor, as we pulled into the apartment parking lot, we were greeted by a girl around our age with a silver lab puppy. That sight struck a chord with both of us. As we resumed our studies at school, things went smoothly. Meeting a diverse range of people, we both found it easy to make friends, especially when surrounded by individuals who shared similar interests. Over the next two weeks, I had the opportunity to participate in two field camps. So much fun! Everything was completely new to me - from handling chainsaws and navigating boats to immersing myself in fireman camp, living in prospector tents for a week, and taking on contests and challenges. It was all right up my alley, and I was absolutely thrilled and exhilarated beyond words!

A couple of months went by, and I was loving life, exploring the outdoors. Will was having a blast too. I used Limewire to download Ray Mears' "Country Tracks" to my laptop, which we both used as a home computer. I would come home for lunch, make myself an omelet, watch a 20-minute episode, then head back to school to discuss it with Brendan and Shawn, my two closest friends there. We all shared a common interest in smoking weed and hailed from the south, which instantly forged a strong connection between us. Interestingly, the only reason I managed to pass orienteering was because Shawn kindly let me copy from him during the test (shhh, our little secret). But I promise, I can navigate on my own now too!

One day, Will looked at me solemnly after a phone call with her mom and shared the news, "They gave Hershey to James Mill," a casual acquaintance we had known for years. I was in disbelief. They mentioned that Hershey wasn't listening and was getting into the garbage, behaviours he had exhibited his entire life. Despite this, they made the decision to give away our (my) dog without consulting us beforehand. I was absolutely devastated by the news. The plan was to reclaim Hershey after a year once we were done with school. However, it's not reasonable to ask for a dog back after someone else has had him for a whole year. I was overwhelmed with emotions - I yelled, cried, and expressed my frustration. Will was also deeply upset by the situation. It felt typical of her parents to make such a decision without considering our feelings.

We decided to visit Windsor one weekend to see Hershey, a choice that I now realize was not wise or sensible, and something I deeply regret. I acknowledge that my actions were selfish, even though it was not my intention to be so. I understand now that even the best intentions can have negative consequences. We called to let James know we were around the corner, he informed us that he wasn't home but that Hershey was in the backyard and we could take him for a walk. I was thrilled at the prospect of seeing him.

However, upon entering the backyard, we discovered Hershey inside a dog house, chained up, with fur fully matted and surrounded by dog shit. My heart broke seeing him in that condition. He seemed to have felt abandoned, yet his joy at seeing us was unmistakable. The sight was overwhelming, and I am tearing up just recalling it. We were shocked by what we found. We decided to take him for a walk at the Ford test track near James' house. Hershey, true to his nature, barked excitedly throughout the walk. Unfortunately, our time together was short-lived as we had to return to school. After our visit, we reluctantly returned Hershey to his dog house, chained him up, said our goodbyes countless times, and drove off, tears streaming down our faces. It became clear to me right away that this decision was a mistake. I resolved to have a conversation with James to see if there was a possibility of getting Hershey back once school was over.

Not long after our visit, I reached out to inquire about Hershey's well-being, only to be informed that he had run away some time ago. Once again, I was devastated. I had a deep love for him. I had fought to save his life when others suggested otherwise. The realization that I had unintentionally abandoned him, despite my promise never to do so, left me heartbroken. I hadn't felt this distraught in a considerable amount of time; it was truly impactful. Despite our persistent inquiries and hopeful anticipation, we never received any updates from anyone. I could only pray that our visit hadn't triggered any negative reactions from Hershey. The uncertainty surrounding his disappearance left a profound ache in my heart. It's a lingering source of pain, not knowing if he truly ran away or if other unforeseen events transpired.

DAY 6 OF 19 — JULY 1, 2025 — 3:00PM

On a flat rock peninsula, surrounded by the soothing rush of rapids on both sides, I find myself seated on my lightweight camp chair, completely bare, engrossed in writing my book. I've been in this spot since 1:30pm, and as the time is now 3:00pm, I feel a sense of peace. My camp is safely set up, and I've enjoyed two refreshing swims today. Despite encountering just one minor hurdle during my paddle, the journey has been rewarding. The only hiccup was unintentionally trespassing at the Flindt Landing outfitters place, as my map indicated no portages in the area.

As I attempted to paddle under the track, I quickly realized it wasn't feasible. Instead, I had to carry my gear up a set of stairs crafted from railroad ties, making my way up and over with my first load. The sound of my footsteps crunching on the gravel beside the railroad tracks triggered a dog's barking.

At that moment, I felt relieved that Wolfie wasn't accompanying me on this journey. While the dog didn't seem aggressive, I simply didn't want to risk having a beloved pet injured during our canoe trip. The presence of bugs, the duration of the trip, and limited space in the canoe were the reasons I decided not to bring Wolfie along. As I reached the top of the small hill where the tracks were located, I caught sight of the large mountain breed dog, barking loudly but showing no signs of aggression, much like most dogs.

I maintained my pace, aware that my presence might attract attention. Despite my discomfort with trespassing, I found myself in that exact situation, a feeling I truly dislike. Sure enough, a lady hurriedly came to see what the dog's issue was. "Sorry," I said, "Just passing through." "Is it just you?" she inquired. "Yes, just me." "Ok, just go on through," she replied. I mentioned that this was the route indicated on my map, and I hadn't realized there was a portage to navigate. She then pointed east and said, "It's actually down there." I asked, "Do you want me to go down there?" To which she responded, "You're already here..."

I apologized once more and proceeded the very short distance past their lodge to reach the river where I needed to launch my canoe. After dropping off my gear, I quickly retraced my steps back up and over the track to retrieve my canoe and food bag. As I walked past the cabin she emerged from, I couldn't help but feel like I was being observed from inside, likely through a window.

As I returned to my boat, the distant rumbling of a train caught my attention. Eager to capture the moment, I swiftly prepared my load for carrying so I could film the train passing by with a canoe on my head. It was quite a unique experience, very Canadian indeed! I waited patiently for the train to pass, balancing the canoe on my head the entire time. Once the train had gone by, I crossed back over to my initial load and swiftly and quietly departed from the lodge.

Looking back, I noticed the impressive setup at Flindt Landing with its cabins and tin boats. Despite paddling for hours without encountering a portage, the weather played tricks on me – raining, then sunny, and repeating this cycle until I decided to stop and retrieve my rain jacket. As soon as I put it on, the rain miraculously ceased for good, bringing a chuckle to my lips. It's funny how that works out sometimes! I had a moment of panic when I thought I had lost my weed, but after a frantic search, I found it in the last bag I checked while standing on a rock by the lake. Phew, what a relief! I'm not certain I could have stayed otherwise.

I'm going fishing tonight, hoping to catch a walleye and make loaded mashed potatoes for supper. It's 5:00pm now, and the weather is all over the place. I've got a fire going to keep the bugs at bay. I texted the outfitter, Bruce, informing him that I would message every three days. He had initially requested a daily check-in, but I prefer every three days.

Every day when I reach camp, I send a message to Will to reassure her that I'm safe and to check that nothing terrible has occurred that would necessitate my return home due to my PTSD from Tony and my brother. More to come about Isaac. Bruce replied with, "Across the tracks, on track and making tracks." I thought it might make a good title for a chapter or page.

The wind never died down, but I went fishing anyway. I lost two lures and almost lost my boat. I was being blown in all directions; without the weight of packs in the canoe, the wind turned it into a sail. So, as I was fishing from the shore, casting my line, the wind suddenly snatched my boat from where I had propped it against the rocks I was standing on.

In a split second, I reached out to grab it, but missed, and watched helplessly as it sped away. Without hesitation, I emptied my pockets, tossed everything in a pile on the rocks, and was about to take a shallow dive into the water to swim after the boat. Which I definitely had to do because all my gear was across the river. I had nothing with me, not even a shirt. Right before I leapt into the water, a gust of wind came from the opposite direction and blew the boat back to me with force. Phew! Close call! I promised myself never to leave it like that again!

I caught two walleye, with the first one being the biggest. As I was taking it off the jig and sharing my appreciation for these locally made jigs on camera, holding my supper in my left hand (my bad hand), the fish thrashed and I lost it — all captured on camera. However, on the next cast, I found redemption as I caught another walleye!

After unhooking it, the fish slipped out of my hands and got stuck in a small hole between the rocks, unbeknownst to me. It was quite a challenge to try to squeeze the fish back up from the hole. I struggled to get a good grip on it, resorting to using my fingernails to pinch the thin tip of its tail. I even had to use my teeth, but unfortunately, the piece I had in my teeth ripped off. I lost my grip on it a few times.

After finally finessing the fish out of the tight spot, I made sure to secure it right away to avoid losing it again. Although it was a bit small, I intended to pair it with some instant mashed potatoes for a satisfying meal. I also managed to catch two other small walleye, all on the jig — truly loving the effectiveness of the jig!

Back at camp, I cleaned the fish, stoked the fire and had a damn good feast. Looking at maps, I may cut a couple extra loops off the trip to make shorter days and add a couple rest days. I can enjoy camp life and write more. Today was a great example of that. I really enjoyed today, and got lots written too. One of the only camps I have been able to hang outside of the tent. Minimal bugs here, especially with the large fire going. Lots of wood too. Great fricking site, bud!

Will and I lived life up in Sault Ste. Marie. We both got part-time jobs. I worked at Pet Food Warehouse, a small pet store. After only a little while, I was promoted to assistant manager. I learned a lot about dog food, dogs in general, fish, and pets of all kinds. I was good at my job, people liked me, and I enjoyed helping people with their pets. I had a longing, though. As a boy in the north, always spending my free time outdoors, I felt the need for a dog. We had become friends with Tammy and Jake, our neighbours who lived two doors down in the apartment on McDonald that we called home.

Tammy was the girl we often saw walking the silver lab puppy, Whiskey, along with their older dog named Katie. These encounters made the desire for a dog even more palpable. We were actively searching. I yearned for a rugged, outdoorsy dog, but above all, I longed for a loyal best friend.

I wanted a dog that I could call my own, a companion for outdoor adventures, but more importantly, a true companion in life.

Tammy texted me at school one day, "Look at the Humane Society website. There's a puppy you will love." When I got home, I looked and saw one lonely German Shepherd - Belgian Shepherd mix named "Sherman." Apparently, his mom was found at the side of the road with eight pups. The Soo (short for Sault Ste. Marie) Humane Society took four, and the Blind River Humane Society kept four. Sherman was the only one left, at least in the Soo. Will and I went the very next day. I still remember, it looked like a puppy's dark blue eyes before they turned brown, looking up at me with that sad puppy face. The millisecond I saw him, I knew I was taking him home, and I was not calling him Sherman. I had Scout's name picked out for a long time already, and boy did it suit him! It all felt so natural; I loved him right away, and he seemed to love me too. He was definitely my dog. He adored Will very much, and she adored him back. The only thing he ever chewed, aside from sticks, was my hat.

IT WAS MY CELTICS baseball cap that Scout chewed when we left him uncrated for a few minutes as a puppy. Despite feeling a twinge of regret, I couldn't be upset with him. Scout was more than just a pet; he was the perfect companion for me. We made sure to take all the necessary steps to be responsible pet owners, something I had not fully understood with Hershey. Scout not only brought joy into our lives but also taught us valuable lessons in caring for a furry friend. We made sure Scout had daily walks, was crate trained, free fed, enjoyed raw treats, and avoided dog parks. Our neighbours' had dogs too and were always willing to look after Scout when needed. This was especially helpful when we went to visit Windsor occasionally. Scout never needed a leash; he stayed faithfully by my side, much like Scrappy did with Brian all those years ago. Scout truly became an integral part of our lives, bringing us so much happiness and companionship. Having the companionship and bond with a dog that I had always wished for was now a reality with Scout. Our adventures took us to Hiawatha Forest, where I would hike into a valley to a spot I enjoyed for smoking and cooking lunch. Scout would walk beside me, often up on the ridge, keeping a watchful eye on me from above. He never strayed far, always staying close by, creating a sense of trust and connection that made our time together even more special. Scout truly became my loyal and devoted companion, making every moment we shared in the great outdoors unforgettable.

Will worked at a local pharmacy and did aesthetician work on the side. Will, Scout, and I had a great time in the Soo. My course was coming to an end, and Will continued until the following September. I finished in June, but I soon learned from professors and locals that the certificate I received from the college was not enough for a serious job. It was not a diploma, just a certification after one full year. I hadn't realized this earlier. It seemed unlikely that I would find a good job outdoors. If I was lucky, I could work at a Provincial Park, starting by picking up litter and then trying to work my way up to something slightly better. I pondered my options, thinking I was an outdoorsman because Scout and I had enjoyed a pretty decent outdoor life with a few adventures under our belts. I admired Ray Mears and knew he had a school called "Woodlore." I noticed they were looking for instructors. Just to let you know, Woodlore is located in the UK.

After writing a resume, I received a reply from a gentleman named Paul Kirtley, who was working for Ray Mears at the time. Back then, I had no idea who he was. Unfortunately, I was rejected, which was understandable. I felt deflated and lost, unsure of what to do next. I now had a student loan of just over $10,000, but to me, it felt like $1,000,000. I left home to attend school, but now I'm struggling to find a job. I even tried applying at the parks in the area, but it seemed like you needed connections to get in. Should I just work at the pet store? Will still had months of school left.

We decided to take a weekend trip in the summer to go camping with Scout up Highway 17 to Lake Superior Provincial Park, specifically Lake Mijinemungshing. It was a similar setup to Rock Lake in Algonquin Park - you could rent a canoe, paddle to a campsite, and enjoy the outdoors.

Our camping trip to Mijinemungshing Lake was a bit of a challenge, similar to the Rock Lake experience. This time, we only managed one trip, and we had Scout with us in the boat. We paddled vigorously against the strong wind and large waves on the expansive lake. As a rookie, I suggested paddling close to shore. It turned out to be a mistake as we were hit hard by crashing waves from the side, putting us in a precarious situation.

We reached a lovely island campsite and stayed there for the entire weekend. I tried my hand at fishing but had no luck. We went for a paddle on a calm day, with the water so still that Scout thought he could walk on it, nearly tipping the boat - a lesson he quickly learned. I also swam out to a rocky island from our campsite. Scout followed me everywhere. He refused to sleep inside the tent, always insisting on staying just outside the door. It was just his nature. I have many cherished memories from my time in the Soo - from college life to the wonderful friendships and impactful professors. One individual, in particular, left a lasting impression on me.

My Dendrology teacher, Don Hall, was like a blend of Obi-Wan and Gandalf - an older gentleman with a wealth of knowledge. He was tall, with grey hair and a short grey beard, and spoke in a slow, methodical manner. Despite his age, he was witty and sharp. Don had a passion for canoeing.

In his classes on Dendrology and Ornithology, he introduced a unique learning method called "bizarre association," where he used silly stories related to the names of trees to help us remember them. For instance, Professor Hall's unique mnemonic for remembering the Latin name "Thuja Occidentalis," which translates to Eastern White Cedar, was quite memorable. He shared a story about a car accident involving his wife and a man with a speech impediment who yelled, "I'm gonna thue ya. I'm gonna thue ya."

This quirky connection helped us recall the tree name Thuja. It may seem odd, but it was surprisingly effective. Having such an innovative and dedicated teacher like Professor Hall was truly a gift and a role model for me. I had the privilege of spending time with Professor Hall outside of school on a few occasions. Will and I visited his home where we enjoyed hot apple cider with him and his wife, Vivian. We spent time watching the red squirrels and black-capped chickadees in their snowy backyard. Those moments outside of school were truly special and added to the great memories I made that year in the Soo.

Will applied for and landed an aesthetician job at Deerhurst Resort in Huntsville, getting ready for when school ended. They even mentioned hiring me for the sports desk there too. We went down and found a house to rent in the Hidden Valley ski community just outside Deerhurst. I bid farewell to everyone in the Soo, expressing that I might never return. Little did I know what the future held. Initially, I found Huntsville challenging, surrounded by private land. Our home was a cedar log cabin with baseboard heaters, which turned out to be quite expensive to heat. We also had a small wood stove, a new experience for me. When we moved in late September, we purchased one cord of wet wood, thinking it would last us a while. It did not!

My days were filled with booking excursions - day trips, horse rides, canoe trips, and hummer rides, keeping me busy from morning till night. I also had to handle sales of chips and pop and distribute towels at the desk, tasks I didn't particularly enjoy. On the other hand, Will thrived in her role at the spa, earning a good salary, receiving generous tips, and even having the opportunity to work with some famous individuals. While I struggled to make friends, Will effortlessly built connections with her colleagues.

Despite my demanding work schedule and limited knowledge of accessible areas in the region, I made it a priority to take Scout out as much as possible. With few options beyond the private lands, we often found ourselves sticking to the ski hill. During the off-season when it was deserted, I would hike to the top with Scout by my side. Watching him run around as I threw his ball down the hill, he would retrieve and drop it on command. Surprisingly, I had never used treat training with him, relying solely on praise training and a pinch collar up to that point.

That year, I found myself smoking a lot of weed as a way to cope with a life that didn't bring me happiness. I began spending more time online, seeking solace and companionship by chatting with people on a weed forum called Budsmoke in hopes of making new friends and finding support. I received a call from my mom informing me that I should come down for the weekend as my nan wasn't doing well and was in the hospital. My nan and I share a very close bond, and I always cherish our relationship. She plays a significant role in my life, much like a father figure, and I hold a deep love and connection with her.

We embarked on the seven hour drive back to Windsor, a journey I hadn't made in quite some time. I was looking forward to reuniting with my friends. My nan, who was elderly and frequently in and out of the hospital, was not in the best of health. Regrettably, I didn't fully grasp the seriousness of the situation. During our three-day visit, I only spent about 30 minutes with her. When I visited her in the hospital, she sensed my restlessness and encouraged me to leave, perhaps to spare me from the somber atmosphere. After exchanging "I love you's" and bidding her goodbye, I returned home the following day. It was a poignant moment. The day after my return, Brian was scheduled to visit.

Brian had grown tired of Windsor, prompting him to make the decision to move to Keene, Ontario. Settling in a trailer on his aunt's property, he pursued his studies in natural resources at Fleming College. With him now living three hours away from me, Brian made the journey to visit, and as always, we had a fantastic time together.

The next morning, at the early hour of 5:00am, my mom called to deliver the heartbreaking news that my nan had passed away during the night. I was stunned and overwhelmed with regret for not spending more time with her during my visit. I couldn't shake the feeling of selfishness and regret for not cherishing every moment with her. To this day, I carry that weight. In her will, she generously split everything between her four children and "her Joey," which was unexpected.

I miss my nan. It's been a long while since she passed at the age of 86. While her mind remained sharp, her body had grown tired. A true Irishwoman through and through, she lived a tough life that left a profound impact on mine. I find myself wishing I had cherished our time together more. It's a lesson I wish I had learned earlier. It was tough having Brian over when I received the news about Nan. We went for a hike in the morning, but my mind was elsewhere. He left that night, and I couldn't hold back my emotions. I was broken. I returned to Windsor for the funeral, where I was surprised to learn that she had been cremated.

While we were still living in Sault Ste. Marie, I was exploring career options and feeling a bit lost. In a moment of inspiration, I decided to write a letter to Les Stroud and mailed it off. To my surprise, a few months later, I received a response directly from Les himself, all the way from Africa! His encouraging words and a signed photo of him in a hot air balloon meant a lot to me. The fact that he took the time to reply, especially from Africa, left a lasting impression on me.

CHAPTER 4

Before we left Sault Ste. Marie for Huntsville, Will had a flare up of her very rare disease called porphyria, often referred to as the "vampire's disease." Porphyria is a group of rare disorders that affect the body's ability to produce heme, a crucial component of hemoglobin. Sun exposure, alcohol, and certain triggers can bring on an attack. She suffered a severe episode while living in the Soo, and despite knowing her for years, I had never witnessed anything like it before. She was hospitalized for two weeks. It was during this challenging time that I came to realize the depth of my love for her and my desire to spend the rest of my life by her side. I cherished our little family.

So I went to the jewelry store and spent $1,600 on a ring (a fortune to me!) as I nervously planned my proposal. The day she was discharged from the hospital, she was still very weak after two weeks of illness. Despite her condition, she expressed a strong desire to be outdoors. Our beloved spot was Chippewa Falls, located north of the Soo on Highway 17. This cascading waterfall originates from the Chippewa River and flows into Lake Superior. It's a popular pull-over spot for fishermen in the spring and fall, as well as tourists travelling along the Trans-Canada Highway.

We embarked on the 30 minute drive, with the ring box nervously tucked in my pocket. I was confident she would say yes. The realization that I was about to propose and embark on the journey of marriage filled me with excitement. We hiked up, not too far, to a rock situated at the centre of the falls. I knelt down on one knee, gazing up at her as I opened the box. "Wilhemina, will you do me the honour of marrying me?" Her eyes welled up with tears as she pulled me to my feet. "Yes! Yes!" she exclaimed, enveloping me in a tight embrace and a kiss. It was an indescribable feeling! She was overjoyed, and so was I. Without hesitation, she called her mom right away.

A few years into our Huntsville journey, my uncle Tom, a man I've always admired and aspired to emulate, reached out to me. He had learned that we were in need of a house. Upon my nan's passing, he had purchased her house back in Windsor for the remaining mortgage amount. Initially, he had allowed his step-grandson to reside there. Unfortunately, the arrangement didn't go as planned, as the young man caused significant damage to the property, prompting my uncle to evict him.

Uncle Tom generously offered to rent me my nan's house for just the mortgage payment, and even invested $1,000 of his own money to spruce it up before we moved in. I was thrilled at the opportunity as I had a deep affection for that house and it was the perfect place for Will, Scout, and me. The address was 1043 Rankin Avenue. From the end of the street, you could catch a glimpse of the Ambassador Bridge leading to Detroit. The neighbourhood where the house was located was excellent. Having lived there as a child and a teenager, returning as a young adult striving to establish a life felt like coming full circle. The house boasted a spacious fenced-in backyard, perfect for Scout to roam and play.

Brian continued to reside at his aunt's place in eastern Ontario, while Eric remained at home with his parents. Tony, Brett, and the rest of the old crew were still in the picture, with some working, some not, and unfortunately, some getting involved in drugs. A few started dabbling in Oxycodone and Percocet, substances that I personally did not approve of. My only indulgence was smoking weed, which had been my sole vice for a long time. I steered clear of the harder stuff.

I stumbled upon an online forum dedicated to bushcraft and decided to become a member using the username "Ranger Joe," a nostalgic nickname given to me due to my deep affinity for the outdoors. The Bushcraft USA (BCUSA) forum quickly became a favourite of mine. Whether in Huntsville or Windsor, I immersed myself in the forum, devouring posts and admiring pictures. Over time, I transitioned from a passive observer to an active participant, engaging in conversations and eventually taking on challenges.

The house that Will and I rented happened to be conveniently located just a five minute walk from Brian and my old hangout spot, The Hut. During my free time, I would take Scout to The Hut, reminiscent of how Brian used to bring Scrappy there. We would engage in activities like building shelters, having lunch, reading, and simply enjoying each other's company in the "bush" of Windsor, creating memories that surpassed those from our time in Huntsville. Who would have ever thought? Crazy.

My passion for bushcraft led me to create my first YouTube video in 2010, filmed in the woods of The Hut! Prior to this, I had shared pictures and written posts on the forum. I always believed that for challenges, videos would be more authentic than just pictures. Despite my lack of knowledge in editing, I decided to shoot the video using a very affordable flip-out camcorder camera. For my birthday, Will's parents had gifted me the camera. Lacking a tripod, I improvised by setting it up on a piece of wood and recording the entire five minute video in one take. If I made a mistake, I had to redo the entire thing from scratch. Little did I know that this humble beginning would mark the start of something truly significant and life changing.

Like my previous job in the Soo, my new job at the Windsor pet store felt like a dead-end, unfulfilling position. However, on the forum, I had been an active member for years, known as a go-getter who truly embodied the bushcraft style. Through this platform, I connected with people from all over the world. I met a guy named Ken D who lived in Windsor. Ken was a professor at the University of Windsor, specializing in marine biology with a focus on benthic invertebrates - small creatures like clams, worms, and crustaceans, in simpler terms.

We went on a few day hikes with our dogs; Ken had a black lab named Beta. Our hikes took us through the tall grass prairie, where Ken would also demonstrate bow drilling. We bonded over practicing making bow drill fires using different types of wood. Our adventures included a canoe trip in Lake Superior Provincial Park, even though we were both relatively new to canoe tripping. I vividly recall Ken carrying his "Holy Cow" branded canoe on the portage. After hearing me complain about my job at Pet Value, Ken offered me a position as a lab tech. He assured me that my college certification was sufficient for the role. I was hired on a contract basis with a higher salary than what I was earning at Pet Value. It turned out to be an amazing job. I would fish for a living and then conduct experiments on the catch back at the lab. It was truly a rewarding experience. Will and I continued to live this way for a few years, hosting family gatherings at our spacious house with a huge backyard. We were back home, leading a comfortable life. However, despite all this, we felt like something was missing.

We decided that we wanted to have a baby. However, Will has a blood disorder that caused her to almost bleed to death when she first started getting her period as a young woman. As a result, she had been on various forms of birth control for years. Now, we were facing challenges in trying to conceive. After visiting the doctor, Will was informed that her years of taking birth control might have impacted her ability to conceive. Despite trying for a year without success, we didn't give up. My mom and Will had been attending church together, with Will finding comfort in it. They began praying for a healthy baby, and not long after, Will shared the joyous news that she was pregnant. I was excited to be a dad. I knew that I would do shit differently.

A few months into the pregnancy, we got married. I wanted our baby, Emerald, to be born within wedlock. Our families pooled resources together to make it happen. We rented the Moose Lodge on Tecumseh, a place I used to pass by on my bike rides to Will's house all those years prior. Our wedding was a very modest and intimate affair. We managed to put it all together for around $10,000. Will's sister, Bri, served as our maid of honour, and I needed to find a best man. I considered asking Isaac, but he was not one to seek the spotlight and felt uncomfortable with attention. Knowing this, I decided not to ask him. Eric was another close friend, but he had been working on his own demons and might not have been comfortable in that role either. I thought of my good buddy Tony as a perfect fit for the role of best man. He was personable, enjoyed being in the spotlight, and I knew I could rely on him. Additionally, he was a friend of Will's from before I knew either of them. When I asked Tony to be my best man, he was thrilled and responded with a big smile, saying, "Sure, Joe! I'll make you proud." And he did just that; we planned the wedding together. Tony shared the news with his parents, and they were excited for him. When we went to try on our suits, I noticed that he was under the influence of something. Those days, he was casually using Percocet and Oxys. I was disappointed to see him in that state, but we managed to sort out our tuxedos together. Looking back, it's a fond memory for me today.

The wedding came and went, and it was a great celebration. Ron and his mom attended, and even Will's Dad seemed genuinely happy. We ended up getting drunk together, with my new father in law buying me shots of whiskey and us sharing hugs. It was a rare moment of closeness with him, and there was a double rainbow that night!

Will drove us home that night, accidentally shutting her dress in the door of our two-door Z24 Cavalier, which I thought was so cool. I had to sell the Jeep in the Soo because gas was $1.40 per litre in 2007, which was too

71

expensive for a guy on OSAP with an all-time 4WD V8. When we got home after the wedding, I, in a happy and slightly tipsy state, counted the money we had received in cards before happily heading to bed. A couple of months later, we welcomed our baby into the world.

Throughout this time, I had been shooting, editing, and uploading YouTube videos. I discovered a new spot 20 minutes outside of Windsor, a bush property that I absolutely loved. Scout and I would visit it often. The reason I started uploading videos to YouTube was to share them on the Bushcraft USA forum. Gradually, I began to gain subscribers on YouTube. People beyond my friends on Bushcraft USA started watching simply because they knew me. In the early days, there was no way to make money from it, not even for a few years after I started. Everything was driven purely by my passion for learning, teaching, and engaging with the community. All my videos were skill-related. Some of them were set to Pearl Jam music, back when that was still allowed. Eddie Vedder's voice became ingrained in my mind for years. Over time, I improved my editing skills and found joy in the process.

One day, I noticed a button on YouTube that said "Monetize Video," and I thought, "Why not give it a try?" That month, I made $50, which I thought was pretty cool. Then I saw the button "Monetize All Videos," clicked it, and earned $200 the following month. That's when I realized, "Hmm, there might be something to this."

I started going to Bushcraft USA meetups in Michigan and Ohio. It was great to meet these guys in person. Guys like "Stuff", O.L.J., Panzer, Suspect Device, DCP, and Donk. I had already met Doug (BushTramp). He lived near London, Ontario. Doug lived close enough to me that we were able to get out together a few times. I really admired Doug - he was older, funny, a Christian man, tough, and incredibly skilled in the outdoors. All of this happened around the same time that Will was pregnant, with some adventures taking place before and some after.

I took Scout out to our woods in the morning, remembering that Will had been complaining of a sore stomach, thinking she was constipated. I didn't think much of it. While I was setting up in the woods after hiking in with Scout, Will called urgently. "Come here now!" She needed to be rushed to the hospital because her contractions were very close together! There were only two hours between Will's water breaking and the baby being born. Thank goodness I was there. A beautiful and healthy girl, Emerald, entered the world! I couldn't help but cry the moment I saw her, and I even got to cut the cord. Will did amazingly well, opting for a natural birth without an epidural due to her blood disorder - she was in full fucking beast mode. She was so relieved, happy, and natural, immediately stepping into the role of the perfect mom. I was overjoyed. Emerald was so amazing; she had my nose from the start! With a dark head of hair, wailing, red, covered in gunk, she was truly beautiful!

That first night in the hospital, I drank my first Red Bull ever. Emerald wouldn't latch onto Will for breastfeeding, so we took turns sleeping. I ended up sleeping in a chair for two nights. When the nurse asked me to dress Emerald after checking on her, I hesitated because I didn't want to bend her arms to put them in the sleeves. I was worried I might break her. The nurse chuckled and reassured me, saying, "They practically bounce." We left the hospital knowing we would be back in a few days for a check-up. We were surrounded by all the support we could ask for, with both families nearby and many people we grew up with, all in the city.

I did a video with Scout and just showed the experience of an overnight bushcraft camp with my dog. Instead of a five minute video about a skill like I usually did, I posted a 20 minute video of just camping, talking to the camera and my dog, showing how to set up a tarp, make a fire, etc. The basics. And it blew up!

It was the first time anything like that had happened to me. I gained a variety of subscribers, received numerous comments, and garnered recognition online. It felt absolutely amazing! Encouraged by this success, I pushed myself even harder. Making some money from it, I was thrilled. I was able to afford a better camera, tripod, and camping gear. I even received an invitation to Missouri.

The owners of Bushcraft USA and many other individuals whom I greatly admired and looked up to were going to be there. I hadn't met this crew in person yet, only the Ohio and Michigan guys. Bindlestitch, also known as Israel Turley, was one person I had connected with online, and he called to invite me. I was thrilled and couldn't wait to go. Along with Israel, I.A. Woodsman was a huge inspiration to me. Terry Barney, a SERE (Survival,

CHAPTER 4

Evasion, Resistance, Escape) instructor, was not only a badass but also an all-around great guy and phenomenal teacher who was conducting a class at the meet-up. I flew from Detroit to Missouri. Israel picked me up, and we drove five hours to the campground for the event.

I had never been in an environment quite like that before. It was all ball-busting, all the time, but at the same time, they were incredibly supportive of each other and genuinely kind people. It had a definite locker room mentality, toxic masculinity and all. Most of them had been enlisted in some form of the military over the years. I learned a great deal, gained a lot of respect, and formed very close relationships. Israel crafted custom knives, Terry was a firefighter who was on the verge of starting a bushcraft school. The group consisted of individuals from all walks of life. Homeslice, also known as Brandon, was essentially a real-life Doogie Howser, a very young emergency room doctor.

My biological cousin, Chantelle, who lived behind us, discovered my identity. One day, she messaged me, revealing that we were first cousins and that my biological father, Jerry, was living nearby. She asked if I wanted her to introduce us. I was in disbelief. Back in high school, I had managed to track down his brother. I went to his house, knocked on the door, introduced myself, and asked if I could have my dad's number. I simply wanted to meet him without any expectations. Unfortunately, I was turned down, and that rejection hurt. So, when Chantelle asked if I wanted her to arrange a meeting, I was surprised but ultimately said yes.

He came over to my house, the same house where my mom lived when he dated her. It was noon, and Emerald was just under two months old. He arrived and requested to hold the baby. I could sense that he had been drinking - not drunk, but he smelled like beer and seemed a bit buzzed. Will handed the baby to him, and I watched closely. The moment he lifted her without supporting her head, I immediately took her back. I didn't make a big deal out of it, just acted swiftly. He left after some small talk, and I felt relieved when he was gone. From that point on, I made a firm decision never to let someone who had been drinking, or anyone who simply asked, hold my fucking baby.

I was deeply disappointed in every aspect. He seemed like a mere shell of a man, and I felt like I was more of a man than him at my young age. It became evident that he was struggling with alcoholism, something I had heard rumours about before. We had a few more conversations, but I made sure my daughter wasn't present. That chapter ended swiftly, providing me with some closure. It wasn't the dream scenario I had envisioned, but my daughter, Emerald, took precedence over any fatherly fantasies. I realized that I was the father figure now, and my focus was solely on her. He no longer held any significance in my life.

I was on a camping trip in Ohio when "One-Legged Josh" arrived after driving up the mountain to get a cell phone signal. He had a serious look on his face. "Joe, you need to call your wife," he said. Will couldn't reach me, but luckily, she happened to call O.L.J. at just the right time. O.L.J. drove me back up the mountain. I called her, and she answered, crying, "Tony's dead." "WHAT?" I screamed. Again, she sobbed, explaining that he had overdosed. It was a devastating blow.

Tony's health had been a concern as he was struggling and had a weak heart. His mom found him in bed, naked and cold. I was in shock and at a loss for words, unsure of how to respond to the tragic news. I had been driven there, so I couldn't even leave. I was unable to mourn for four days, and it weighed heavily on me. When I finally got home, the reality of Tony's passing hit me hard. I had a deep connection with him, and we were close. My heart ached for his parents and Brett, his lifelong best friend. Tony's love for music and his talent on the guitar always resonated with me. He was a bright light in my life for a while.

Tony's funeral was incredibly tough. His parents were devastated, and I found myself constantly shaking my head in disbelief. It felt like such a tragic waste of a life because he was truly a good person. The drugs didn't define him; they were a way for him to cope with the deep sense of abandonment he felt from being adopted. He never harmed anyone through theft or violence; he was just trying to navigate his own pain. I could empathize with his struggles, as I truly cared for him. Tony was a unique and special individual, and his loss was deeply felt by all who knew him. Rest in peace, man.

In the years leading up to this, I had developed a strong friendship with Kyle from Ohio. We first met at a Terry Barney bushcraft school class called "Midwest Bushcraft," and we instantly clicked. Kyle recognized me

CHAPTER 4

from the forum, and despite a slight age difference (with me being a few years older), we found common ground. Unlike many of the other guys in the group who were not in the best physical shape and preferred simpler camping trips, Kyle and I shared a passion for more challenging adventures.

Kyle and I shared a similar personality, where it is impossible for us to sit still for long periods. Our bond grew stronger over our shared passion for genuine adventure - from canoe tripping to backpacking and building shelters. Despite living three hours apart, with Kyle in Ohio, we made plans to reunite and embark on more outdoor escapades together.

We went on a couple of canoe trips, both of us still relatively new to the experience, with Kyle being even less experienced than I was. Kyle and I embarked on a week-long trout fishing trip in Algonquin at the perfect time for trout. Our journey began with paddling up Opeongo Lake, the largest lake in the park, amidst a blizzard. As we pushed through the snow, someone from the dock shouted, "I hope you have life insurance!" We shared a nervous chuckle in response.

Despite our efforts, we didn't catch any trout throughout the entire trip. Tensions ran high as we yelled at each other, and we even faced a close call of almost capsizing at Windy Point. A sudden gust of wind sent our canoe flying, landing 20 feet away in the frigid water. Thankfully, two other canoeists happened to be passing by at that exact moment and came to our rescue. Despite the chaotic situation, we found humour in the madness and embraced the adventure. This mishap only added to the memorable experiences we shared. This trip was just one of many more adventures I had with Kyle.

I had been filming all of my adventures, and Kyle also had a channel. People loved watching, and my subscriber base grew to 30,000. New bushcraft channels were emerging daily, such as Scrambled O, Black Owl Outdoors, TA Outdoors, and MCQ Bushcraft, just to name a few. While I was making minimal money from filming my adventures, I was still working at the University of Windsor and going on as many trips as possible. My boss, Ken, was incredibly understanding. As long as my work was completed or I could catch up quickly, he allowed me to take days off. It was the perfect arrangement. Unfortunately, Scout could never join me on canoe trips. Scout, my 90-pound companion, always tried to retrieve every time I cast a line, whined when in the canoe, making it a bit challenging. Despite this, we embarked on other adventures together. People adored him, and his presence undoubtedly helped grow my channel.

ONE DAY ON THE forum, someone posted an advertisement they saw for a new survival show. With shows like "Naked and Afraid," "Dual Survival," "Survivor," and "Survivorman" already popular, the survival genre was thriving. The new show advertised, "Live off the land for as long as you can. Win big!" The working title was "The Last Survivor," and I was immediately drawn to it. Excited by the concept, I applied and eagerly awaited a response. After submitting two videos that met their requirements, I went all out in showcasing my skills. The weeks of waiting in anticipation finally paid off when I received the call - I was accepted! They sent me all the necessary information, and I was scheduled to attend an in-person tryout with a group of other participants. The tryouts were set to take place in New York at a location called Bear Mountain.

Among the 18 guys trying out, most were rugged men, and I found myself as the smallest among them. Their gruff demeanour and imposing size left me feeling intimidated. However, amidst the group, I noticed Mitch from his YouTube channel Native Survival, a fellow participant from Massachusetts. Among the participants were army veterans, serious individuals, and even a writer with a larger build. Everyone was American except for me and a participant from New Brunswick. After a big meeting filled with discussions, the next day brought the real test - surviving for a day and night in the wilderness. As they lined us up, one participant was taken at a time, and each time, that person didn't return. Now, it was my turn.

At the start of the talks the previous day, we were instructed to always carry our survival kit with us during the trip. As I walked up and noticed the wet ground, a sense of foreboding crept in. Turning the corner beyond some bushes, I came face to face with the hired survival expert, a cameraman, and a producer, all gathered in front of a lake. I smiled as they instructed me to jump into the lake. Without hesitation, I waded in until the water reached my shoulders. Then, I heard them say, "Ok, come on out." Turning around, I marched back to the shore. They followed up with, "You're staying out here all night. Build a shelter and a fire, or you'll freeze." Despite it being summer and knowing I wouldn't freeze, I understood that this was the test I had been anticipating.

Moving swiftly, I made my way to the spot where the previous participants had begun their tasks, completely soaked from the lake. As person #8, I hiked up the ridge, seeking sunlight and dry wood. Pulling out my survival tin from my pocket, I took care to protect it by wrapping it in a heavy-duty Ziploc-style bag. Despite being soaked, everything else in my possession remained bone dry. I took out my 550 paracord and gutted it, creating seven strong strings along with the sheath, each 10 feet long. In addition to the paracord, I had a mylar blanket, a handheld "chainsaw," a firesteel, various small tools, and a couple of fishing hooks.

I made "buttons" on the four corners of the space blanket with duff (decomposing organic matter) from the ground, tied off to the trees with my 550 inner guts and made a quick, down and dirty lean-to shelter. Looking around, I seemed to be doing better than most who started before me. Next was a fire.

Uncertain of how long I would be out there and feeling a bit chilled, I was determined to show everyone that I was up for the challenge. Using a sharp rock and my firesteel, I sparked some grass, gradually adding small twigs until I had a roaring fire by the time the producer and survival expert came around to check. As I saw them approaching, I made a conscious effort to appear relaxed. Shirtless, with my shirt drying on a stick next to me, I sat by the long fire on a makeshift bed of leaves under my lean-to. Their impressed expressions were evident and I couldn't help but smile. Picking up my Altoids tin survival kit, I revealed the salamander I had found while scavenging for materials to build a bed frame. "Should I go fishing with this?"" I quipped, showcasing my resourcefulness. They told me I was the first person to have a fire. I had done well and was very pleased with myself. We had to camp in bivvies, slaughter rabbits and trout, eat crickets, and all kinds of other fun stuff. Then, the next day, they told us the show is going to be called Alone® and "The winner wins $500,000 USD." My jaw dropped.

When I returned home I couldn't wait to share my success with Will. After weeks of anticipation following the tryouts, I finally received the call - I had been selected! The news filled me with excitement, and everyone around me shared in my joy. Ken and Joe were incredibly supportive, but it was my mom who harboured some apprehension. Will, as always, had unwavering faith in me. Beating out the competition and proving to myself that I had what it takes was a moment of immense pride.

DAY 8 OF 19 — JULY 3, 2025 — 8:00AM

I am currently reclining in my tent, penning down thoughts for my book. I arrived here around 6:30pm last night after a full day of canoeing. It was an exhilarating day on the water once again!

The day began on a high note as I stumbled upon a world-class campsite shortly after departing from my favourite spot of the trip so far. Along the Flindt river system, I encountered three exceptionally beautiful sites within a 30 minute paddle distance. With just three casts, I managed to reel in three fish, enjoyed the pool, navigated thrilling drop rapids, and explored camps at each picturesque location. The experience was so remarkable that I am already planning to return and explore a small loop in this area.

After the exciting discoveries along the river, I encountered some long paddle sections. I've decided to challenge myself by relying less on my GPS for navigation, unless absolutely necessary. I want to avoid paddling against the wind aimlessly or making irreversible wrong turns. This decision serves a dual purpose: conserving the limited power I have left on the device and honing my map-reading skills. By embracing this approach, I aim to become more proficient in navigating the terrain and make the most of my remaining resources.

I also noted that certain sections of this journey may not be downloaded on my GPS, emphasizing the importance of practicing my map-reading skills. Despite my progress, I couldn't shake off the apprehension I felt when I first spotted a challenging section on the map a few days ago.

The label "Portage Rough" and the extended portage line appeared daunting, especially compared to any others encountered thus far. The fact that this portage was uniquely labeled as "rough" added to my sense of unease, as no other section bore such a description. So obviously, it was a slight concern. After navigating a few small rapids, joyfully bypassing some sections, and paddling into ferocious headwinds, I arrived at the "rough" portage.

I had a positive intuition from the start. Spotting a lodge on the lake, I held onto the hope that they might have cleared any obstacles or tricky spots along the way. As I neared what I presumed to be the take-out point for the beginning of the portage, I pondered the meaning of "rough." My uncertainty dissipated as I noticed a line of rocks extending into the water, guiding me directly towards a trail. Noticing straight lines in nature is quite rare, as they are typically man-made. "Hmm, a good sign," I remarked aloud, and indeed it was. The portage path traversed across bedrock for the middle section, while the beginnings on either side were slightly muddy but not overly challenging. It seemed that the descriptor "rough" likely referred to the length of the portage.

Having gained experience in Algonquin, Temagami, and Killarney, I felt well-prepared for this adventure. This flat, one kilometre portage was a welcome challenge for me, especially compared to shorter ones that require frequent navigation and boat entry and exit. It was a relief not to have to worry about it all day. Despite battling a fierce headwind on the lake and passing by two campsites to reach the final one before the portage, I managed to set up camp and enjoy a well-deserved dinner.

A nice enough site. I liked it a lot more this morning. I'm sure it has to do with the cooler temperature, no bugs, great firewood, and a nice view on this foggy morning. It'll warm up. I can feel it. I set my tent up on top of a termite mound, I had no other spot. Today, I have an 800 metre portage ahead that's labeled as "800 blowdown, not travelled well." Let's tackle it head-on! As I embark on day eight of my journey, it's starting to sink in that I've been out here for a while now. The first six days seemed to fly by. Nevertheless, I feel optimistic and fully prepared for whatever the day brings.

After I tapped out on *Alone*, I had to stay for a week to film again. It was torture, and I felt depressed. I had believed that this was my one opportunity to make something of myself, to provide a better life for my wife and baby, and to break free from living paycheque to paycheque. That's all that both of us had ever known as kids. I wanted to do better for my kid, like every good parent does. I blew it. I'd love to share every intricate detail of all the things that happened while on *Alone* which lead to me tapping out, but I signed a non-disclosure agreement (NDA). The decision to leave was completely mine.

When I got home, Will greeted me with loving open arms - no shame, guilt, or anger from her. I had quit my job at the university because, for all I knew, I was going to be gone for months. Ha ha, yeah right! My whole family and all my friends were very supportive. Nothing but sympathy and admiration for actually getting as far as I did. I was very depressed, and I think for the first time, I knew it.

I had 30,000 subscribers on YouTube at the time of the show's release; back then, this was a good amount for my genre. I had to sign a contract for *Alone* that I wouldn't put videos out until they aired the show, so nobody could tell if I was home or not, to avoid spoiling the show. In those few months, I watched people who came out after me surpass me in subscriber count. There was nothing I could do but wait. It lit a fire under me. I felt like I had something to prove to YouTube, to myself because of my experience on *Alone*, and because I believed I belonged higher up the bushcraft YouTube ladder.

After the show aired, I faced a lot of trolling online - much more than I expected. It felt like people were acting as though I had taken food out of children's mouths. I received numerous emails, saw videos about me, and read Reddit threads discussing me. People came up with some crazy theories, with some even doubting that I came as close to a bear as I did. They thought it was superimposed or something. I took it really hard. It was tough enough to let myself down by failing miserably, crying, and tapping out on the History Channel. The build-up to what I wanted to do, what every outdoors person wants to do, is to test yourself, to see if you can sustain yourself.

It was tough watching those first two or three episodes. To be honest, I've never watched the rest of that season or any of the following. The hate I was getting was overwhelming. Trolls seemed to come out of the woodwork. I made a video explaining my experience. I took a small break, but I couldn't stay away for long.

I got my job back at the university and went all in on YouTube. Long-form videos became my signature. I believe I was a trendsetter in that regard. I was able to keep people engaged on the platform for longer periods, which YouTube appreciated. From the very start, when it was just a hobby, I did it out of love and to be part of a community, which I've said many times.

It took seven years to reach 100,000 subscribers, a huge milestone that I was proud of. It only took one year after that to hit 500,000; the snowball effect is real. I started making real money, and I was hooked. I invested in better camera gear and took an online editing course, putting in a lot of effort into filming and editing. People commented multiple times that they loved my personality and that they would watch me do anything. It was effortless for me to talk to the camera. Initially, I was making videos for myself and my online forum friends to see. So, talking to the camera always felt natural, like speaking directly to them when I said, "Hey guys!" It was as if I was having a conversation with them. Eventually, I was able to quit my job to pursue YouTube full time. It was a crazy but exciting decision!

My uncle Tom offered to sell me the house for the remainder of the mortgage, $60,000. I jumped at the chance; it was my family home. $60,000 was a steal for a three bedroom house. My uncle Tom had helped me so much at the start of my adult life. I really appreciate, look up to, and try to emulate him now. He might be the only male Robinet left in the family, other than me. I need to call him when I get home! Seriously.

My canoe tripping had taken a huge leap. I was constantly travelling for camping trips, spending time with Kyle, Doug, and Ken. We went camping together frequently. One spring, we booked a canoe camp in Killarney Provincial Park. Kyle and I had never been there, but Ken and Doug, being older, had. This was the biggest and most real canoe trip for all of us to date, although looking back, it wasn't a huge trip. It lasted one week, with lots of movement every day, two canoes, and four guys. Killarney is known for its crystal-clear water, white quartzite, and steep, long portages. The canoes were very heavy, and so were the packs; all of us overpacked like crazy.

I have a vivid memory of all of us passed out on the portage trail in the middle of the forest, lying on top of our packs, completely exhausted on day five. It rained heavily all day, with steady downpours from before we woke up until after we went to bed that night. Despite the challenging weather, we were determined to stick to our schedule and planned activities. So, we got up, had breakfast, and set out paddling into the rain. Despite wearing rain gear, even the best gear gets soaked through after hours of sitting in a canoe. It turned out to be a seven hour travel day. Unfortunately, I got hypothermic. The cold, windy day and being soaked from early on took a toll.

Towards the end of the day, we had to backtrack a portage for some reason. I don't even remember doing it; they told me the next morning. By the time we reached camp, I could only stand in one spot and shiver. Ken, with whom I was sharing a large tent, set it up and helped me inside. Once inside, I could only stare at my sleeping bag still in its stuff sack. I knew I had to strip down and get in, but I just couldn't physically do it. I sat on the ground, as the tent had no floor, contemplating my sleeping gear. Doug made me a cup of soup and made me drink it, which helped. Thanks to that, I was able to gather my thoughts, get into my sleeping bag, and finally get some much needed rest. That experience was the most hypothermic I have ever been, and it was tough. But now, I have learned valuable lessons on how to dress properly to avoid such situations in the future.

The following spring, we all decided to embark on the same trip. Prior to that, Kyle and I undertook our most ambitious adventure yet, which we planned ourselves (with Kyle taking the lead as I was still struggling with reading maps and trip planning). It was an eight-night excursion in Algonquin, commencing at Cedar Lake on the north end of the park. Our route took us on a substantial loop, navigating the Nipissing River before returning to Cedar Lake. For this journey, we rented a Swift Keewaydin 17, the same model we had used on our very first trip from Opeongo. Both of us paddled in tandem, making for a memorable experience. The trip was truly unforgettable, and Kyle and I often reminisce about it when we chat. Just last month, we embarked on our first trip together in two years, following my accident. During that recent adventure, we fondly recalled our Cedar/Nipissing trip. Despite still being relatively inexperienced, we were learning and gradually mastering the art of navigating through challenging journeys. On our way up, as we drove past the Swift store in Bracebridge/Gravenhurst, we decided to make a stop. The store showcased a variety of beautiful boats that caught our eyes.

One type struck us as odd, but intriguing. Something called a pack boat, an open top kayak basically, with a detachable yoke, paddled with a double blade, a solo boat that weighed 28 lbs. We looked at it quite a bit and got the rundown. We loved the idea. We basically needed one another or someone else who wanted to do the type of trips we liked, to go on a canoe trip. We needed two people to paddle. Kyle resided in Ohio and held a typical 9-5 job, while I had more flexibility in my schedule. Initially, I saw this as an opportunity for new adventures, but when I saw the price tag of $5,000 for the solo boat, reality set in. Considering my financial situation and responsibilities to my young family, it was clear that I wasn't in a position to invest such a significant amount in a single purchase.

During the trip, Kyle and I discussed the pack boat extensively. By the time we were heading home, Kyle had made a firm decision to purchase one for himself. While I was genuinely happy for him, I couldn't help but feel a tinge of disappointment. I knew that with his new boat, he would have the freedom to embark on solo adventures whenever he pleased, leaving me slightly envious. After dropping me off at my home in Windsor, Kyle continued his journey across the bridge to Ohio. He later shared a couple of videos showcasing his new pack boat and even went camping a few times on an Ohio river. Eventually, he set his sights on conquering the Lady Evelyn River. That's when an idea struck me. If I invested in a pack boat, I could join Kyle on the trip. I had never been to Temagami but had heard wonderful things about it. It became clear that I needed my own boat to make this adventure a reality.

I sent an email to Swift, introducing myself, outlining my plans, and requesting an Adirondack Pack 13.6 in exchange for promotion. I offered to provide extensive promotion for their product. Initially, they did not respond, which left me feeling disappointed. However, after a week, they finally replied and apologized for the delay. They mentioned that they had a meeting to discuss my proposition. They had never ventured into such a promotional arrangement before. The agreement was that I could acquire one at cost in exchange for promotional efforts. I was thrilled and enthusiastically accepted the offer, opting for the red kevlar fusion model. The boat was ready just in time for Kyle and I to collect it on our way to the Lady Evelyn trip. When I laid eyes on the boat, I was impressed by how cool it looked. Its lightweight construction was exactly what I believed I needed, especially after struggling with the portages during our previous trips in Killarney. With the kayak-style paddle, it felt like even a child could effortlessly maneuver the boat.

On this first trip with my pack boat, I thought that since it only weighed 28 lbs, I could bring more or heavier items in my pack. I was accustomed to carrying a much heavier boat, but the weight distribution and the height of the pack made the canoe not sit comfortably on my shoulders during the portages. This, combined with the terrible black flies and getting sick from their bites (something called black fly fever), catching only one fish in nine days, and the challenging portages made for a memorable adventure. After one portage, we had to rappel our canoes down to the water. It rained for two days, and I lost my fishing rod right after catching one trout. Despite the rough conditions, it was another memorable adventure with my buddy Kyle. Tripping with pack boats turned out to be a learning curve compared to some of our previous trips, like backpacking in Dolly Sods, West Virginia. During the frigid winter in Michigan, we built a huge shelter to survive the extreme cold. I even had to put my foot inside Kyle's armpit to prevent losing my toes during a four-night winter trek.

Continuing to create videos in Windsor, I had the pleasure of taking Isaac out on a couple of adventures. One memorable occasion involved hiking into a spot where we cooked bacon over hardwood coals. Isaac declared it the best bacon he had ever tasted, and considering his love for bacon, that was quite a compliment. Our excursions also included canoeing in the Detroit River and exploring Peche Island. During our time on the water, Isaac managed to catch a pike. Although the grilled fish didn't turn out as expected, Isaac's joy and satisfaction were palpable. His happiness at catching the fish was truly rewarding for me. I felt compelled to introduce him to as many "manly" activities as possible.

Being 10 years his senior and with no father figure in his life, I took on a significant role in raising him. I often babysat him, and he became more than just a little brother to me. I always felt a sense of responsibility towards him and Abby. Our day trips together spanned over the years, but as he grew older, he developed his own circle of friends. I had my own life, and Abby welcomed her first daughter, Angel, shortly after Emmie was born. We were all transitioning into new phases of life. While we continued to have family gatherings at my house, Isaac's presence became less frequent over time. When he did visit, he would often sit quietly, his eyes reflecting a different demeanour than I was accustomed to. It became apparent that his mental health was deteriorating.

He had begun smoking weed around the age of 17 or 18, which was not ideal given his predisposition to conditions like psychosis. Unbeknownst to me, he was struggling with these issues. I wasn't even aware of his psychosis, and I don't think he was either. He started smoking at school and eventually confided in me about it, leading to a moment where I joined him in smoking. I used to give him weed regularly, as it seemed like a normal thing to do based on the environment I was in. In Windsor, it was common practice, especially among guys his age. To me, it was just weed, nothing out of the ordinary. However, for Isaac, it had serious consequences. He ended up being admitted to a psychiatric ward at one point. There was an incident where he accidentally set my mom's house on fire while smoking weed in his room. Thankfully, nobody was hurt, but it deeply affected him.

While I was out in the bush in Windsor, Kyle called me one day with exciting news - he had landed a job in California and would be moving soon. I congratulated him and expressed how genuinely happy I was for him. However, once we hung up, I couldn't help but shed a few tears. Kyle had evolved from just a camping buddy to a close friend, and the thought of not seeing him again was difficult to bear.

One day, I came across a new YouTube creator showcasing the beauty of Algonquin and the art of catching brook trout. This skill, which had always eluded me, ignited a profound longing within me. The dream of catching brookies and cooking them in the wilderness symbolized the true essence of a northern bushman to me. Hailing from Windsor, where such adventures were rare, the enchantment of brook trout in their natural habitat was truly mesmerizing and almost exotic. I noticed that he had a solo boat, so I decided to reach out via email to propose a collaboration for a video. My idea was for him to guide me on catching brook trout in Algonquin, while I aimed to bring more visibility to his relatively small channel. To my delight, he responded with a positive affirmation. Our first outing was a success - I caught trout and promoted his channel. As we continued to spend time together, I felt our bond growing stronger. We embarked on several trips together, and I even introduced him to Doug, further solidifying our budding friendship.

CHAPTER 5

During that period, I came across an Instagram page called Red Lake Outfitters, which seemed to be excelling in the realm of social media. Intrigued, I delved deeper and discovered that they offered authentic wilderness canoe trips. Notably, renowned figures like Ray Mears and Paul Kirtley had ventured there for their adventures. With a sense of optimism, I believed that by reaching out to the owner, I could potentially secure, at the very least, a discounted trip. I shared this exciting opportunity with my new YouTube creator friend, who expressed interest in joining the adventure. Harlan, the owner, promptly responded, eager to delve into the specifics. Before long, everything was set in motion - we embarked on the nearly 30-hour drive from Windsor to Red Lake for what would be my inaugural fly-in canoe trip.

🔥🔥🔥

DAY 9 OF 19 — JULY 4, 2025 — 10:00PM

Paddled for nine hours today. The day started out lazy. I couldn't decide whether to stay in bed or get up early to start paddling, knowing I had a big day ahead of me either way. I was up and gone by 7:00am, not too early and not too late. I headed to the fast water "rapid" where I caught the two walleye for last night's dinner.

I ran the first rapid, portaged the second, more rocky one. The portage went smoothly, and I also remembered from the night before that there was a good paddle after that. I could sense that the weather was changing. The saying "red sky in the morning, sailors take warning" proved true. The entire sky darkened, not just the clouds. The wind picked up, a tailwind, and then the sky opened up. It rained steadily for a good few hours. I decided to head north at the junction of Brennan toward the falls and up to Bruce's "secret" lakes. I had never been up there, but I had been through Brennan Falls last month with Kyle.

The more direct route is Brennan, but I wanted a little more adventure after the sun came out. I saw a caribou swimming across the lake in a narrow channel; he noticed me and quickly turned back. It's such a beautiful area. The portage was a bit tricky to locate but not too challenging. My right eye was almost swollen shut; there must have been black flies in the tent last night. Yesterday was amazing, a great site, but I stayed up late for a nighttime adventure to catch walleye, so I crashed hard. I made it to a site marked "WC" for World Class on Bruce's map. I'd rate it a three out of 10. It was extremely slanted, windy, and far from the water. Definitely one of the worst sites so far on this trip. My sleeping area is NOT flat.

I've been smoking too much weed during the day, I need to cut down. I'm getting burnt out and running low, lol. I had pulled chicken for supper; it tasted good but it was mushy. I can't afford to use flatbread for it, so I just ate the mush, no biggie. I texted Bruce to tell him I was changing the route and to check in. I was supposed to be doing it every three days. He said that someone had found my yellow backpack I lost in Thunder Bay with Kyle! He was going to pick it up on Monday. Crazy! I have a lot of bug bites now. I feel pretty good though. I might have enough food to last. Here's hoping!

It was a good trip with my new YouTube buddy, Shawn. It opened up my eyes to the real wilderness. I caught tons of fish, dealt with heavy winds, and previously burned portages. All in all, a good trip. There was a bit of a weird vibe between Harlan and my new buddy when we got out, but we left soon after, and I thought nothing of it. Turns out that my new friend was jealous that Harlan was going to pay me for promoting him. He even mentioned this to Harlan. Harlan, feeling awkward, told my YouTube friend that he would pay him for some written articles and pictures. This had happened before we left for the trip, but I knew nothing of it until after. Weird, I thought, but whatever. All the while, my YouTube channel kept growing, which meant the comments were coming in abundance.

By this point, the number of haters had increased. Despite facing criticism for taking on sponsorships and being labeled a sellout, I was learning to develop thicker skin. I've always struggled with caring too much about others' opinions of me. In my most successful year yet, I managed to bring in an impressive $600,000. Six hundred thousand dollars. I couldn't believe it. As the success continued, I began buying cars for my family and Will's family. I was able to help out everyone I could financially, and it brought me immense joy to do so. Additionally, I now had an unending supply of Percocet.

I moved into Will's parents' house full-time. Their eating habits were vastly different from what I had been accustomed to for the first 16 years of my life. Living with Nan, there was a lot of home-cooked, healthy meals. However, entering Will's household was a different experience. Food was purchased daily instead of the weekly grocery shopping routine I was used to. Every day, her dad would go to the cheapest grocery store to feed a large household. They never asked me for much, so I can't complain too much. However, the lack of food in the house and the quality of what was available was suboptimal. It often came down to junk food, chips, or Pop-Tarts for breakfast with Pepsi to wash it down, or cheap pork chops for supper. I didn't complain. As a young man not accustomed to such freedoms, it felt like a luxury to have sunflower seeds for breakfast! This routine continued throughout the entire time I lived with them, spanning over years.

My first problem was a hemorrhoid. Just a little pain in the ass. It absolutely sucked. I rode my bike everywhere, and it got worse. Over the years, I got into snacking all night long, always with the munchies. You'd never tell by looking at me, but I ate junk food non-stop for years. I got used to living with it. Then, still eating like an idiot, I was diagnosed with IBS (irritable bowel syndrome). A nervous stomach, internal hemorrhoids, and diarrhea would occur whenever I got stimulated or excited. I could be planning a canoe trip, looking at maps, and even years later, I would have to run, not walk, to the toilet. Dealing with these issues for over 15 years led me to start taking Percs, as I knew they could help with binding you up.

They had a profound impact on me. I was immediately drawn to them and found myself hooked for years. Despite attempts to quit, I would often relapse. Transitioning to Tylenol 1s proved to be even more challenging to break free from compared to Percs.

I had a hookup from an older guy on my street who had them prescribed but never took them. I would buy 500 at a time and end up consuming them regularly. The fear of running out before getting more was the only thing that made me ration them. This behaviour started to affect my canoe trips. While I could last all day on them, not having enough to last the entire trip would prevent me from going. I was deeply hooked. I found solace in Percs as they regulated my bowel movements, allowing me to engage in activities like map-reading without the fear of diarrhea. However, I eventually slipped into heavy drinking, justifying it as a reward for my hard work and success. This led me down a path where money was no longer a concern, indulging in cocaine and alcohol at night, while relying on Percs during the day. This pattern persisted for a few years until I discovered that Isaac was also struggling with similar issues, and we ended up doing it together.

I lived this way while continuing to create videos on YouTube, which kept growing. In 2017, we discovered that Will was pregnant again. She had left her job when my income started to increase. Our daughter Emmie was in grade school, and Will desired to be at home when Emmie returned from school. I shared the same sentiment and was delighted and proud to be able to make that a reality. We were financially comfortable. Will was not only a skilled aesthetician but also an exceptional mother. We consider ourselves very fortunate.

This time, we had a gender reveal party. Will had been carrying this pregnancy differently, mentioning that it felt different too. I was convinced we were expecting a boy. Abby already had a second girl, and Bri, Will's sister, had two girls of her own. It was about time for a boy! That year, we had both families gathered at our home on Rankin. Will was a few months pregnant. Everyone attended except for Isaac. And then, pink! Another girl! I couldn't believe it at first, but I was filled with joy. Emerald would have a lifelong companion. I didn't want her to grow up alone. I was grateful for Abby and Isaac. In this world, who else can you trust but

CHAPTER 5

family? Parents age and pass on, but siblings are your lifelong friends and family.

I had been on a solo trip, and as usual, after four or five days, my brain started to function better than ever. I think the most clearly out there. During this time, I came up with the name Autumn. She was expected to be born in September, my favourite time of the year, and I believe it is a very beautiful name. I also made the decision to quit using drugs to become a better father, work harder, and not be enslaved by the opioids that took the life of the best man at my wedding and many others. I cleaned up completely, which was a challenging process. The lifestyle was readily available, given the money I had and the easy access to Percs on my street. Opioids are malevolent; they transform you into someone you never thought you could become. I did it for my daughters, for my career, and most importantly, for my love of the outdoors. Being free from the grip of addiction allowed me to truly enjoy camping once again.

What a fucking day! I've been travelling for 12.5 hours today. Currently, I find myself winded on Lower Wabakimi Lake, just two kilometres away from my intended destination for a two-night stay over and a much-needed rest day. That was the plan. Last night, I stayed at Bruce's world-class site. This morning, I set off just after 7:00am, navigating through a series of small, buggy, and rarely used portages back to back. Half of the day was spent in a beautiful area, although it was tight and rocky. Unfortunately, the bugs overtook any sense of calm, peace, or enjoyment. I found myself yearning for a big open lake with a breeze. Finally, around 1:30, I reached such a spot. I took a break on an island site for a hot lunch, my first warm lunch other than fish on this trip. It was rejuvenating and much-needed. I could only stay for 30 minutes as the bugs were relentless. I can't even sit still right now due to the incessant black flies. I have to stop writing for now. I'll be back later, hopefully at camp in my tent.

I didn't make it far as the waves were crashing over my boat, making it quite precarious. I even had to put on my life jacket. I only managed to travel about 300 metres from my initial stop. Surprisingly, the bugs are just as relentless here, despite the strong wind. It's so strange. Just two days ago, I thought the black flies were on their way out, but today was the absolute worst. My face, forehead, neck, and ears are covered in welts.

I hurried to set up my tent in the midst of the strong winds. Despite my efforts to be swift, there are still about 50 bugs inside my tent. Enduring over 12 hours of travel, navigating challenging portages, and braving strong winds on vast lakes, all to secure a rest day tomorrow. I recalled an island named Stonehenge, a place I've visited twice before, once with Kyle last month. I wanted it for its spaciousness, offering ample room to relax and a flat area perfect for pitching my tent. Stonehenge seemed like the ideal place for a rest day, but sometimes plans don't unfold as expected. It's another valuable life lesson — we can't always plan too far in advance because life happens.

I'm just rolling with it. I'm camped here on the side of a lake, its not Stonehenge but the ground is flat enough. It's 9:00pm, and I had a cookie for supper. I plan to sleep in tomorrow and then paddle the two or so kilometres to Stonehenge to set up camp there. It will still be a rest day, just a short paddle of 30 to 50 minutes.

Today was the longest, hardest, and most frustrating day yet. Oh, there's also smoke from a forest fire here now. I was concerned because it came in so fast, but Bruce says it's from Manitoba, so that's a relief.

This trip is only the second time I've been out in the wilderness longer than this. My first extended trip was twelve days in Wabakimi, where I was picked up on the 12th day. Another memorable journey was a 10-day trip with just 10 items, ending early on the 10th day.

The initial week of this current adventure flew by, but now I find myself eagerly counting the days until I see my girls again. Despite the fun, I can't shake the feeling of missing them and the weight of being away for too long. And despite the emotional rollercoaster today, I know I need this time for myself. The sound of black flies hitting the tent mimics the patter of rain. Time to put this down.

We stayed in touch with Tammy and Jake from Sault Ste. Marie. They visited us for a couple of nights when Will was first pregnant with Autumn. They had purchased a house outside the Soo and were truly enjoying it. During a solo trip, I came to the realization that we needed to move out of Windsor for the sake of my career. I also felt strongly that I didn't want to raise my girls there. I also needed to get away from all the people and all the drugs that came with them.

In the summer of 2018, Tammy called. She said that her neighbour, who was American and never there, was planning to put the house for sale. She knew that we had been looking. So Emerald, Will and myself took a drive up to the Soo to visit Tammy and Jake and check out the house next door. We all fell in love with it. The property was by the water, spanning two acres. It was a beautiful place, nicer than anything we had ever owned. Given that it was 2018 and the real estate boom hadn't yet occurred, the price was just right. It felt like fate. Everything fell into place seamlessly and swiftly. We sold our Windsor house for double what I had paid, and I was absolutely stoked.

CHAPTER 6

Will gave birth to our youngest daughter (you will always be my baby), and she was incredible right from the start. The moment I laid eyes on her, tears welled up, much like when Emmie was born. This birth was more challenging, yet again Will opted for a drug-free, all-natural delivery. It was intense; I was there in the room once more. At one point, they had Will on all fours during the process. She nearly crushed my hand, gripping it with incredible strength. Autumn was a perfect little girl, albeit with a slightly smaller nose - a detail that made me chuckle. Right away, I noticed that the inner corner of her right eye seemed almost hollow, lacking the usual pink fleshy part. I mentioned this to the doctor, but it felt like he dismissed it. After four surgeries later, I can't help but think I was onto something. Despite it all, Autumn was an exceptionally easy baby.

In October, our family made the move up north. We travelled in two vehicles - Will and Emmie in her Jeep Liberty, and Autumn, Scout, and myself in the Grand Cherokee. Along for the ride were two cats and two pet rats. Thanks to Will's sister's boyfriend, John, whose parents owned a trucking company, John and a driver transported our belongings for us. Just as we were loading the final items into the Jeep, my neighbour, who had Percs, approached me and offered some to take with me. Thinking it might be wise to have them on hand "just in case," I purchased them for the first time in a year. Unfortunately, this decision led me back into addiction just as we were moving away. We braved a blizzard during our late October drive north, which served as a harsh reality check. That winter, we faced over 10 feet of snow - quite the adjustment for us.

🔥🔥🔥

DAY 11 OF 19 — JULY 6, 2025 — 10:45AM

Finally, the rest day I've been waiting for! Day 11 marks my first attempt to relax since Day 9 at that "world-class" site. It was a letdown. The site was buggy and small, located far from the water on a tiny, murky lake. After nine hours of paddling and portaging to reach it, I felt the urge to leave as soon as I woke up.

To navigate through some of the most underused, hard-to-find portages, I found myself in and out of the boat what felt like a hundred times. Near the end of my day, I took a wrong turn, costing me almost an hour of backtracking to locate my portage. Then, I got windbound just four kilometres away from my destination, Stonehenge. This island offered a bug-free environment, as far as I can recall, having camped there during a previous trip with Mike and revisiting it last month with Kyle.

While navigating through the portages, I was constantly harassed by black flies, undoubtedly the worst part of the entire journey. It took me 10 days before they really got to me. Now, my face resembles that of the Elephant Man, Joseph Merrick. The situation was so dire that I couldn't even wait out the wind on the lakeside where I had to make an emergency stop. The bugs were relentless, persisting even in the gusting winds — truly the worst of both worlds! Waking up this morning, my face was unbelievably swollen!

Knowing that Stonehenge was just a short paddle away and the wind had yet to pick up, I quickly packed up camp without breakfast and set off on the paddle towards the open water. It was a vast lake. Unlike the previous night where I was nearly capsized, with water splashing over the bow, this time I encountered only a gentle rocking of waves, creating a completely different atmosphere.

As I was breaking down camp at 6:00am, I found myself once again being swarmed by black flies, their bites targeting my face. I realized the importance of taking a break from these relentless bugs, as my intolerance for black flies could easily escalate into a state of lethargy, with spiderweb-like blood tracks up my swollen legs — a situation I definitely wanted to avoid, especially during a three-week solo mission!

I swiftly made my way over to Stonehenge in just an hour. There, I set up camp and prepared some scrambled eggs from Happy Yak. While the name might be spot on, I have to admit, it was a bit gross but definitely easy and filling.

After a late morning spent setting up a comfortable new camp, I took the time to hang everything out to dry — food, gear, everything that had gotten damp. I relaxed, took some Benadryl, smoked a bowl outside, revelling in the fact that I didn't have to hide from the bugs because there were none around. Just four kilometres away from where I had woken up being attacked, I found myself in paradise. No bugs, just a gentle breeze and the warm sun shining down on me. This was exactly where I had been longing to be for the past three days — a place of rest and relaxation!

After 10 full days of travel, I had done at least six-plus hours of daily paddling, except for day two where I managed maybe five. Days nine and ten were particularly long, with nine and twelve hours of paddling, respectively. I truly feel like I've earned this rest day! It's currently 10:45am, and I decided to turn on my Garmin inReach just to let Will know that I'm doing well and taking a break.

At 9:30am, I received a text from Bruce informing me that there is a fire south of me on an island and a massive one just to the east. I smell no smoke, nor see any in the sky. The sun casts a very strange orange glow, but none of that smoke stuff is happening here. So the wind must be in my favour. I'll inquire tonight and see what Ol' Brucie says.

For now, I am going to enjoy a day of rest: writing, relaxing, and maybe swimming. I haven't eaten fish in the past two days, I've been too busy moving. I didn't even take out my rods from their holding place in my canoe at all yesterday. Not the norm for me!

During that winter, we were hit with over 10 feet of snow. It felt like being thrown into the deep end with a brand new baby and no support from family or friends. The town was an hour away, and the closest gas station was a 30-minute drive, but we knew it was meant to be. Our neighbours from the Soo in 2007 had become our next-door neighbours in 2018.

With the harsh winter, readjusting to life up north and Emmie changing schools, it all took some time to settle. We even considered moving back to Windsor, but we persevered, and before long, it felt like home. I could easily embark on trips from there, without enduring the eight-hour-plus drives to reach Algonquin. Stepping out my door with Scout or my new 4-wheeler, I could camp anywhere. Crown land was abundant, a new experience for me!

Scout and I explored for about a month, then in late November, he started acting strange, lethargic. I didn't think much of it because he was 11. I had always hoped he'd live a long life for a large breed dog. I'd always say, "If I get 12 years out of him, I'll be happy." He shit in the house that day, something he never, ever did. He was so well-behaved, except when he would steal my firewood as I split it. But that's a great memory now.

I got mad at him and yelled at him for defecating inside. Later that day, he was still not himself, and I started to worry. I felt around him and noticed that his glands under his ears and around his jaws were swollen. I literally thought he had a cold and his glands were swollen. I always did call him part human. The next day he was no better, so I called the vet. I brought him in, and pretty quickly after checking him out, the vet told me that he had lymphoma. It was a serious, fast-acting type of cancer, and he had about two weeks to live.

CHAPTER 6

I couldn't believe my ears; he was perfectly fine just two days ago. I couldn't comprehend how it all happened. The vet explained the situation to me, but I could barely hear him over my tears as I held onto Scout. After asking what I could do to help him, I learned that it was just a matter of time before he would be gone.

Devastated, I drove home with Scout for the last time ever, crying the whole way. Will was distraught, as was Emmie. Scout was such a huge part of our lives, a real member of the family. It hurt knowing that Emerald was about to feel real loss. I was going to lose my best friend. This dog was irreplaceable. I vowed to do everything I could. I thought that I had saved Hershey's life when the vet said that I couldn't. I could make Scout's life last as long as possible and keep him healthy and happy. I did tons of research, like I had for Hershey.

I learned about the potential benefits of Rick Simpson Oil or full-spectrum CBD oil in treating or slowing down the progression of lymphoma. Some pet owners have shared success stories of using these oils with their dogs. Given my familiarity with smoking and oil-making, I understood the importance of properly heating the oil for decarboxylation to enhance its absorption in the body. THC is not safe for dogs, so DO NOT do this. He was about to die, and I was desperate. After trial and error with dosages, I finally got it right. Half of a grain of rice size, administered in his mouth like a pill, would help him sleep. I switched to a raw meat diet for him, providing a variety. Miraculously, he ended up living another month and a half longer than expected. We got to spend Christmas with him.

One morning, he was back to having accidents inside, lying on the kitchen floor. I struggled to get him up, our eyes meeting in understanding. I knew the time had come. Making the decision was not difficult for me, as I was well-informed about his condition. I recognized that it was the end, and I couldn't bear to see him suffer. I knew I had to let him go that day. Oh man...

I called the vet, and we prepared a blanket in the Cherokee. Carrying him to the car was a heavy task. Will and I drove together, leaving Tammy to stay with the girls. The journey felt endless. He had another accident in the back seat, leaving a lasting reminder. Despite our best efforts to clean, we would catch a whiff of Scout's "goodbye gift" whenever it got hot for a year after. Arriving at the vet, I carried him, knowing that easing his pain was the only way to help him. I really wanted it to happen quickly. It wasn't physically hard but most definitely one of the worst things I've ever had to do.

As the vet entered and informed me that the moment was near, he offered for me to step out of the room. I couldn't fathom leaving Scout in his final moments. I held him close, trying to remain composed so as not to distress him, though he seemed to understand. His unwavering gaze locked with mine. The vet administered the shot swiftly, and his body relaxed, going limp. It was a difficult but necessary act, bringing peace to him in the end. They tried to tell me to leave, but I stayed, holding his head and hugging him around the neck as he lay on the sterile silver table, not in the woods. I hoped he remembered our time in the woods and all the fun we shared. Just like that, he was gone. I left, feeling a mix of relief that he was no longer in pain but also completely lost once again.

I felt abandoned once more, this time by another close male, even if canine. The drive home was difficult; Will and I just cried and cried. He was our original baby, a once-in-a-lifetime dog. He helped shape my career, saved my baby's life and brought Will and I closer together.

While I was away filming *Alone*, Will took Scout for a regular walk around the block with Emerald on Windsor's west end. She approached a house with an American bulldog like usual. On this occasion, the gate was open and the bulldog lunged at Emmie. Scout ended up getting mauled in the face as he used his body to shield Emmie, who remained untouched. Scout, on the other hand, needed stitches. Damn I miss that dog now. Fuck!

I brought Scout from the north to Windsor, then back up north, only for him to pass away a couple of months later. Where is the justice in that? Grieving while on Percs was incredibly tough. I had to drive back to Windsor for more. I had plans to wean myself off, something I had successfully done years before. However, after Scout's passing, I no longer wanted to come off them. The medication subdued my true feelings, even from myself.

I drove down to get more; I did that a couple of times. With around a million subscribers on YouTube, Shawn, as mentioned earlier, invited me to his cabin, which he had now centred his YouTube channel around. Gone were the days of canoe tripping and fishing videos; it was all about cabin building now. Doug joined us as we all watched my subscriber count roll over to one million. One million subscribers - what a ride! Not many outdoor channels had reached that level of success at the time. I felt proud and elated about it. Shawn created a video about our visit titled "One Million Subs." However, there was no mention of the million subscribers belonging to me, nor was there a picture of me in the thumbnail. It seemed odd that he was using it to attract views once more, but I didn't think much of it at the time.

I decided to wean off the Percs once again, mainly because they were interfering with my camping plans. Doug and I embarked on a memorable journey, crossing Algonquin Park from west to east by canoe and portage. It was an incredible trip. Swift seemed pleased with our adventure and offered me a boat for free. I loved my original boat so much that I got the same model in green this time. I agreed to sell my OG original red one to my buddy Doug. I was genuinely excited for him to have one.

Doug and I were like polar opposites. Come to think of it, Kyle and I are as well, but we make great friends. I knew Doug could keep up with my pace; he even set the pace at times! We had a fantastic rapport. The idea of camping in solo boats together was thrilling. I sold it to him for $1,000, a number he had mentioned. I got my new green one with the words "The Emerald Grace" on it for Emmie. Doug and I embarked on numerous canoe trips and backpacking adventures together. Now, I have a fleet of Swift boats, so they must really appreciate the arrangement we have.

Unfortunately, Shawn and I had a falling out. I discovered that he was quite sneaky and underhanded. It seemed like he always believed that others were plotting against him or had hidden agendas. I playfully tagged him in a steak challenge online, which was a men's health challenge organized by another YouTube channel. During my challenge, I wore a Red Lake Outdoors green hoodie that Harlan had kindly given to me. I particularly enjoyed the hoodie because it fit me perfectly. Being on the smaller side, most clothing items tend to be too big for my frame, but this one was just right. I wore it frequently, including in the video, a detail I might have overlooked if it weren't for what I'm about to share with you.

I nominated Shawn and another guy to participate in the video challenge. I believed it would be a positive change to offer him some new content ideas beyond just focusing on cabin-related videos. His channel had experienced rapid growth, but he expressed to me his frustration that it had become predominantly cabin content. While I was in the midst of nominating him, I accidentally burped. I was enjoying a steak outdoors during a camping trip. Personally, I never really pay much attention to natural bodily functions like burping or farting when I'm outside. However, my unintentional burp ended up offending him.

A few days later, he released his own video without mentioning me at all. I could sense that it was intentional from the way he said, "I was nominated by someone," carefully avoiding mentioning my name. Despite our years of friendship, I was deeply puzzled and hurt by this turn of events. Eventually, I decided to call him and directly ask what was going on.

He was furious with me. He accused me of burping on purpose and wearing that sweater because he and Harlan were in a feud at that time. He claimed that I deliberately chose to wear it to provoke him while nominating him. I was completely taken aback by his accusations. Despite the tension, we attempted to move past it. I reassured him that I had no ill intentions. Why would I even mention his name if I didn't care for him? I wouldn't have made a video involving him if I didn't want him to participate in a community activity. It felt like silly high school drama. This marked the definitive end of our friendship and any potential for future collaborations. I felt overwhelmed with frustration over the situation. Perhaps our personalities simply didn't mesh well. By that point, Kyle had already left, and Doug was down south. The forum had become monotonous, with none of the old crew members present. Still residing up north, I found myself knowing hardly anyone in the area.

By that time, I had immersed myself in frequent camping trips. I even constructed a massive fort in the woods, which became a popular feature on my channel. However, my main focus remained on spending time at home with my wife and two daughters. I steered clear of hard drugs, rarely drank, but was still smoking weed. As usual, I found myself feeling quite bored overall. I longed for a camping companion. Kyle and I continued our tradition of embarking on an annual trip together, a practice we uphold to this very day.

I also had another canoe buddy, Mike Morton. We first crossed paths years ago when I operated my own bushcraft school. He and his brother made the journey to attend a class we hosted in North Bay. Given their proximity to Toronto, I assumed they were eager to learn. Mike and I immediately clicked. He was also a member of the BCUSA forum. We kept in touch and embarked on canoe trips together, typically once a year, a tradition that also continues to this day. We are currently in the midst of planning another trip for this year, and his buddy Adam will be joining us as well.

I found myself without a camping buddy who was always ready to go whenever I was, so I decided I needed a dog to accompany me. I had previously done training with Scout and noticed many working breed dogs during our sessions. One particular Dutch Shepherd caught my eye – a brindle beauty who seemed completely attuned to its owner's every gesture, word, and whistle. I was captivated by the appearance and temperament of the Dutch Shepherd breed. After all these years, with financial stability on my side, the time had come to welcome a new dog into my life. I had my heart set on getting a Dutch Shepherd, and I already had the perfect name in mind. Just like with Scout, I had already chosen the name for my next furry companion. Since he would be joining me on canoe trips, I decided to call him Tripper.

Well, it was quite a surprise to learn that "tripper" is another term for the sexually transmitted infection (STI) gonorrhea in some parts of the world. I discovered this after sharing a video of my puppy. While I didn't mind the coincidence, others found it amusing. My initial search for a Dutch Shepherd breeder in Ontario yielded few results, and I couldn't find any available in Canada in the near future. Eventually, I discovered a breeder in Oklahoma.

The lady's name was Keeley, but I can't recall the kennel name. During our phone conversation, I clearly outlined my preferences - a male Dutch Shepherd puppy, preferably smaller in size, with a brindle coat, and a good listener. I ended up paying a hefty sum, around $5,500 USD, for the puppy and his transportation to Michigan, where I planned to pick him up.

Everything was set in motion, and I was filled with excitement at the thought of welcoming a new companion. The pain of losing Scout still lingered, but the anticipation of a new furry friend helped soothe that sting.

I was leading an active and mostly healthy lifestyle, yet I felt a sense of loneliness without a dog by my side. I desired for my children to experience the joy of growing up with a furry companion, a privilege I never had but always longed for.

The day finally arrived when I drove to the States to bring him home. As I approached the counter, a crate awaited me. The attendant lifted it onto the counter, and as I peered inside, I gently whispered, "Hey buddy. You're home now. Welcome." He whimpered and retreated to the back of the crate, seeking refuge as far away from the door and me as possible. My heart sank, realizing he must have had a distressing experience flying at such a tender age of nine weeks. Later, I discovered that young puppies shouldn't be flown, a mistake or oversight on the breeder's part. As I carried the crate to my truck, I continued to speak in soothing tones, reassuring him that he was safe now. "You're going to have an amazing life, little guy," I whispered, filled with hopeful plans, intentions, and expectations for Tripper.

Tripper proved to be quite a handful right from the beginning. About a week after bringing him home, I embarked on a six-hour drive for a camping trip. Knowing he was still too young for such an adventure, I left Tripper in the care of Will and the kids. Just as I was nearing the camping spot, my phone rang, and it was Will sounding frantic. "I lost Tripper," she exclaimed. "What?" I shouted in disbelief. "How?" Will explained that Tripper had darted outside without a leash, and Emmie had chased after him.

Filled with worry and anger, I was too consumed to hear her words clearly. "I'm coming home now. Call me if you find him. DON'T CHASE HIM!" I bellowed, my voice laced with frustration during the drive back. The weight of the situation pressed heavily on me. I had only just welcomed Tripper into my life, already forming a deep bond with him, envisioning a future filled with adventures. It was heartbreaking that he hadn't even been with us for a week. Throughout the journey home, I pleaded with God, praying for a call to come through, informing me that she had found him. Sadly, the phone remained silent, and my hopes were left unanswered the entire drive home.

I raced home in record time, the sky transitioning into dusk as I arrived. After a brief stop at home, I set off down the road in the direction Will had mentioned he went nearly seven hours earlier. With the windows down, I drove slowly, the darkness of night enveloping the surroundings. Intermittently calling out for him, I spotted a pair of bright, glowing eyes low to the ground on the road, approximately 100 metres ahead of me. Swiftly turning off my truck, I hopped out, a mix of excitement and calmness in my voice as I softly called, "Tripper, here." However, by the time I had stepped out of the truck, he had already darted down one of the long driveways on my street.

The driveway was flanked on both sides by dense, towering trees, casting shadows in the enveloping darkness. Despite the limited visibility, I caught a glimpse of his tail disappearing down a particular drive. Opting for a brisk walk instead of chasing after him, I followed cautiously, determined not to startle him into running off once more. As Tripper vanished from sight, I continued along the driveway, eventually arriving at a summer home that seemed unoccupied at the moment. Without hesitation, I began to explore, making my way to the back of the property.

Approaching the large, low deck, I crouched down to get a better view. Peering around the corner at the back, I spotted him nestled as far back as he could go. In the moonlight, his eyes reflected a soft glow, two small orbs close to the ground. Without hesitation, I began to army crawl towards him, repeating soothing words, "It's okay, bud. I've got you. You're safe," in a calm and reassuring tone. I didn't allow him the opportunity to flee. In what seemed like a split second, I reached out and held him firmly, feeling his small body in my arms. Surprisingly, he didn't struggle or attempt to break free. It was evident that fear had caused him to soil himself, a poignant reminder of his vulnerability. My heart ached for this frightened little soul, igniting a fierce determination to shield him from harm and provide a loving home. This incident only strengthened my resolve to care for him and share countless adventures as a canoe companion.

Blessed with disposable income and seemingly endless resources, I had everything I desired and so much more. My plan was to enlist a professional to train my dog to become the perfect canoe companion. His spirited nature was evident as he interacted with the fire, displaying a fiery enthusiasm that often led him to bark at the flames and playfully nip at the smoke. His exuberance even extended to the point of grabbing burning wood from the fire, risking his whiskers in the process. When it came to being in a canoe, he would tremble uncontrollably. Whether from anticipation or sheer excitement, his behaviour hinted at a deep-seated uneasiness.

I must take responsibility for the oversight; this dog was a working breed. I had envisioned canoe tripping as his calling, a role he could truly thrive in if we had dedicated ourselves to it from the start. Regrettably, I failed to realize that engaging in this activity only once or twice a month wasn't enough to truly qualify it as his primary occupation. Recognizing his need for routine and consistent activity, it became clear that my dog craved a daily purpose. While I envisioned him as a passenger in the canoe, he seemed more inclined to take the lead and paddle it himself. A true working dog at heart, his strong instincts were accompanied by some challenging behavioural issues. Acknowledging the need for professional help, I embarked on a thorough research journey to find the best solution within a reasonable distance. After careful consideration, I discovered that the top-rated option in the vicinity was Sunnybrook Boarding Kennels in Barrie.

It was a decision to entrust my dog to a comprehensive training program, a "leave the dog there" arrangement where I would return after two months to a fully trained companion. During our initial conversation, the staff at Sunnybrook Boarding Kennels assured me that their experienced trainer, who had personal experience with Dutch Shepherds and Malinois, would be an ideal fit for Tripper. This assurance put my mind at ease, knowing that Tripper was in capable hands. At around one and a half years old, Tripper began his training journey under the guidance of the skilled trainer. The trainer's expertise and rapport with working breeds instilled confidence in me. The investment of $6,500 for the two-month training program felt like a worthwhile commitment to Tripper's development and well-being.

CHAPTER 6

I agreed to return four times during those two months for training sessions under the trainer's guidance. I remained true to my commitment, dedicated to transforming Tripper into a well-behaved, trained, and contented dog. Together, we covered the basics and addressed my specific training goals. Additionally, I brought a canoe to the facility for the trainer to use with Tripper. On paper, the plan appeared to be effective and promising. Tripper excelled in basic commands such as come, sit, down, and stay - showcasing his aptitude for learning. Prior to his training program, I had successfully taught him the command "boat," which meant hopping into the canoe. This training session was even documented in a YouTube video, highlighting my proficiency in dog training. Tripper consistently proved to be an attentive and obedient companion. My ultimate goal was to help him become calmer, alleviating any stress, anxiety, and nervousness he may have experienced. I believed that providing him with a structured environment, like the two-month program at Sunnybrook Kennels, would greatly contribute to achieving this goal.

I was truly amazed by Tripper's transformation upon his return at the end of the training program. His responsiveness was outstanding - a simple command like "down" would prompt him to drop to the floor with unwavering dedication. He gave his all, putting in 110% effort in everything he did. Tripper's overall behaviour had significantly improved, making him a better companion in every way. Taking him on a canoe trip post-training was a delightful experience, as he displayed improved behaviour compared to before. Surprisingly, he showed a gentle and caring side when interacting with Autumn. Tripper's newfound reliability meant he no longer required a tie-out when outdoors, and he eagerly accompanied me on all my trips to the woods. Despite some lingering issues post-training, my love for him only grew stronger, appreciating the progress he had made and the bond we shared.

Once again, I was away for just one day, not far, when Will called me in a panic. I could tell between sobs that Tripper had broken his leg. But it turned out to be much worse - he had shattered his elbow. The family was outside, and he was in the woods in front. "All of a sudden," Will said, "I heard him crying like I have never heard a dog cry before. I got up to see, and he came hobbling on three legs, his front left held up in the air, crying. He collapsed in my lap, so I carried him inside." The vet explained that he had a degenerative bone disease due to poor breeding practices.

So, there were surgeries we could try, but the vet warned that another break could happen again and it would not be cheap. Anxiously, I agreed. We also needed to consult an out-of-town specialist for the procedures. I obtained the doctor's number and had a conversation with him. Tripper would require a titanium plate, screws, and pins to stabilize his joint. Additionally, we would need to plan to preemptively break the other one and fix it before it breaks on its own. The vet understood that we lived a camping lifestyle, and another accident could occur out in the bush. He made a valid point. The total cost was over $15,000, which was a significant amount. Despite the financial strain, my love for Tripper and my desire for him to recover and have a companion pushed me to agree to the surgeries. The first surgery was performed promptly, followed by a long period of rest and extensive home care. Gradually, Tripper started to put weight on the operated leg. It was a challenging time with constant oozing, draining, and changing of gauze. We knew we would have to go through it all over again for the other leg.

Tripper's behaviour changed significantly after the surgeries. He became very fearful of things, shaking like a leaf in the truck, a behaviour he had never exhibited before. He started seeking solitude in his crate more often. The trip to Espanola for his second surgery seemed to have a profound psychological impact on him, causing him to lose trust in us. I dedicated a lot of time to working with him once he had fully recovered. I made a conscious effort to take him out to the Fort frequently to help him regain his confidence and trust but it wasn't sustainable and we were spiralling hard. He was in pain and he was painful to watch. I just wanted this nightmare to end.

BY NOW MY YOUTUBE career was thriving. I mean it was really thriving. I was gaining more recognition than ever before. I had already appeared on the show *Alone*. My kids were doing well, my wife was happy and I was drug-free (except for the occasional indulgence when we visited Windsor, which usually involved one night of drinking and coke - as a special treat, of course). Life was truly good.

I was approached by a National Geographic production person who had seen Tripper and me on my YouTube channel. They were casting for a new show featuring people and their dogs. Was I interested? Absolutely! Ever since my experience on *Alone*, I had been eager to get back on TV. I had even tried applying to a few unconventional ads in the hopes of getting back on screen. I believed that promoting my YouTube channel on TV would undoubtedly give it a significant boost. This opportunity felt right up my alley, so I enthusiastically agreed. They informed me that a film crew would be coming to my house to shoot the first part of the show. The highlight would be a week-long canoe trip to test if Tripper could handle it now. Winter camping would provide a change of scenery and a new camping experience. I was thrilled! Another chance at TV, this time with my dog by my side - it felt like the perfect fit!

CHAPTER 7

The family geared up for our second TV appearance - and Autumn's first experience with it. As the crew arrived, we exchanged introductions, and I found them all to be cool dudes. What truly took me by surprise was the moment they shared that they had previously worked as part of Les Stroud's (Survivorman) B-crew. They were the go-to team for Les whenever he needed camera operators for drop-offs, pick-ups, b-roll, or safety. It was a surreal full-circle moment for me – my ultimate hero, my favourite outdoor personality, the very reason for my passion, Les Stroud's former camera crew was now on board to film our adventure? Mind blown! BOOM!

My joy was short-lived. The initial shoot at the house went smoothly. However, Tripper's leg was still recovering from the second surgery. He continued to hobble, his leg swollen, and he appeared calmer while lying down. The second shoot, where we embarked on a canoe trip, proved to be challenging. Tripper managed well on the portage trails, but once in the canoe, he would whimper loudly and shake uncontrollably.

During the campfire at night, Tripper reverted to his usual neurotic self, enthusiastically grabbing and barking at the flames. When I attempted to fish from the canoe as the crew requested, he nearly tipped the canoe in his eagerness to chase after the lure. I felt frustrated by the situation and somewhat embarrassed. Despite the challenges, we completed the entire trip, and surprisingly, Tripper seemed to improve as the journey progressed. On the last night of the shoot, we arrived at the vehicles late, opting to sleep in our trucks, with Tripper off-leash the entire time. Standing in the bed of my raised truck, I commanded, "Up." Without hesitation, Tripper jumped up, settled down, and slept next to me throughout the night. In the morning, he was still by my side, a moment that felt like progress. We ventured out in the winter with the crew and repeated the trip. Unfortunately, Tripper's behaviour was still challenging, mirroring our previous experience.

For about 12 years, I consistently maintained my winter camping routines and continued filming videos year-round. I believed that this dedication was what kept people engaged with my content. Adapting to the changing seasons, I showcased camping, home life, and canoe tripping videos that resonated with my audience. Watching other canoe camping videos in winter often left me yearning for my next adventure, even though it seemed so distant. One video that caught my attention featured a guy camping with a black lab, a scenario I found appealing, especially when combined with canoe camping. By this point, I was growing weary of YouTube; it seemed like everyone was just following the same formula. Creating content had started to feel more like a job than a passion. However, don't get me wrong, my love for canoe tripping remained unwavering. In fact, as I write this, I'm on Day 11 of a solo trip, my fourth or fifth journey this season. I still find immense joy in both experiencing these adventures and capturing them on film, whether it's to educate others or allow them to live vicariously through my experiences.

During the winter months when the allure of staying home beckoned, I would deliberately wait for a blizzard to appear on my radar. This strategic move allowed me to venture out camping in the midst of the snowstorm, aiming to create content that could potentially go viral and generate significant income. Surprisingly, this tactic continued to yield results beyond my wildest expectations. The peak of my earnings consistently occurred around Christmas, particularly during the months of October, November, and December. In January, payments would significantly decrease.

In 2019, I managed to make $150,000 in those three lucrative months, allowing us to live quite comfortably. However, I must admit, I was not wise with my newfound wealth, having never experienced such financial abundance before. I indulged the kids, splurged on vacations, treated myself to a new truck, and invested a large sum into a monster 4-wheeler, a decision that attracted criticism when featured in one of my videos. The allure of those hefty paycheques became somewhat addictive, as I became increasingly aware of what resonated with my audience on my channel.

One day at home near springtime, I was checking my messages on Instagram, a routine I often followed. As I scrolled through messages from people I didn't follow, a familiar profile picture caught my eye - it was the guy with the black lab. He had reached out a few days earlier, inviting me to join him on a canoe trip with his dog. Given that I didn't have any canoe buddies at the time and knowing that he seemed capable in the wilderness, a significant advantage since I had observed him in action, I felt intrigued by the opportunity. It was indeed a smart vetting practice on YouTube to ensure he wasn't a bit off. I enthusiastically agreed to the invitation, looking forward to the adventure. The guy with the black lab, who had a modest following on his channel, expressed his surprise that I responded to his message. He had simply taken a chance and reached out. Our connection blossomed quickly, leading to a budding friendship.

I had to leave Tripper behind as he had become aggressive towards other dogs and was displaying unruly behaviour, even growling at Will. Though worried, I had to focus on my duties. This situation led my friend, his dog, and me to spend a significant amount of time together. My friend's non-traditional work schedule, stemming from his discharge from the Army due to an injury, perfectly matched mine, creating a unique bond between us.

I led a home-centred life and would go camping about four times a month. Much of that time was spent with my friend and his dog. Tripper's behaviour continued to deteriorate, causing me concern as I had to leave for several days at a time or even longer. I feared that something might happen in my absence. I attempted to address the issue by staying home and working with Tripper, as well as hiring another trainer to assist at the house. In total, I ended up spending over $30,000 on Tripper. By the way, did I mention that I was careless with money? I never thought it would end.

After exhausting all my efforts with no success, I ultimately made the difficult decision to rehome Tripper. I had tried everything I could, investing not just money but also time, effort, love, and compassion. I believed that the best course of action was to find a new home for him with someone who understands the breed and could provide him with the good life he deserved.

I immediately thought of the trainer from Barrie. He had expressed his fondness for Tripper and mentioned wanting a Dutchie for his teenage son. He had even told me to reach out if I ever considered rehoming Tripper. Although I had initially brushed off his offer, now I found myself calling his number. Unfortunately, his response was, "No, not interested, already got one." I respected his decision. I thought of all the dog people that I knew. I reached out to them through calls, emails, and texts, hoping to find someone willing to take Tripper who would be prepared for a Dutch at that time. I wanted to be selective and ensure he went to a good home. I extended my search to all the working breed enthusiasts I could think of or find. Unfortunately, I received minimal responses, and some of the replies I did get were "No."

One day, while I was outside splitting firewood, Tripper nipped at Autumn's face. She had approached him as she always did, to sit and watch TV. When Will informed me of the incident, my heart sank. I realized he had to leave. Despite the significant investment of $30,000 in him, my family's safety came first. It was a tough decision, as we all loved him dearly and didn't want to part ways with him.

After pondering for a few days, I made the difficult decision. On a day when I knew the family would be away all day, Tripper and I visited our favourite spot, the Fort in the woods. We strolled around for a couple of hours as I weighed my options. Following our walk, we quietly got into my truck, and I drove him to the animal shelter. It was a heart-wrenching moment. I felt terrible, the weight of the decision heavy on my heart. I deeply regret everything. I regret the decision to bring him into our lives, not being more patient with him, acquiring him online, and ultimately having to take him away from our family. The entire experience was incredibly painful for all of us, including Tripper. I feel immense guilt for abandoning that poor dog, knowing firsthand the pain of being left behind.

When I returned home, Will could see right through me, as she always does. After spending over half a lifetime together, she has a way of understanding my emotions. She sensed my distress. I took her to our bedroom and poured out the truth, breaking down in tears. A week later, I mustered the courage to tell the kids. Surprisingly, they seemed oblivious to Tripper's absence. "Have you guys noticed that Tripper isn't here?" I asked. "Oh yeah!" they replied in unison. Autumn was now old enough to speak, and she started talking early too! I explained to them that Tripper was always anxious and not enjoying his time with us. I shared that I found a farmer who had other animals for Tripper to play with and run around freely all day. Initially, they felt sad for a few hours, but then they seemed to accept the situation and moved on.

I fabricated a story on YouTube, claiming that Tripper had passed away due to surgery complications because I felt like a failure, and the negative comments on YouTube are hurtful. My intention was to protect myself and my family. I regret deceiving everyone, but at that moment, I felt it was necessary for my well-being. Dealing with the guilt was challenging, and I resorted to this as my coping mechanism. I felt ashamed of the situation - the financial burden, the surgeries - it all weighed heavily on me. Having lived my adult life in front of a camera as an outdoorsman, I found myself at a loss for words. What was I going to say?

Feeling the pressure to maintain visibility and relevance in the online world, I realized that being forgotten was a real possibility. Balancing camping trips, raising my two daughters with Will, and managing a YouTube channel became my daily routine. Alongside these commitments, I ventured into a couple of side projects. One of them was BAM SON! spice rub, a fantastic camp seasoning that gained popularity and sold successfully. We also created merchandise that resonated with our audience and sold well. I collaborated with a clothing company called RevolutionRace, who provided us with boxes of clothing for both me and Will, and compensated us generously for about two years. Additionally, I delved into the world of camping gear, introducing camping grills, signature knives, and cooking pots made of titanium for the optimal strength-to-weight ratio for camping enthusiasts. I also had the opportunity to collaborate on my own backpack design with The Hidden Woodsman. There may be more ventures that I am overlooking, but these were some of the exciting projects I was involved in.

One day, Kyle called from California. He was getting married and asked if I would stand in for his wedding. Overwhelmed with honour and emotion, I tearfully said, "Yes! Of course!" Will and I arranged for plane tickets, and my mom and Joe came up to watch the kids. The experience was wonderful, and I cherished every moment, feeling closer to Kyle than ever before. When I spoke with his parents, they expressed how much my friendship meant to Kyle and how we had become good buddies. It was truly heartwarming to be a part of such a special occasion. Kyle had other very nice guy friends, but none of them camped like we did. It was a special bond, and I agreed with them. I felt so honoured to stand for him, and we all had a great time celebrating his wedding.

After the wedding, Will and I rented a car to drive along the coast back to San Francisco, where we would catch our flight home. The scenery was breathtaking, unlike anything we had seen before. I had visited Kyle once before, years ago, but that trip had taken us to the mountains, not the ocean. This time, we indulged in more touristy activities like marvelling at giant sequoias and driving up a small mountain, making the journey even more memorable. Our night in San Francisco was truly an experience to remember! The city's eclectic atmosphere was evident as we strolled through the streets. From the sight of luxury cars like Lamborghinis on one street to witnessing unfortunate scenes like someone defecating in public on the next, it was a stark contrast that left us feeling a mix of awe and sadness. It was a moment that made us realize the diverse and sometimes challenging realities that exist within a bustling city like San Francisco - far removed from the Canadian wilderness I was accustomed to.

Back at home, still enjoying the company of my black lab buddy, Richard, a full year had passed since I had to part ways with Tripper. Watching my friend with his dog reignited a longing in me for a furry companion of my own. However, I felt hesitant about getting another dog after my previous experience. I had rushed into getting Tripper shortly after Scout's passing, attempting to fill the void left behind. I was determined not to repeat that mistake again.

I found myself casually browsing online for dogs available in Ontario. I had narrowed down my search to a mix breed, leaning towards something like a Shepherd mix. The idea of a German Shepherd/Labrador mix sounded ideal to me. While I had always dreamed of having a white Shepherd, they were hard to come by at the time, and I preferred not to focus on a specific breed or purebred. I had a few options in mind but hesitated for a while, afraid of making the wrong choice when it came to selecting a new furry companion. The dogs I had my eye on seemed to get adopted quickly, time and time again. This pattern continued for a while. Will was aware of my longing for a dog, and we both understood that Tripper was a challenging exception, but we were confident in our ability to train a dog. We had previously gotten Emerald a dog named Beauty, and we enjoyed her company for nearly a year before Tripper left our lives.

Will finally encouraged me, saying, "If you really want a buddy, just get one." Despite my fears and past experiences, I knew deep down that I truly wanted a furry companion. After some searching, I came across an

Australian Shepherd/Border Collie mix, a blend of two breeds I adored. The mix seemed to have the perfect size for canoe trips, a great temperament, and was known to be good around kids. Excited about this find, I placed a $500 deposit and reached out to the owners, expressing my intention to choose one in person. Their response was a simple, "Ok." I failed to follow up with them; my uncertainty about the breed choices held me back. I left behind the $500 deposit without reaching out again. Regrettably, the same scenario repeated with another Collie mix, another $500 down the drain, and once more, no communication from my end. It was all on me. Feeling frustrated with myself, I eventually decided to give up the search.

During a camping trip with my Richard and his well-behaved dog, Cooper, I couldn't help but notice the strong bond between them. Cooper's obedience and love for his owner were truly inspiring, and it made me realize how much I longed for that connection. That moment solidified my decision - I was getting a dog. After an extensive search, I stumbled upon a new post from North Bay featuring a litter of puppies, complete with pictures of both the pups and their parents. The dad was a unique German Shepherd/Husky mix that resembled a Rottweiler mutt, while the mom was a small, sweet-looking German Shepherd. Among the litter of pups, they all took after their dad—black with dark brown markings, floppy ears, and a slightly pudgy build, except for one special pup. This little one stood out with its all-white fur, a touch of grey down its back, a pink nose, and two upright satellite dish ears! It was the closest thing to a white German Shepherd that I could have hoped for.

Now, the Husky part scared me after my experience working in two pet stores, dealing with all types of dogs in person and hearing horror stories shared by customers. Huskies could be, and will be, a problem, but he was only one-quarter Husky. I did a quick calculation, but I could be wrong. How challenging could it really be? Despite the occasional horror stories from Husky owners, there are just as many heartwarming tales of love and the charming personalities of these dogs. With that in mind, I eagerly sent the money and embarked on my journey to North Bay the very next day.

DAY 11 OF 19 (STILL) — JULY 6, 2025 — 7:00PM

It's still Day 11 here in Wabakimi, and it's 7:00pm. I'm still at my rest day spot, the stunning Stonehenge campsite island on lower Wabakimi Lake. I was concerned that today would drag on, but quite the opposite happened. I usually struggle with just sitting around on these trips, but with this being such a long journey and having completed 10 consecutive days of travel with a book to write, the day flew by.

I had a late brunch of eggs, followed by another Happy Yak meal of beef stew at five, and now I'm enjoying pepper beef and rice from Alpine Air. In between meals, I managed to swim three times, dried out my gear, organized my food supplies, sorted out my gear, and rationed out both food, weed and supplies. I'm all set on both food and supplies, but I better not get delayed in being picked up, or I might get a bit hangry and cranky. I'm paddling out to Highway 527, train in and then paddle my way out, all on my own terms. With my gear in order and food arranged, my pack feels much lighter. I'm ready to move tomorrow, though it's only about a half-day journey, so I'll take my time leaving here in the morning.

I found my notes from the last trip here with Kyle, highlighting a really nice camp marked on my own GPS. The note read, "Really nice camp; huge walleye!" Although we didn't camp there on that trip, I made a mental note of how great it would be to stay there. So, I've decided to camp there tomorrow. It's not far, but since I cut off an extra northern loop, I'll have to backtrack to get back on this route. With only one rest day in 11, I can afford a shorter day tomorrow. I plan to stay there for one night; that will mark night 12! Time is flying by on this adventure.

CHAPTER 7

Today was fantastic! A much-needed and much-appreciated break. Right after writing that last line, I stepped out of my tent to tidy up my campsite. It's a great habit I should practice back home too. As I clean up and message Will on the inReach, I glance up to the west and notice white smoke billowing up towards the sky. It seems pretty close. It's a sight I've never seen before; usually, it's just in the air or a subtle glow in the sunlight. The smoke I see is from an actual fire, not too far away. After rereading the message, I reached out to Bruce once more. There's a fire on an island in Wabakimi Lake. I'm currently at Lower Wabakimi Lake, about 12 kilometres to the east. It feels quite close.

There is also a fire east of me outside the park. I pray that the wind does not pick up. I feel like I should move as far from here as I can tomorrow instead of getting up late and only moving a short distance. I think I'd rather put distance between the fire and myself. I'd prefer to be near the takeout early and just camp near the Kopka Waterfalls for a few nights, write, and be ready to evacuate if necessary. I don't want to feel rushed on this trip, but I also don't want to risk not seeing my family again. We'll have to wait and see how things unfold; Bruce doesn't seem too concerned, but the wind will play a crucial role. If I push myself and avoid a headwind down Smoothrock, I believe I can reach the takeout in about four nights. Sticking to the big lakes seems like a good plan in case of fire or the need for a plane evacuation. I'm feeling about 30% worried, but only time will reveal what's in store. Let's stay positive and see how things go!

DAY 12 OF 19 – JULY 7, 2025 – 5:30AM

I didn't burn in a fire last night, so I'll be able to finish this book. Nice! It's super calm outside, with the birds singing enthusiastically. The chill in the air is invigorating. I haven't gotten out of bed yet to check the smoke. A loon's call adds to the peaceful morning. I'm excited to start moving today. I'm not sure how far I'll go yet, but I'll go with the flow. Just as I began writing this morning, I had to rush to the bathroom for a quick, satisfying poop. Nature's call, right?

The best part is that I didn't see any billowing smoke, nor did I notice any orange glow or smell anything unusual. I believe I should be okay. I began working on an emergency evacuation plan last night, not exactly what I had in mind, but definitely better than the alternative. I'm uncertain about my destination or how far I'll travel today. I'm contemplating whether staying on the big lakes is crucial for fire safety; it's definitely beneficial for fewer bugs, as I'm still dealing with facial swelling. Unfortunately, I won't be able to escape the bugs for another 8 - 9 days. It's surreal to realize it's already Day 12. Today marks the longest solo journey I've ever undertaken, reminiscent of being picked up by Bruce around noon on Day 12 four years ago. Pretty fricken cool, bud!

The sky has a pinkish hue. As the saying goes, "red sky at night, sailor's delight; red sky in the morning, sailor's warning." With that in mind, I have two different plans for today. If I reach the epic site I've marked on my GPS and it lives up to my memory, I'll likely stay, especially if I don't depart from this camp early this morning. My Garmin inReach just alerted me at 6:00am - I should check it out.

I received a message from Will about the northern lights forecast. She must have sent it after I turned off my device last night. I usually keep it off to conserve battery, only turning it on for about an hour at the end of the day. Before starting my day, I wanted to check for any alerts from Bruce as they could potentially impact my plans.

I was feeling apprehensive; I still didn't know if I was making the right choice in getting a Husky/Shepherd puppy. I drove in silence for the six hours it took to get to North Bay. When I arrived at the house, I noticed they had kids, which was a good sign. I was invited around back where the puppies were playing freely on the deck, which was enclosed by a locked gate, providing a good amount of space for them. The small Shepherd mom was friendly, and they welcomed me inside to start looking at the puppies. I was surprised that nobody had chosen the white one yet, as he was the only one with that unique colouring. The rest of the puppies were all pudgy and had a Rottweiler-like appearance, which wasn't really my style. The white one looked like a wolf. I caressed him, and he didn't jump all over me but also didn't run away. He simply turned a bit so I could scratch his butt instead of his head.

It was a different experience compared to Scout; this new puppy didn't lock eyes with me and hold my gaze like Scout did. Nor did he show the same fear as Tripper, who would cry and try to hide. But there was something special about this moment. It felt right, like it was meant to be. Despite my doubts about deserving another dog after losing Scout and giving up Tripper in such a short span of time, I found myself sitting in my car, reflecting. Ultimately, I couldn't deny the feeling that this new dog was meant to be mine. So, I gathered my thoughts and went back to bring my new furry friend home.

I inquired if the puppy had a name yet, realizing I hadn't pre-selected one as I had done for my previous two dogs. They mentioned that the kids had been calling him Wolfie due to his appearance. I couldn't think of a more fitting name than Wolf or Wolfie, which felt affectionate and appropriate. I was committed to giving this dog the best care possible. I had brought a crate with me, ready to start this new journey with Wolfie. During the long drive home, whenever Wolfie would whine and cry, I made a point to ignore him completely. Once he quieted down, I would pull over and take him out for a short walk or a bathroom break. This routine continued for half of the journey. By the time we arrived home, it was already 10:00pm.

Wolfie showed remarkable progress in crate training during the ride home, which made me pleasantly surprised, overjoyed, and proud of my furry companion. Upon arriving home, I grabbed a bone from the fridge, took my canoe, and headed to the lake. I placed the bone in the canoe, settled Wolfie in, and paddled around the lake for an hour. As we paddled, Wolfie stayed relaxed, his focus on his bone. He briefly looked around, showing a calm demeanour despite being recently separated from his family, enduring a long drive, and now on his first canoe ride in the dark. He was just chillin'! That night, my heart was full of love for this amazing pup.

I spent a lot of time working with Wolf on training and behaviours. He's such a chill, aloof dog. He communicates by "woooing," almost like a howl but more like Husky talk. I love it; he has so much personality. He immediately got along with Emmie's dog, Beauty. He was great with the kids and didn't seem bothered by Tammy and Jake's huge, barking German Shepherd outside. He only cared about food and going outside!

The plan was to bring him out with myself, Richard and his dog, so Wolf could see how a great bush dog acts and learn from him. We did a trip in the French river together, Wolf was still not full grown. Even though Wolf was still somewhat of a puppy, he was already paddling and portaging like a pro. When we met up with Richard and his brother, who were already out there, Wolf immediately hit it off with the black lab. They had a special bond and got along famously. Unfortunately, our time together was cut short when I later received a text informing me of the black lab's passing. I was devastated for my buddy, knowing how much they meant to each other.

Even though the original dog plan fell through, Richard still wanted to camp. So, a couple of weeks later, we embarked on an ice-out canoe trip to Algoma, near where I live. We were paddling in two canoes, with Wolf accompanying me and Richard paddling solo. At one point, we pulled up next to each other in the lake to have a chat. I could see Wolf contemplating something. Just as I was cautioning Richard to be careful as Wolf might jump into his boat, that's exactly what he did. Thankfully, he didn't capsize. It was a close call in the icy water, but Wolf's bold move showed me that he wasn't afraid to take a leap of faith.

The summer before getting Wolfie, I was eager to embark on a big trip unlike any I had done before. I had heard about Wabakimi in Ontario, the largest natural canoeing preserve in the world, and I was determined to do a solo fly-in trip there. Despite having only done it once before, I was ready for the challenge. On our last fly-in trip, Kyle and I had encountered a fire up north, which left us stranded. It was a crazy experience. The plane couldn't land to pick us up, so we had to make do by catching fish for food and waiting anxiously for rescue.

Wabakimi wasn't supposed to be as forest fire-prone. It was known for being wetter, not dry and arid, which meant fewer fires but a lot more bugs. I reached out to Wabakimi Outfitters and that's when I first spoke to Bruce, an elderly man who was a wealth of knowledge about this lesser-known park. Despite his speech being a bit challenging to understand due to having only half a tongue, we managed to communicate effectively. After discussing my plans with him, we settled on a route: a solo plane ride into Burnt Rock, a lake located in the northwest section of the park. Heading due east for half the trip and then south for the pickup two weeks later sounded like an adventure of a lifetime. I was pumped for this challenge, my biggest undertaking yet, and there was a lot of planning to be done. I decided on double carrying, with two backpacks - a heavy one to carry alone and a lighter one to carry along with the canoe. I made sure to pack two fishing rods, planning to rely on fish for food, although I brought most of my food supplies with me. It was going to be a test of my skills and endurance, but I was ready for the challenge!

Using my Swift Prospector pack boat was a smart choice. I've noticed they've started converting all types of canoes into pack boats now, but this one had a much larger capacity to accommodate all my gear. Before I knew it, I was hitting the road for the nearly 12-hour drive up to near Armstrong, Ontario. The anticipation was building, and I couldn't wait to start my epic adventure in Wabakimi.

It was an amazing trip. I created a really good video from it and became hooked on that place. Embarking on a longer solo journey, I was completely self-reliant. I got along well with Bruce, and this current trip marks my seventh or eighth visit with him in the last four years. I spent 12 days on that trip, concluding at Cliff Lake. It was a delightful surprise for me. The lake was surrounded by cliffs, rising straight up to 200 feet at some points, adorned with Indigenous petroglyphs on the walls and home to blue walleye. The place exuded a spiritual aura. Bruce shared with me that numerous individuals reached out to book trips, eager to experience a journey akin to the one I had undertaken and showcased in my videos. He expressed how my promotion significantly boosted his business. I felt a sense of pride and honour, knowing that my efforts had made a meaningful impact.

Wolf was great in the bush, he always wandered off, his nose was trouble, but he always came back. At home he was the same but there was more trouble to get into than there was in the real wilderness. Funny, eh! I was at home snowplowing the driveway. I always liked having a dog with me outside when I did yard work. I just enjoy seeing a dog, laying there watching me or running around. Just having a dog present with me when I was outside felt right.

After a while of ploughing, I realized that I hadn't seen Wolf for some time. It was not unusual as he was allowed to wander two houses down in the same direction. He would often go next door to see if there were any old dog bones left by the neighbours' dogs, Cash and Winter. I called him, but there was no response. I then shook a bag of treats, a sound that usually had him racing home like a Greyhound. Wolf is undeniably food-driven, unlike any dog I've had before.

The treat trick didn't work either. No sign of Wolfie. I searched next door and the following house, but no one had seen him. I decided to hop on my snowmobile to cover more ground quickly. Riding down the street in the direction he usually went, I spotted two other snowmobiles approaching. I waved at them to stop and asked, "Have you folks seen a white dog with pointed ears?" They responded, "Oh, Wolfie?" as they removed their helmets, revealing themselves to be my other neighbours from three doors down in the opposite direction of where I was searching. "He visits us often. We always give him treats." "Oh," I replied, realizing why he always went there. "Well, let's go check." They had been out riding for half the day. Upon reaching their house, nobody was home; only their dog, Louie, an elderly mixed Shepherd. I turned to head back, but they were already

CHAPTER 7

facing the right way and reached their house before me. As I arrived, I saw the man leading Wolf out of the house by the collar. Perplexed, I halted, dismounted my sled, and took off my helmet. "Did you put him in there?" the man inquired. "What? Why would I do that?"

Through deduction, we pieced together what had occurred. Their door had a latch, not a doorknob, and it wasn't locked. Wolf likely jumped on the door, causing it to open. He then let Louie out, who was outside when they arrived, and closed the door behind him. So, Wolf essentially broke into their house, released their dog, shut the door, and started helping himself to whatever he could find!

It was truly baffling for all of us. I offered my apologies and promptly brought Wolfie back home. Huskies sure have a knack for getting into some crazy situations. While he had a few minor incidents before, like rummaging through the neighbours' garbage, this escapade took the cake. From now on, Wolfie will be on a tie-out lead whenever he's outside at home. No more free-roaming for him. Despite the neighbourhood being bustling with dogs, I'm committed to being a responsible pet owner and a considerate neighbour. So, Wolfie will be staying on leash while at home to ensure everyone's peace of mind.

In the bush, Wolfie tends to stir up more worry and fear in me than any other dog ever has. There are moments when he disappears for what feels like an eternity, only to nonchalantly reappear as if nothing out of the ordinary occurred. It can be quite frustrating after calling and searching for him. He's had run-ins with porcupines twice now. If he catches a whiff of something repulsive (which he finds delightful), he'll undoubtedly explore and possibly consume whatever it may be. However, he always manages to find his way back.

He and I had been on some great, real adventures by the time he was one year old. He shares the fish I catch. I'll eat the fillets, and he eats everything else - head, tail, bones. I just don't give him the gills. I'm not sure why; it just seems right. He is so strange, though. I used to give it to him raw, and he loved it. Now he won't eat it unless I put it in a frying pan or on the fire for like two seconds. I don't cook it for any specific amount of time; he just wants it cooked. This is the same dog that will actually eat my poop if I don't cover it with a rock while camping. On one occasion, he caught a wild turkey and began devouring it while it was still alive. He truly embodies his animal instincts, yet he has this unexpected preference for his fish to be cooked. Fancy pants, right? Despite his wild antics, we formed a deep and fast bond. He has turned out to be everything I've ever desired in a dog. He's independent and capable, yet remarkably gentle with zero signs of aggression, even in the face of barking dogs. He simply looks away, unfazed and indifferent. I trust him completely around my family and any child without a doubt. He exudes an air of aloofness, is content in his own company, and eagerly anticipates our camping adventures - a steadfast companion always by my side. I cherish him deeply; he almost feels like Scout reincarnated. There have been moments where I've accidentally called him Scout more than once. I am immensely grateful that I chose him. After all the uncertainty and deliberation, it's clear that I made the right choice. Our bond is unwavering and continues to flourish with each passing day.

Richard and I kept going out together, sometimes with Wolf and sometimes without. In May 2023, we embarked on a fantastic trip down the Sand River in Lake Superior Provincial Park. We were dropped off by an outdoor business called Forest the Canoe. Getting to Sand Lake at the beginning of the river was quite a challenge, and the thought of having to drive back to retrieve a truck was not appealing, so we opted to pay for the drop-off service. It's interesting to note that the train used to transport canoeists to that location, but unfortunately, it no longer does. I wish it did. Hint. Hint.

The first section rarely gets paddled or fished, which is what we were after, brook trout! It was a great trip, lots of fish, lots of rapids, amazing scenery and two large waterfalls. I'd highly recommend the trip. We got done that trip early. In only two nights. A habit we had gotten into. Move, move, move. We both enjoyed that type of canoe camping. Since we were done early and had such a great trip, we thought, let's go try Bobowash. A lake near my place. I'd heard great things about the trout there.

We stopped at my place, dropped off Wolf, did a little food and gear switch and we were off for another trip. We drove, paddled, portaged, caught fish and had a great day. We had just set up a nice camp and were getting ready to go out to fish again for the night bite, it was 8:00pm. I didn't have my inReach with me because he had his. If I needed it I could use his.

Richard called out to me from his canoe, "Hey, you need to go home." Perplexed, I responded with a confused "Huh?" He continued, "Will spoke to Natalie (his girlfriend) and informed her about an emergency at home. You have to head back immediately." A sense of dread washed over me as I realized that something serious must have occurred.

I began hastily tossing my gear into my backpack, skipping the usual meticulous packing routine. Tears welled up in my eyes as I frantically tried to gather everything as fast as possible. The need for answers consumed me. "What is it?" I demanded, my voice strained with emotion. "I don't know," he replied. "Find out!" I yelled, almost hyperventilating, as I hurriedly got into my canoe, ready to embark on the day-long journey back home, a journey that had already been a full day's worth of driving and paddling. As I paddled away, I heard, "Joe." "What?!?" I responded. "It's your brother, man," he said. "Dead?" I asked, the words barely escaping my lips. "I'm sorry, man," he replied. "FUCK NOOOOOOOOOOOOOOOOO." The moment the message came through, I knew it was about my brother. The fear I had carried for years had finally materialized.

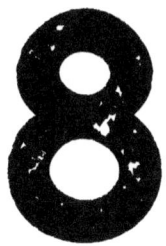

I WAS THRUST INTO panic mode, a sensation I hadn't experienced since parting ways with Tripper, but this time it was a million times more intense. The news of my little brother's passing hit me like a ton of bricks. Oh my God. Panic gripped me fiercely. I abruptly left my friend, who was attempting to gather his things and accompany me. He caught up to me eventually. We managed to get out in just two hours. Although he offered to drive alongside me, I felt the need to make the journey alone. I had to go swiftly.

It was my worst nightmare realized - someone I held dear, someone with whom I shared a deep bond, was gone. He lay lifeless on the floor of his bachelor apartment. The weight of regret and sorrow washed over me. I should have been there for him. Whenever he was struggling, whether in a haze of substances or battling a psychotic episode, he always reached out to me. It was always me he turned to, even coming to me in person when I lived in Windsor. Me. Not anyone else. He relied on me when he needed help, and now, after being away from Windsor for so long, I wasn't there for him when he needed me the most. He had no one to turn to when he was struggling. Increasing his cocaine use, someone unknowingly gave him fentanyl. He tragically passed away. Unaware of its presence, he didn't stand a chance. Just days before, we were discussing future plans. He wasn't seeking death; he was simply trying to silence the voices in his head with alcohol and cocaine. Which obviously is not the answer. He had gone through so much. I knew he was always searching for something. A father figure? A higher power? The predisposition to psychosis from his biological father, coupled with heavy marijuana use in his teens and escalating to severe cocaine and alcohol abuse until his passing, only exacerbated his struggles. It made things worse, and I could see it all too clearly.

As time passes, it's important for me to cherish the moments I have with those who are dear to me. I am grateful for the Bushcraft USA Forum, as it has introduced me to wonderful individuals like Doug, Ken, Kyle, Mike, and Terry. Through this community, I have not only honed my outdoor skills but also developed valuable interpersonal skills and gained a deeper appreciation for diverse cultures.

Isaac always wore a cheerful expression and demeanour around my kids. He adored them, and they adored their Uncle Isaac. He would joyfully carry them on his back, regardless of his own feelings. He consistently showed kindness to everyone, particularly his nieces. He referred to Mom as "Ma." They shared a special bond, of that I am certain. Isaac was a kind-hearted individual. I recall a time when he selflessly gave his last $5.00 to a person in need on the streets when he was young. He did not choose the challenges he faced, yet he bravely navigated them for 30 years. He showed immense resilience but perhaps needed more support. It's natural for me to question why he endured such hardships. Why him and not ME?

DAY 12 OF 19 (STILL) — JULY 7, 2025 — 7:45PM

This morning I left camp around 9:00am after staying in bed to finish filling up the first notebook I brought to write in. I brought three. So far, I've filled up that one and have depleted four pens. I left feeling sad, after finishing that notebook with the death of my brother Isaac. Today marks the longest trip I have ever been on solo. I feel all over the place.

My previous 12-day Wabakimi trip would have ended today, so I'm experiencing a mix of emotions this morning. It feels bittersweet. I had set plans last night for today, but the smoke was too intense. I adjusted my plans as the smoke cleared once again. Not even a hint of it remained. Why do I feel such a sense of urgency? I cannot predict how Day 13 will unfold. There's no need for me to rush, but I have the option to hurry if I choose to.

Today, I chose to go with the flow, and I'm so grateful that I did. I discovered an incredible campsite with stunning fishing opportunities, now saved on my GPS. I considered staying here for the day. Despite reaching this spot after just two hours of travel, I felt content with stopping. When I marked this location last month with Kyle, the bug situation was much more manageable. It remains a beautiful spot, but the bugs are relentless. My face is still swollen from their bites. Each day, I seem to be facing more attacks from these pesky insects. The bites behind my ears seem to have bites of their own now. It's bites upon bites, lumps upon lumps, bugs upon bugs. Despite the bug situation, I remembered another spot marked on my GPS that read "Huge Walleye Deep at Waterfall," and there was a campsite noted on my map in that exact location. I made my way to that spot after a series of back-to-back portages, which are notably easier now that I'm in a more frequented area of the park and my packs are considerably lighter. Over the past 12 days, I had hoped to build some muscle out here in the wilderness.

Wearing my head net all day has been a lifesaver. It definitely helps keep the bugs at bay, but somehow they still manage to sneak inside, eager to join the adventure and feast on my skin. They're persistent little creatures, aren't they? And they're quite resilient too. Dealing with them can be a challenge. You have to wait for a breeze, flip the head net inside out, and then flail your arms like you're trying to stop traffic just to get rid of them.

I made my way through a few short 300 metre portages, carrying my gear, and eventually arrived at the waterfall where I spotted two tin boats. In each boat, there were two guys fishing for walleye. This spot marked the entrance to Smoothrock Lake. It seems like a popular area with several lodges around. Companies often send their customers and clients here for what they promise to be "good fishing" at this location. I felt a bit disappointed, not because they were there, but because I didn't want to set up camp only to have motorboats coming to fish at night or early in the morning.

On my second carry, I encountered four gentlemen from Mississippi after losing a lure during my trek. I could sense they were from the southern part of the United States, but I asked to confirm. They appeared impressed by my three-week-long solo "trip" — in every sense of the word. They were using live bait and catching big walleye.

I had planned on having fish for dinner today, so I took my shot at the first cast, but all I caught were snags. Here I am, celebrating my longest camping trip without catching any fish today. Luckily, I have one last pack of lunchmeat. It's 12 days old, but it still seems okay to eat. It feels like a good plan to finish up that lunchmeat before it goes bad.

The next two days, I paddled down Smoothrock, visited a site where Kyle and I had stayed before.

The wind wasn't too strong there. Fuelled by my sandwich, I still felt energized and eager to keep moving. My original plan was to navigate down the east channel of Smoothrock, a long lake that can get pretty windy, especially paddling from north to south. This route meant paddling across the entire width of the top of Smoothrock.

Navigating in and out of island loops would have been a lot of work as the wind picked up in my face. I'm going to stay out here for the duration, until I am happy with the work I have done on the book — the reason I am here. I don't feel like having huge travel days anymore. I'd rather spend two nights at a couple of cool spots. After tonight, I'll have eight nights left until my three-week duration is up. I want to stay the full three weeks for my own ego, bragging rights, and just to have a cool story to tell. That's my plan, and I'm sticking to it. Right now, I'm off the map I have because I had originally planned for the east channel, not the west. Today, I paddled blindly for a while. I was very tired and hungry, and the headwind made paddling quite challenging.

Around 5:00pm, feeling exhausted, I glanced to my right. I had been scanning the shores with my eyes, searching for a suitable camping spot. I spotted an old rock fire ring, a clear indication that someone had camped there before — it seemed like it could be a decent spot. Tin boats zoomed by, creating a large wake that made it challenging for me to get out and unload my canoe. I'm pretty sure they weren't even aware of my presence. I looked around and found a half-decent, relatively flat spot for my tent, and I was sold. For dinner, I enjoyed a large meal of chicken stir-fry with rice — mmm, it tasted just like home. After organizing my food, I settled into my tent with some Benadryl. Tomorrow, I have a rough plan to paddle only a short distance on Smoothrock, maybe two hours or so. I'm looking forward to having spaghetti for dinner tomorrow at Spaghetti Island. The day will be dedicated to writing.

DAY 13 OF 19 — JULY 8, 2025 — 1:35PM

I did indeed paddle to Ol' Spaghet Isle. It started raining last night, and I was awakened by the sound of a motor boat or possibly a plane. In the pitch-black darkness, I assumed it was a motor boat, which still seemed strange to me. Glancing at my watch, an old Casio Pro Trek Tough Solar that Will got for me in Huntsville back in 2008, I saw that it was midnight. I closed the vestibule to my tent and managed to fall back asleep, although I woke up to pee five times throughout the night. It was the worst sleep I've had on this trip, and I'm not sure why. Perhaps it was all the water I drank after supper. Today was kind of an easy day for me.

Today, I paddled for about eight or nine hours without any portaging. While trolling, I managed to catch two pikes and kept a big one to eat later. I only had an oatmeal cookie for breakfast before leaving camp. I departed later than usual because it was still raining until around 8:30am. Upon setting up on Spaghetti Island, I wasn't very pleased to find the second campsite with huge cans of cooked chicken with labels from Indiana empty and half-charred in the fire pit. I bet it was the first guy I saw; he came this way. Gross, in every way. This site was used heavily. I searched for a flat spot for my tent and ended up on the other side of the island. I found probably the flattest spot of the trip — bonus! The first pike I caught came up to the boat and grabbed the Little Cleo out of the water. Pretty cool.

I am having a hard time going back to writing the book. It's 1:36pm. This is incredibly difficult for me to put into words. I find myself seated outside in the warm sunlight, my shirt off, surrounded by an unusual absence of bugs and wind. The atmosphere is perfectly serene, eerily quiet except for the gentle buzz of a lone fly and the distant chirping of a few birds. Despite the tranquility of the scene, tears flow freely, evoking a raw emotional response that somehow feels strangely fitting.

It was my ultimate nightmare realized. I had already encountered numerous perilous situations, even personally extracting Isaac from a crack house on two separate occasions. I was the one he reached out to when he was experiencing an episode. I would do my best to calm him down during those moments. He used to come to my house in Windsor, completely depleted of drugs, alcohol, or battling psychosis, sometimes all at once. However, I eventually moved away. I fucking left. Even now, I carry a sense of guilt. I was his confidant, his first point of contact in times of need. Yet, I made the difficult decision to leave to improve my family's life. I understand the reasons behind my choice, but the weight of leaving him behind, especially knowing the extent of his struggles, still lingers within me. I realize now that I could have offered him a place to stay with us. We had the space and the means to support him. Even if he might have initially declined (which is likely), I believe I could have pushed the matter and convinced him. After all, he was my little brother, and I feel a deep sense of responsibility towards him.

The truth is, fear gripped me. With two daughters and a wife at home, my concerns were amplified. While I had unwavering trust in my brother, the thought of him experiencing an episode while I was away camping, or getting involved in drugs in the Soo and bringing potential trouble to our home, weighed heavily on my mind. The risk felt too great to take. Looking back, I regret that decision. I have a deep understanding of my brother, but the fear of the unknown clouded my judgment. He truly embodied kindness and gentleness, a memory that lingers in my thoughts frequently. The difficult choice to part ways with a beloved pet for the greater good of my family weighed heavily on me. Considering the potential risks of bringing what felt like a "liability" into our home while I was frequently away seemed like an insurmountable challenge. Despite the logical reasoning behind my decision, the regret is profound. I can't help but wonder about the impact it could have had if I had insisted on him living with us. While the outcome remains uncertain, the possibility of sharing more time with him tugs at my heartstrings.

My mom was the one who found him. How devastating that was. The news hit me hard; if I had been there, it could have been me discovering him. The weight of guilt and selfishness consumed me. He had collapsed alone in his shitty apartment, his passing unnoticed for some time. The thought of my dear mom experiencing such a traumatic event was unbearable. He was her baby; the pain she must have endured was beyond comprehension. He had been using coke, alone, as he often did. Someone had introduced fentanyl into the mix. The duration and extent of his drug use remained unknown to me. I couldn't fathom how long he had been laying there on the floor before his passing. He had left this world alone, likely filled with fear. My brother Isaac was not a bad person; he had battled severe demons in the form of depression, psychosis, and schizophrenia. There might have been more struggles that I had been unaware of. Despite his inner turmoil, he had never caused harm to anyone. He had a gentle demeanour; his nieces would always gravitate towards him at family gatherings, climbing all over him with affection.

In his apartment, as I sifted through his belongings, I found very little. There were no personal artifacts to speak of, except for two cherished pictures: one of my girls and one of Abby's girls, a heartfelt card they had all created for him, and a pocket knife I had gifted him a decade ago. Despite the countless drunken nights he had endured, that knife remained in his possession. It was a poignant reminder of the bond we shared. Knowing that he loved and looked up to me added another layer of sorrow to the situation. Will, the family, and I embarked on a swift journey through the States to return to Windsor in just six hours. The experience felt surreal, as if we were moving through a dream.

When we arrived in Windsor, I immediately sought out my mom. We embraced, both of us overcome with tears. The reality of the situation was almost too much to bear. My mom had been staying at my sister Abby's place with Joe and Abby's girls. We all gathered together, sharing our grief and trying to make sense of the tragedy. My mom had tasks to attend to, such as purchasing clothes for Isaac to wear at the showing. It wasn't an exaggeration when I mentioned that he had very little to his name. Years before, he had been in such dire straits that he resorted to selling his groceries to fund his drug habit. This left him with nothing of value, no nice clothes, and very little to his name. When I went through his apartment with my mom, the stark reality of his situation hit me like a ton of bricks. It was a shocking and heartbreaking realization of just how little he had in his life.

I felt the strong urge to accompany my mom to buy clothes for Isaac. We made the decision to go the next day. After our emotional visit, attempting to eat amidst tears, we eventually departed. I dropped the family off at a hotel since none of our relatives had space for us in their homes or apartments. Following this, I headed to Eric's place. We shared drinks, both of us sobbing as he comforted me like a true friend would, shedding tears alongside me. I ended up spending the night there, too inebriated to drive back.

The next day, I accompanied my mom to pick out some decent clothes for Isaac. As we wandered around, engaging in conversation and trying to hold back our tears, we eventually settled on an outfit, possibly from Sears. The specific store didn't really matter in the grand scheme of things. Isaac probably wouldn't have worn it even if he had the chance; he was more comfortable in his usual attire of sweatpants and a flannel shirt. Isaac was a big guy, easily over 200 lbs. I affectionately called him my "big little brother" because he would playfully lift me onto his shoulders, and I thought it was hilarious.

Isaac was always singing made-up songs, radiating contentment. He admired and looked up to me, even though I didn't have much time for him or Abby when they were young. I made a conscious effort to make amends for that later on. There was a time when Will called me in a panic, informing me that the police were on their way to take Abby, who was just out of high school. I was residing on Rankin in the west end of Windsor with Will. When my mom called to inform me about the situation with Abby and the police, I was taken aback. It seemed that Abby was grappling with a surge of teenage angst, and my mom, feeling overwhelmed, had resorted to calling the authorities because Abby refused to leave the house. While I hold immense love for my mom, I couldn't help but disagree with her actions in this instance. However, I also acknowledge that I haven't experienced the challenges of being a mother trying to raise a teenage girl, which undoubtedly presents its own set of difficulties.

When I learned about the situation with Abby and the police, I knew I couldn't let things escalate further. Understanding my sister's tendencies, I was concerned she might end up in serious trouble. I immediately shared the news with Will, who wasted no time in urging me to go and bring Abby home. Without hesitation, I set off to retrieve her. Abby ended up living with us for about a year. My love for my sister runs deep, and I would go to great lengths to support her and her daughters. I hope she truly understands the depth of my devotion to her. She is the only person I trust implicitly with my own daughters. The bond between the cousins, five girls in total, is incredibly strong, and they get along wonderfully.

Not only with Abby, but I also made an effort with Isaac to demonstrate that I am a better person now than I was when they were younger. I was frequently tasked with babysitting them, and unfortunately, I was unkind at times. I would have friends over, make them promise not to tell, and then proceed to ignore Abby and Isaac. Now that I am older, I can see that I was a truly awful teenager. I did my best to support Isaac in any way I could. I remember taking him to Peche Island, where we cooked Pike over hardwood coals on a folding grill. Despite my efforts, he remarked that it wasn't as tasty as bacon. He would often ask me for weed, and I tried to be a caring brother to both him and Abby. However, looking back, I can't help but feel like I fell short. My heart goes out to my dear sister.

We opted not to hold a funeral for him, as that's what he would have preferred. Instead, we had a small gathering with only our immediate family in attendance. The experience was incredibly difficult. Seeing my baby brother lying lifeless in a casket was heart-wrenching. The sight of his face, altered by the mortician's makeup, with his lips sealed shut and his skin cold to the touch, was haunting. Despite the overwhelming sadness, I felt compelled to speak. It was, without a doubt, the saddest moment of my life. The pain of losing him was far more intense than any previous losses, surpassing even the grief of losing Tony, Nana, Scout, or Tripper. His passing was especially devastating because he was young and hadn't had the chance to truly experience life. It was evident to all of us that he was deeply troubled and suffering. The burden of voices and hallucinations became overwhelming for him. Unfortunately, his coping mechanisms of turning to alcohol and drugs, like booze and coke, proved to be ineffective and only added to his struggles. Despite our collective love and support for him, he was caught in a cycle of pain that he couldn't break free from.

We didn't linger at the gathering for long, maybe half an hour at most. As we were leaving, I confided in Will, expressing, "This is not the way I want things to be for me." Will, always attuned to my thoughts and emotions, reassured me with understanding. A couple of days before, I had reached out to Ron, the biological father of Isaac and Abby, to inform him of the situation. His response, "Oh no. When is the funeral?" left me feeling conflicted. I made the decision to ask him not to attend, explaining that it was a private affair for family only. His understanding reply, "OK. I know how you feel, I lost a brother too, you know," struck a nerve within me. The urge to scream, "YOU JUST LOST YOUR FUCKING SON!" was overwhelming. It was a moment of deep frustration and pain.

I couldn't comprehend it at all. Ron re-entered Abby's life with a desire to reconnect with his granddaughters and daughter. Despite his efforts with Isaac, Isaac remained distant. I couldn't fault Isaac for his reluctance. After all those years of absence, it was hard to understand why Ron had stayed away. A divorce with his wife shouldn't have severed his connection with his children. I will never understand what kind of "man" would abandon his kids. You would have to kill me or put me in jail for life to keep me away.

That night, I found myself in a state of distress, turning to alcohol and making impulsive decisions. I attempted to retrieve Isaac's phone from my mom, driven by a desire to uncover information about his drug use. The idea of confronting the dealer with violent intentions crossed my mind, envisioning a scenario where I would take matters into my own hands. In the heat of the moment, I lashed out in anger, directing my frustration at my mom and Joe, creating unnecessary tension. However, upon reflection with a clear mind, I realized the dangerous path I was heading down. I understood that resorting to violence would only lead to devastating consequences, a reality that was not part of my intentions. It was a moment of turmoil and recklessness, but ultimately, I recognized the need to step back from such destructive impulses.

During our week in Windsor, amidst all the challenges we were facing, I began noticing small bumps appearing on the left side of my forehead. Concerned about my health and aware of the limitations of the healthcare system in the north, I decided to seek medical attention at a clinic. However, the diagnosis I received was that the bumps were likely a result of the hot weather and stress-induced sweating. While I respect medical professionals, I couldn't shake the feeling that this explanation didn't quite align with what I was experiencing. Ok, if you say so. We made the drive home, unsure of what to do next. I resorted to the only method I knew to make sense of the entire situation. It remained surreal, yet growing more tangible with each passing day. To process everything, I organized and reserved an ambitious, high-mileage adventure in Algonquin. In my experience, if you seek a challenging journey through vast wilderness and strenuous portages, Algonquin is the ideal destination. Specifically, venturing off Highway 60 to the northwest region offers the best access.

DAY 13 OF 19 (STILL) — JULY 8, 2025 — 6:00PM

Today has been a day of indulgence and relaxation. I savoured a large pike upon my arrival around noon. Later, at 3:00pm, I delighted in a bag of Uncle Ben's rice. Now, at 6:00pm, I just finished paying homage to Ol' Spaghet Isle with a delightful supper of spaghetti topped with Parmesan cheese. It was absolutely delicious!

I cut my hair off today with a belt knife. It was the longest it had ever been, but it was time. The bugs were using it to hide behind my ears and wreak havoc in that area. I didn't want to keep it tied up in a bun under a hat anymore; it was becoming quite bothersome. I truly cherished my long hair, as I had been growing it since before my accident. However, that's also why I decided to cut it. Out with the old Joe, and in with something new.

I was surprised by how strong my hair was. It required me to saw through the ponytail with my razor-sharp knife before it finally gave way. I trimmed it meticulously, taking my time, and the process was quite lengthy. Despite being a knife cut, I honestly think it looks decent. It feels so much better not having that mop of hair on my head. It's probably the last time I'll ever have hair of any significant length. I was concerned about regretting it, but now I realize I don't care at all.

Tonight marks Night 13. Honestly, this campsite is truly amazing – fantastic for swimming, flat terrain, and surprisingly, no bugs! Although there were some when I first arrived and set up, they seem to have magically disappeared. I've spent most of the day outside my tent, writing and basking in the sun without any black flies bothering me. It's been awesome! Despite all this, I must admit I am feeling homesick. I have to remind myself not to plan on getting too close to the take-out point too early. I know that if I'm near the take-out and finished with my writing, I'll be tempted to call for the pick-up. I absolutely must complete the book out here, at least the story part. My publisher, Brian Aspinall, and I will discuss the finer points, adding more detail where needed and refining the writing style. I'm considering incorporating some of the journal entries into the book.

Tonight, I plan to stay away from writing for as long as possible. Tomorrow, I aim to leave early as I have a rapid to navigate before the exit of Smoothrock. This will be followed by at least five consecutive portages, leading me to the "Walleye Kitchen" where I'll be staying for two nights. I've visited this spot before with Mike. It's located after the "Fantasia Portage," a one-kilometre portage that is truly stunning with thick moss covering everything.

Earlier, I spotted a red canoe passing by Spaghetti Island with two guys on board, likely looking to camp at my island. Upon seeing me and my gear, they decided to head across the lake to secure a spot. If by chance they are heading the same way as me tomorrow, which I highly doubt, I'm determined to reach Walleye Kitchen before them to fish and secure the campsite. I'm confident I can beat them there. They managed to get a spot near me for tonight. Tomorrow marks two weeks alone in the wild!

After spending just one night at home, I embarked on the roughly 8-hour drive to Algonquin. I worked tirelessly for three days, battling the relentless black flies and mosquitoes that were out in full force as May transitioned into June. The bumps on my head continued to worsen, evolving into an intense burning and itching sensation. To make matters worse, my left eye began to swell, worsening with each passing day. I have a bad reaction to bug bites, especially black flies. So, I initially thought it could be that. However, when I noticed those small red dots that had now turned into red blisters, I realized something was amiss. I decided to take a detour and paddled myself out through Maple Creek, then drove straight to the nearest hospital.

I was anxious while driving, my eye had swollen completely shut, and my face and head burned like never before. I feared that due to the numerous bug bites, the doctor would attribute it to a severe reaction to the bites... However, that was not the case. As soon as I walked in, he took one look at me and promptly declared, "You have shingles."

I felt relieved that the doctor acknowledged it wasn't just bug bites. However, I grew anxious about his next words."It's a viral issue; you need antiviral medication and antibiotics within 72 hours of onset of signs and symptoms," he explained. I had waited almost a full week. He warned me that I could lose my eye if the medications didn't act swiftly. "Holy smokes," I exclaimed, shocked by the seriousness of shingles. I knew it was painful, but I had no idea it could be this serious.

It was clear to the doctor that my shingles outbreak was triggered by the stress of my brother's passing, a burden too heavy for my body and mind to bear. I remember tiredly driving the rest of the way home and spending days in isolation as I had heard it could be contagious. Now, I bear scars in the middle of my forehead. My face has transformed in just two years, reflecting the toll of grief. The mourning process is complex and unpredictable. Grief is a fucked up, unpredictable journey, capable of striking at any moment.

A COUPLE OF MONTHS slipped by. I had dedicated some time to recuperate from the shingles episode. Before that, upon my return from Windsor, I crafted a YouTube video to inform my audience about Isaac's passing. It had become a routine for me to share my personal life through videos. From marriage, kids, and three dogs to now grappling with death, life had taken a poignant turn.

I received a portion of Isaac's ashes in the mail from the funeral home. Isaac and I had been eagerly planning a canoe trip to Quetico for a year. We were waiting for the right time when we were both healthy and ready to embark on this adventure together. It was thrilling to imagine him joining me on a trip that I cherished and was eager to share with him. Now, I wonder if he would have been able to handle it. His interest in something I loved was both exciting and bittersweet. It's a realization that our planned canoe trip would never come to fruition, adding to the weight of regret for not making it happen sooner. As a gesture of remembrance, I considered taking some of his ashes to scatter in a picturesque location - a place I would have loved to show him in person. I can only imagine how that experience might have altered his outlook on life, potentially offering him the same solace and renewal it has brought me time and time again.

CHAPTER 9

About a year before his passing, I began abusing codeine. Initially, I turned to it for the typical reasons - to address issues with my gut and my rear end. Initially, I used it to prevent accidents like the Percs used to. They helped me avoid situations where I might have bowel issues if I got too excited or suffered from severe hemorrhoids. These hemorrhoids made it excruciatingly painful to poop, a discomfort that would only subside over time if I soaked in a bath. This was particularly challenging while camping was my profession and I had to consistently produce new videos each week.

Codeine was easily accessible and effective in managing my issues. The most conflicting aspect was that I wouldn't run out and experience withdrawal symptoms, which could hinder my camping activities. I could simply purchase more at Shoppers Drug Mart. It may sound unconventional, and I feel uneasy admitting it. However, I was aware that codeine is water-soluble and that you can purchase Tylenol 1s over the counter. It was simple to extract codeine into a liquid form, a quick and convenient process. Eventually, I reached a point where I disregarded the extraction method and started consuming handfuls of pills at a time. I became addicted to them over a few months, and this pattern persisted for years. The continuous supply was both a convenience and a curse. However, by ingesting the pills, I was consuming a concerning amount of acetaminophen, which is detrimental to health, especially the liver. What initially started as a means of help ended up causing harm in the long run.

After Isaac's passing, I received his ashes and arranged a solo trip (accompanied by Wolfie) for a fly-in excursion to Wabakimi. The purpose was to scatter some of his ashes at a couple of breathtaking locations that I regret not showing him while he was alive. Wolfie had never experienced flying in a plane before. We embarked on a 12-hour drive to Bruce's lodge, Wabakimi Outfitters near Armstrong, Ontario, for this meaningful journey. We spent the night at the lodge and took off the next morning with NDK Airlines, right from Bruce's backyard. Wolfie did remarkably well, until about three-quarters of the way through the flight when he started panting heavily. I comforted him, and as we landed, the unloading process began.

I had to lift Wolf out and into the canoe as we began our week-long trip, starting a bit north of the prime section of the Kopka River. It was on this journey that I paddled a two-person canoe solo for the first time, opting for a rented Souris River Quetico, which was symmetrical and allowed for paddling backwards alone. The rear seat was ideal for paddling in a boat like that, providing the necessary space for Wolf and my two large bags. I primarily used a double-bladed paddle, only occasionally experimenting with a single blade, albeit with less success.

The trip led us to a couple of incredibly scenic spots, including one by a picturesque waterfall. I will be revisiting this spot in a few days, planning to spend two nights there. It will undoubtedly be an emotional experience but also deeply meaningful to me. The desire to have a conversation with him was and is still strong, and the memories created in such a special place will be cherished. I told him I was sorry and that I had always and would always love him so damn much. I expressed regret for letting him down and not being there when he needed me most. After the trip was done, it was back home to my loving family, where some home time was needed.

Before leaving Bruce's place to head home, I purchased a Royalex Bell Yellowstone Solo canoe from him. Richard, mentioned earlier, along with his friend Jay and myself, were gearing up for a significant trip in the fall. We were planning to navigate the Bloodvein River in Woodland Caribou Provincial Park, with the possibility of extending the journey all the way to Manitoba or James Bay. The other two guys were seasoned whitewater adventurers, whereas I had yet to experience the thrill of a true whitewater trip. Joining these skilled paddlers filled me with excitement as I looked forward to learning from their expertise. Despite still grappling with the loss of Isaac, I eagerly anticipated the camaraderie, bonding and teamwork dynamics that awaited us on this upcoming journey.

I had a prior business connection with Albert from Goldseekers Canoeing. When I reached out to him, I explained our plan to leave the vehicle with him for drop-off at Lund Lake. Our itinerary included paddling through the park, exploring the Bloodvein River in the northwest pocket, visiting Musclow or Barclay Lake, and then embarking on a river journey towards Manitoba.

I arranged a shuttle back with Albert for just the cost of gas. We had some discussions about the logistics, including who would drive and where we would stay the night before the long journey. Although I initially wanted to drive my truck and stay in a hotel, we ended up in Jay's vehicle and sleeping in the truck. I chose to go with the flow, recognizing that as the newcomer, it was important to adapt to the majority decisions.

The plan was for the two of them to drive up to my place, which was on the way to our destination. We would load three canoes onto Jay's truck and then continue the journey north to Red Lake. The idea was to spend the night in the truck on the way and start early in the morning. When they arrived at my house, I met Jay for the first time and found him to be a nice guy. I sought help in rigging up my canoe a bit, as I was inexperienced in whitewater paddling. When I asked for assistance, the response I received was a bit curt, with a simple, "Just do it, I don't know." Despite this, my canoe was quickly rigged up, albeit in a somewhat dismissive manner. My intention was to foster a sense of camaraderie and connection with my companions. After bidding a heartfelt farewell to my family with hugs, kisses, and expressions of love, we all packed in and prepared to embark on our journey together.

As we set off, we retraced the route they would have taken if I hadn't joined, which was only a 30 minute detour from the 16 hour planned drive. I immediately admitted my lack of experience, stating, "I have no idea what I'm doing, guys. I'll definitely take a back seat on this trip and follow your lead." I know I set the wrong tone.

While I've had my fair share of camping experiences with various groups of guys, including grown American Military men known for their banter and sometimes toxic masculinity, this trip was unlike any other. From the moment we hit the road, I sensed a shift in the atmosphere that made me feel uncomfortable. It was as if I had been transported back to high school, where I felt the pressure to conform or risk being overlooked, a situation I was not willing to tolerate. Being true to oneself and feeling accepted for who you are is essential in any group setting.

Despite feeling uneasy during the truck ride up, I persevered throughout the days that followed. Arriving late at Red Lake, with bedtime fast approaching, I once again proposed the idea of getting a hotel room, suggesting we split the cost three ways, with me even offering to foot the bill entirely. However, the group decided to opt for sleeping in the truck instead. "I've decided to pitch my tent outside. I just can't sleep in here with two dudes and no room," I declared. Despite their laughter and teasing, I remained firm in my decision, simply wanting to get some rest. Unfazed by their reactions, I set up my tent near the truck, close to a garbage bin, on a small patch of grass behind the grocery store. Knowing that Red Lake can be a bit sketchy, I politely asked if they could move the truck closer to me for safety, but once again, they responded with jest.

After a good night's sleep in my tent, I packed up and settled back into the truck, only to be met with a palpable sense of awkwardness. With plenty of time to spare and no rush to meet the outfitter, we had the flexibility to stay anywhere along the way. Richard and I had shared many nights together at each other's homes or in hotels, so I couldn't understand why this situation felt so tense. As we had hours to kill in the morning, I found myself already contemplating the idea of bailing out. The lingering discomfort and tension in the air made me question whether continuing on this journey was the right choice.

Being excited for the white water portion of the trip, I had already convinced myself that my unease was all in my head. As we wandered around downtown near the float planes taking off, each of us engrossed in our cell phones and keeping to ourselves, the disconnect between us became more apparent. Finally, it was time to head to Albert's place to begin the journey to the put-in spot. As we set off, carrying the heaviest boat I had ever portaged, I made a conscious effort to keep pace with the group. Our interactions were limited to small talk at best, with occasional grunts being the only responses I received from either of them. The lack of communication and camaraderie during this crucial part of the trip added to the growing sense of isolation and discomfort I was experiencing.

After enduring four or five days of discomfort and regret, I found myself seriously reconsidering my decision to join the trip. The internal struggle had been weighing on me for a full day, and as we settled into camp one morning, I made the difficult decision to speak up: "I'm going to bail. I shouldn't have come. I have too much going on at home, and I feel like I need to go back." I chose to hide my feelings in this manner because I didn't want to dampen the mood of the trip for my companions, who seemed to be enjoying themselves together. It was a tough choice, but I prioritized getting myself out to ensure that everyone could continue to have a positive experience on the journey.

CHAPTER 9

It's possible that my expectations were high, but I firmly believe that if I were in a situation with two friends who didn't know each other, I would go the extra mile to ensure that I didn't inadvertently favour one over the other. I would strive to create an inclusive environment where everyone feels like an integral part of the team, fostering a sense of unity and camaraderie among all members. Prioritizing equal engagement and making each individual feel valued and included is key to building strong relationships and a positive group dynamic.

I would definitely engage in some friendly teasing, but always in a lighthearted manner. I am confident in this approach because I have experienced it multiple times before. For instance, with Joel and Brodie, who are best friends and graciously include me on their annual spring trip, or with Adam and Mike, who have now expanded their yearly adventure to include me as well. In these friendships, there is no sense of inadequacy, exclusion, or hurtful teasing. It's all about good-natured banter and camaraderie, without any of the negative dynamics reminiscent of high school drama.

I revealed my intentions to go home, only to be met with unexpected sincerity from both of them urging me not to leave. Their genuine concern and encouragement resonated with me, and for the first time, I felt a sense of connection and camaraderie. With their reassurance ringing in my ears, I made the decision to stay. "Aw, screw it, let's go." Seeking the approval and acceptance of my male peers has always been a significant aspect of my life, even if it's a vulnerability of mine. So, with newfound resolve, we set off towards our first rapid, united in our shared adventure.

As I arrived at the roller-slide next to the rapid, I was struck by an idea for a fun video moment. Being the first to reach the spot and observing the size of the rapid, I decided to ride my canoe down the slide and into the water, thinking it would make for a cool shot. The rapid seemed too daunting for me to paddle through, so the slide offered a thrilling alternative. As I splashed into the water, laughter bubbling up from within me, I felt a genuine sense of joy for the first time in days. However, when I turned around, I saw both of my companions confidently navigating the rapid together. In that moment, a realization dawned on me - they shared a bond that I, as the third wheel, couldn't quite penetrate.

In that moment of realization, I knew that my journey with them had come to an end. I made the decision to inform them that I was heading back to camp to arrange for a plane ride out, even though it meant flying back from Thunder Bay without a car. Leaving my gear and canoe at Albert's place, I proposed that they could still catch a ride back for the cost of gas and drop off my belongings at my home on their way. Reflecting on the situation, I found solace in the fact that I hadn't driven there myself. Though my companions may not have had much to say in response, they understood the gravity of my decision and respected my choice to part ways.

After parting ways with my companions, we made a pact that I would message them once I was safely out using my inReach device. True to my word, I reached out to them upon my return. The journey back home came at a significant cost, totalling around $3,000, but in hindsight, I would have paid double for the escape from my ordeal. Upon my arrival, I confided in Will, sharing the details of my experience, and to our mutual surprise, we realized that our perceived closeness with him and his girlfriend was not as genuine as we had believed. Our shared memories, such as attending a Burt Kreischer show in Sudbury and Will's online workouts with her, along with Richard's interactions with my kids, all seemed unexpectedly distant in light of recent events.

As I waited for the anticipated call, it finally came a day later. "Hey, Jay and I are almost at your place," they said. "Ok, see you soon," I replied. Despite the turmoil and inner conflict I had experienced, I had already resolved not to bring up the true reason for my sudden departure. All I wanted was for everything to be copacetic, and in that moment, I still harboured a glimmer of hope that we could remain friends and move forward together.

As I reflected on my emotions, I grappled with uncertainty, questioning whether my feelings were genuine or simply heightened by the weight of recent events. Despite my inner turmoil, I extended a handshake to both guys as they departed in their respective trucks, swiftly dropping off my gear and boat. Within moments of their departure, a text was sent: "Send that $350 to Jay." Those few words marked the end of our interaction, leaving me to ponder the depth of our connection and the abruptness of our parting.

Having previously agreed to split the cost of the trip, the sudden request for payment felt out of place. Money had never been a point of contention between us, as we were both financially comfortable. Our interactions had always been characterized by a casual approach to expenses, taking turns covering various costs without keeping track or discussing it. Richard was well aware of this unspoken understanding. Feeling the need to address the situation, I gave him a call.

"Hey, I didn't ride back with you guys from Manitoba to Red Lake, nor back to my house," I said. "Ya but your fucking gear did." he snapped. The conversation quickly turned confrontational, with his sharp retort triggering my outburst. I raised my voice, demanding to be heard. "Shut the fuck up and listen to me. I paid $3,000 to get home," I exclaimed, trying to convey the gravity of the situation. However, his dismissive response only fuelled my frustration further. I unleashed a torrent of emotions, laying bare all my feelings and grievances, detailing every action or inaction that had led to this breaking point. "Yeah, but I didn't force you," he cut me off. I exploded. I poured out everything. I shared all my feelings, everything he did or didn't do. He realized he had been acting like a completely different person on this trip. I ended up paying more than what was requested of me just to be done with this situation.

We had been camping together for years, he was always the same guy, but this time he was acting completely different. As for the money situation, I told him, "I got a deal from Albert for gas money, that should count for something. Plus, you were passing by here on your way home. It's not about the money, it's about the fact that you texted me that and then snapped at me. You were clearly only concerned about Jay getting paid, and that seemed to be your sole focus." I said. He actually apologized. I responded, "That's fine, but I'm done. I'm going to spend time with my family, and don't worry, I'll make sure to pay Jay." We said "OK" and hung up, another friend lost. I should have noticed some signs back then, but I see them clearly now. Years ago, I shared an idea with him. With the abundance of outdoor creators on Instagram and YouTube in Ontario, many of whom I knew, I wanted to plan a winter meet-up, reminiscent of the ones I used to attend during the BCUSA days. More on that later.

DAY 14 OF 19 — JULY 19, 2025 — 3:15PM

I woke up a few times during the night to pee. I can't wait for urethra surgery, and I plan to have it this winter, finally. It was a full moon, shining brightly in my tent area. It was so nice. I fell back to sleep easily. I planned on getting an early start to paddle Smoothrock while it was still calm, just in case the red canoe guys were coming this way too. I wanted to get to the Walleye Kitchen before them.

I enjoyed a quick oatmeal breakfast. I had set up everything the night before — arranging twigs for my Ganesha twig stove with my pot nearby. It only took five minutes, and I was able to eat while organizing my gear in the boat. By 6:00am, I was already on the water, savouring the peaceful calm of what is typically the daunting Smoothrock Lake. I burned a quick bowl, as custom, and started my paddle. No double blade on Smoothrock? What!?! I single bladed the whole paddle today! About four hours in total. Two hours through the main part of Smoothrock and Spring lakes, through the Fantasia portage.

After paddling a little while longer, I arrived at a portage around a set of gorgeous rapids and an extremely nice, lush, green campsite right at the start of the portage trail. I contemplated staying at this site. Not being able to shake the thought that I had been wanting to stay at Walleye Kitchen, I then saw red canoe paint on a rock and another in the water next to the takeout — lots of red. Those guys were sitting a bit low. What if they came here last night and were now at the Walleye Kitchen? I would have to pass by and miss camping there.

I scoped out the site by the port. A flat spot for a tent, no black flies, swimming, fishing, scenic, a spot to hang my tarp to get some shade. Ok, I'm sold. I was planning on staying at the Kitchen or right by there for two nights anyway, this was close by, so it's pretty much the same thing. I have no idea if it was those guys in the red canoe I saw or some previous trippers, but I am loving this site. It was meant to happen for sure.

I set up my tent, a tarp, and lounged in the sun. I went for two swims, all while taking breaks from writing. I had chicken dumplings for lunch. I'm comfortable in my tent, the sun went behind the clouds a while ago. The deer flies were eating my back and my ankles out there, so I am laying in my tent, writing a not so enjoyable part, counting the days now.

I sense that I have the energy for about four more nights. While I am hesitant to depart prematurely and potentially regret it, the proximity to the takeout and the near completion of my book present a compelling dilemma.

So that is why I can only move a short distance for a couple of days until I reach the Kopka and perhaps discover myself at the two-night spot, Isaac's spot... But, at the same time, I don't want to miss any more time with my family, especially when the girls are on summer break. And for what? Bragging rights? To say that I completed three weeks solo? Yeah, probably!

I told Richard that I wanted to set up a content creator meet-up. He may have suggested a group on Instagram, but that was the extent of his involvement. I believe he was just the first person I shared the idea with. I created a group on Instagram called "Ontario Outdoor Content Creators Meet-Up" and invited many well-known individuals, most of whom I had previously camped with or met in person.

Everyone seemed excited and happy to be a part of this group. We all discussed where to go and what to do, and it was decided that we would meet up in March for a winter camp. The planning process was great. However, what struck me as odd was that I heard a couple of people mention how cool it was for "Joe and Richard to set this up," and then more about how great it was for "Richard to organize everything." I brushed it off and didn't think much of it at the time.

I don't want to come across as boastful or belittle Richard, but without my initiative in creating the group and inviting the creators, it's unlikely that anyone would have joined. I had good relationships with everyone, which is why I extended the invitations. I admit that not inviting Shawn was intentional, and looking back, I realize it was a petty move on my part. The reason everyone joined and attended was due to the invitations and organization efforts. You can ask them yourself. As for Richard, he remained a friend throughout the camp. Our interactions were consistent with our past camping experiences, and we continued to get along well in group settings.

As winter arrived, my thoughts naturally turned to spring, a time of renewal. However, the loss of Isaac continues to weigh heavily on me, and I'm uncertain if I'll ever fully heal from that loss. Spending more time at home, I focused on creating winter base camp videos, but I noticed a slowdown in activity on YouTube. The constant challenges of winter camping in harsh conditions, like blizzards, had taken a toll on me, and I was feeling burnt out.

I experimented with stealth camping inspired by Steve Wallis, hoping for similar success, but unfortunately, it didn't yield the results I had hoped for. Additionally, I found myself relying heavily on T1s, not just for my stomach issues but also to cope with the emotional pain of losing Isaac. While the medication initially provided some relief, I began to realize that it was becoming more of a problem than a solution. Rather than improving my digestive issues, it was starting to have negative effects on my health. I began experiencing symptoms of acetaminophen poisoning, leading to severe and frequent diarrhea, which was taking a toll on my liver and likely other parts of my body. Despite the harmful effects, I continued with my habits enthusiastically. I found myself drinking more heavily than ever before, day after day. Reflecting on my actions, one might expect that I would have learned a lesson from Isaac's passing, but instead, I was consumed by grief and sought solace in substances.

During that winter, I found myself spending a lot of time at home and online, feeling bored and restless. I started looking into dirt bikes and motocamping as a way to add some excitement to my routine. It reminded me that I already had a motorcycle sitting in my garage. A few years back, I had taken a trip to Toronto and treated myself to a Honda CB500X, a smaller bike that had been waiting for its next adventure. The Honda CB500X, capable of both on-trail and off-road travel, was equipped with camping gear, making it perfect for motocamping adventures. My love for motorcycles traces back to when my mom married Ron, who had a motorcycle during the early years of their relationship. He used to take me for rides, and as a seven-year-old boy, I thought it was the most manly and awesome thing ever.

When I had some extra cash to spare, I made the decision to purchase the Honda CB500X without hesitation. I drove to pick it up, and with some effort, we managed to load it precariously into my truck. Back at home, my buddy and his two sons helped me unload it. I had never ridden a motorcycle before. Unfortunately, the bike ended up sitting in my garage for years as I never found the time to take a motorcycle course. Those were the peak years of YouTube for me, constantly balancing between camping trips and editing videos. The cycle of camping, editing, and repeating went on year after year.

The bike remained untouched, gathering dust in my garage. During that winter, I began to feel a shift was needed for my YouTube channel. The views were dwindling, and I wondered if perhaps people were growing tired of watching me camp after over a decade, or if they could sense that it had become more of a job for me rather than a passion. Despite this, my love for canoe tripping and capturing it on film remained unwavering - still to this day. I genuinely enjoy the experience, but during the winter months, everything felt forced as I eagerly awaited the thaw for the ice to melt and the adventures to begin anew.

Feeling the need to revitalize my YouTube audience, I saw motocamping as a potential gateway to a new viewership. With my current audience dwindling, I believed this new adventure could attract fresh eyes. After days of online research and video watching, I made the decision to purchase a dirt bike to learn on come early spring when time allowed. Before the ice melted off the lakes, I planned to teach myself how to shift gears and ride, drawing on my experience with 4-wheelers, snowmobiles, and side-by-sides. Confident in my ability to learn from online tutorials, I was determined to master this new skill.

Excited about my new venture into dirt biking, I purchased a Kawasaki KLX 300 in excellent condition. When I went to pick it up, the seller recognized me from YouTube, a common occurrence by now. It seems my online presence was reaching far and wide. Even my kids, who accompany me to the grocery store, roll their eyes at the recognition, not quite grasping the coolness of their dad being recognized in public. That or I'm just simply not cool to their generation. In early April, I picked up the Kawasaki and dedicated a few days to teaching myself how to ride. Before long, I felt like I had mastered it. I was thrilled with my progress and the confidence I had gained in such a short time. Shifting gears smoothly and exploring the trails with ease, I was enjoying every moment of my newfound skill on the dirt bike.

Within a week of mastering the dirt bike, I felt confident enough to take my Honda motorcycle out on the road without any mishaps like before. As I geared up in my motorcycle jacket, boots, and helmet, I started off slowly in my driveway. Once I hit the road, it felt like I was floating, living out a dream. I spent the entire day riding, relishing the freedom and thrill of the open road. Taking Will for a ride, I enjoyed the feeling of connection as she gripped me with her thighs and held onto me tightly when I accelerated. "I am a man now," I said, jokingly.

As spring of 2024 rolled around, Autumn was in Senior Kindergarten and Emmie was in Grade 6. Both of them had settled in quickly, making friends easily in the neighbourhood where we had been living for six years already. It's truly remarkable how time flies by. People always used to mention how fast time goes, but witnessing the growth and development of your own children really puts that concept into perspective. Time passing in the context of your children's milestones and achievements truly hits differently. Autumn had found her very best friend forever, Emma-Roo. The two girls were inseparable at school, so naturally, the next step was to arrange playdates and sleepovers. It was a match made in heaven! We were so fortunate. You can't choose your kids' friends or their parents, but we truly lucked out with this one. Emma's parents, Marc and Kaitlyn, along with her older sister Sophie and my buddy Cain, the youngest and only boy in the group, quickly became part of our extended family.

They are a great family, and we quickly hit it off. Sophie and Emmie, Autumn and Emma, Will and Kaitlyn, and us three boys - Marc, Cain, and me. We had the kids over for sleepovers, and they did the same at our house. It was wonderful to make like-minded, similarly aged friends. The fact that they were close by made it even better. The immediate trust we shared with each other regarding our children says a lot.

I had the motorcycle itch somewhat scratched for the time being. I still had plans for motocamping. In fact, I even recorded a video, brimming with excitement, announcing my upcoming adventure. However, my focus had shifted to the eagerly awaited ice-out season. Ice-out trout fishing took precedence above all else during this time of year. That particular year, I had a fishing trip lined up with Doug's brother, Carl. I had met Carl a couple of times before. He was a nice guy who had a passion for fishing and was quite skilled at it, but his expertise lay in fishing from a boat in southern Ontario or angling for Steelhead in rivers. He preferred wading in the water rather than fishing from a canoe in the remote back lakes.

He had the itch and ended up purchasing an Esquif Adirondack, a solo canoe weighing under 50 lbs, which was perfect for him. I have a multitude of fantastic backcountry lakes and routes within just a few hours from where I live. We made plans for him to assist me with trout fishing. While I had become quite skilled at it by now, I was always eager to learn from someone I respected in the craft. I was tasked with showing him the ins and outs of canoe tripping and the best spots to explore. We organized a trip for a few nights and set out in early May. It was truly incredible, and I brought Wolfie along for the adventure. Both of us managed to reel in some impressive splake, brookies, and lakers. The highlight of the trip was the stunning display of the aurora borealis on the second night, and I was able to capture it on film!

Before this trip, in late April, I embarked on my first adventure with Joel and Brodie, who make it a tradition to go on an ice-out trip every year. Joel and I had camped together before and had discussed the idea of ice-out trips. Brodie, Joel's longtime best friend, was more than happy to join in. They have had great success fishing for brooke trout in Little Osler Lake in Algonquin. On my end, I've had my fair share of success fishing in the Petawawa River in Algonquin as well. Among the three of us, we devised a route that includes both of these destinations. It's a long journey in terms of kilometres, but definitely worth it. The three of us had a fantastic time together, with no tension or jealousy, just friendly banter and mutual assistance. We caught plenty of trout, except at Little Osler, eh, fellas?

After those trips, I was approaching my 40th birthday on the 19th of May in 2024. Since returning from the trip with Joel and Brodie, I had significantly reduced my alcohol consumption and cut back on the T1s. I was still taking them, but I was gradually trying to reduce my dependence on them, which seemed like a daunting challenge. I spent my time building and repairing things in the garage. I was feeling quite positive for the first time in a while. I mentioned this to Will, and she agreed, saying she could see the difference in me. However, it seemed like my streak of good fortune was about to come to an end. It felt like every time I gained momentum, a significant obstacle would appear in my path.

A few days after returning home from the trout trip with Carl, we planned to have a barbecue that evening for dinner, with Marc and his family coming over for burgers. The kids weren't fans of steak. Earlier that day, around noon, Sophie, their oldest girl, and I went for a 4-wheeler ride to gather wild leeks, a spring delicacy.

It was a wonderful day, as far as I can recall. Emmie was enjoying a birthday party at her friend's house. Marc and the rest of the family joined us, and we gathered around a crackling fire just as I got the call to pick up Emmie later in the day.

Upon returning, I noticed my bike standing there, beckoning to be ridden. Filled with excitement, I impulsively hopped on without a helmet. With a burst of energy, I took off from the driveway, feeling the thrill of the moment, fishtailing down the road. The evening was transitioning into a cool, dewy dusk as I rode off into the fading spring light. Regrettably, my memory fades at this point, leaving me with no recollection of the events that followed. I'll defer to Will to provide the details and fill in the gaps.

10

BY WILHEMINA ROBINET

THE DAY OF JOEY'S accident was incredibly surreal. It started as a typical spring day in May with friends but quickly turned into one I would never wish on anyone. I was at home with our friends and the kids when Emerald came in and said, "Dad left on his dirt bike." As the evening approached, I didn't expect him to go far or be out for very long. Our friend Marc went outside immediately to check if Joe was nearby on the property. A few minutes later, Marc returned and inquired about what was at the end of the street. "Are there any trails he might have taken his bike down over there?" he asked. I informed him that there weren't any trails. However, Marc was convinced that Joey had gone in that direction. "Can I take the 4-wheeler just to be sure?" he asked me.

Marc had a sense of unease about the situation. While he was out looking for Joey, his wife Kaitlyn and I were preparing their kids to go home, unaware of the unfolding events. Suddenly, Marc returned looking pale and panicked. "You two, in the truck NOW!" he exclaimed.

I could sense from the expression on his face and the urgency in his voice that something terrible had occurred. My heart sank, and I quickly instructed Emerald to watch the kids. We jumped into Marc's truck and drove halfway down the road. There he was, lying lifeless about six feet from his bike. Without hesitation, I leaped out of the truck and sprinted towards him. He was making strange facial expressions while curled up in the fetal position, clearly unconscious.

I yelled for Marc or Kaitlyn to call 911, realizing I had left my phone at home during the frantic escape. Kaitlyn bravely made the urgent call to 911 using Marc's phone, while I held Joey close, wrapping my entire body around him. He lay near a shallow ditch, his body drenched and shivering uncontrollably. It seemed like he had been there for at least 20 minutes.

Kaitlyn had to backtrack down the road to find a cellphone signal. As she spoke to the paramedics, she quickly retrieved a blanket from our house. Meanwhile, Marc carefully supported Joey's head to keep it still as we wrapped him snugly in the blanket. Kaitlyn stayed by his side, monitoring his pulse while we waited for the paramedics to arrive. We noticed blood underneath him, but we were cautious not to move him in case of a potential neck injury. Nearby, there were large rocks and boulders, adding to the urgency of the situation.

After about ten minutes with no ambulance in sight, my concern grew for the kids at home who must have been scared. I quickly called our neighbour Tammy, explained the situation, and asked her to go sit with the kids. Her husband Jake also came down to offer assistance. "The kids are all crying," he mentioned, but my attention remained solely on Joey, hoping for help to arrive soon.

After about thirty minutes had passed with still no sign of an ambulance, Kaitlyn made another call. We reside in a very remote area, and the ambulance was still struggling to reach us. It had been dispatched from a hospital over an hour away. Suddenly, Joey began to regain some consciousness but was extremely disoriented. We instructed him to stay still, and I held onto him tightly, the three of us working together to soothe him. As he started to shift, I noticed more blood - there was a lot of blood.

By that point, it had been about forty minutes since our initial 911 call. Joey had been in that position for just under an hour. When the paramedics arrived with a neck brace and board, they struggled to get Joey onto it as he was confused and agitated, not comprehending the situation.

It took all of us, including the paramedics, to carefully position Joey on the board and into the ambulance.

As the ambulance left for the nearest hospital, I hurried back home to check on the kids. It was clear they had been upset, so I tried my best to downplay the seriousness of the situation until I had more information. "Dad had a fall off his bike and had to go to the hospital," I explained, holding back my own emotions. I didn't want to alarm them further. "You'll be staying with Marc and Kaitlyn tonight so I can be with Dad at the hospital."

My neighbour Tammy kindly drove me to the hospital as I was too overwhelmed to drive myself. Upon arriving, I could hear the medical staff trying to communicate with Joey. A nurse passed by the doors, completely covered in his blood, which was a distressing sight. I hadn't received any updates yet and was anxious to speak to someone about Joey's condition. The Ontario Provincial Police (OPP) had arrived and required a statement from me. Despite being shaken up, I tried my best to recount the events, but the questions were challenging to answer amidst my emotional state. I couldn't help but cry and repeatedly ask about Joey's well-being. The OPP constable showed great compassion, offering to arrange a health status check for me and suggesting we could speak later when I was more composed.

After some time, a doctor came out and requested that I accompany her alone. As I passed through the double doors, the noise abruptly ceased, enveloping me in an eerie silence that left me feeling apprehensive. She led me to a private room where she disclosed that Joey had been sedated to manage the swelling in his brain and head. She explained that his intense screaming was due to the pressure on his skull and that he was being readied for transfer to another hospital. No tests had been performed but she was fairly certain he would never be the same. She asked me if he had any mental instability because he wasn't wearing a helmet. It was clear they were assessing his risky behaviour and wondering if this was possibly self-inflicted. She then inquired about our family and children. I shared that the kids were doing okay, but our extended family lived over 12 hours away. I will always remember her suggestion for me to go home to be with the kids, implying there was no hope for Joey. Overwhelmed, I returned to the waiting room, where I tearfully recounted the conversation to Tammy. Despite the emotional turmoil, I had still not had the chance to see Joey.

By 10:30pm, I made my way to the parking lot to call Vickie, Joey's mom. It was evident she was asleep, and I struggled to find the words through my tears. "Joey was in an accident, and it's bad," I managed to convey amidst my sobs. Vickie assured me she would gather her things and head up as soon as possible. I then called my parents, who agreed to be on standby until we had more information. Upon returning to the hospital waiting room, Tammy mentioned that Jake could drive me the 45-minute journey to the new hospital once Joey was ready to be transferred.

Upon arriving at Sault Area Hospital, I checked in and was briefed on the ongoing tests and evaluations. I made periodic calls from the waiting room phone, receiving the same updates each time. It felt like an eternity before I was granted entry, waiting for three long hours. Joey was situated in the critical care section of the ER. As I entered the room and laid eyes on him, the sight was heart-wrenching. Tears welled up once more as I took in his appearance. His face was swollen, marked with open wounds, and his body covered in road rash. The medical team had to carefully cut his clothes off, and he lay there heavily sedated.

As I sat beside Joey, the doctor started detailing the extent of his injuries: significant swelling and a lacerated kidney. They had conducted MRI scans of his brain, spine, and torso, along with x-rays of all his limbs. Miraculously, he had no broken bones. However, due to the severity of his injuries, including the lacerated kidney and head swelling, he required immediate transfer via air ambulance to the ICU at the Sudbury Trauma Centre. The clock had ticked past 3:00am by this point.

While Jake took a nap in his truck in the parking lot, I stayed by Joey's side. I called his mom once more to share the latest update. She made plans to join me in Sudbury and would set off in the morning. Throughout the night, I found solace in conversing with the nurses. They emphasized how fortunate Joey was to be alive and particularly lucky to have escaped any broken bones. I assisted in cleaning and bandaging his wounds, which were so deep that it required the effort of multiple individuals. The morning fog caused delays, and it wasn't until around 10:00am that Joey could be airlifted. I was given the option to accompany him, but I chose to return home to be with our children. I was also reminded to pack a bag, as the length of our stay in Sudbury was uncertain.

Jake drove me back home that morning, where Marc was waiting with our daughters. I embraced Marc tightly, expressing my gratitude for his intuition. "If it weren't for your gut feeling, who knows how long Joey might have been out there alone," I told him. I took some time with the girls as I packed, ensuring to explain to them that their dad needed to rest at the hospital where he could receive proper care. I wanted to shield them from any further trauma. I reassured them that their aunt Abby would be coming to stay with them, providing comfort and support during this challenging time.

When I called Joey's sister Abby earlier that morning, her emotions were raw. "Will, I can't lose another brother. I can't lose him," she expressed, her voice filled with anguish. Abby shared that she, along with Vickie, their mom, would come up to stay at our place while I was in Sudbury with Joey. As Kaitlyn and I began our drive to Sudbury, I attempted to catch some sleep in the car, realizing I hadn't rested in the past 24 hours. However, my mind was consumed with endless "what if" scenarios that kept me wide awake, making it difficult to find peace even in moments of quiet travel.

Upon our arrival in Sudbury, we found Joey in the ER. The staff promptly attended to Kaitlyn and me. Joey had been under their care for a few hours, and his wounds showed signs of improvement. Despite their efforts to remove his wedding ring, his swollen hands posed a challenge. In that moment, it dawned on me that Joey had several significant trips planned, including one with Kyle in just a few days. I promptly reached out to Kyle and briefed him on the situation. Kyle offered reassurance, promising to handle all the necessary cancellations with the outfitters, alleviating some of the logistical burdens.

After Joey was settled in his room, the primary physician shared with me the difficult decision to place him in an induced coma to facilitate the healing of his brain and head injuries. Additionally, Joey was put on life support to aid his body in the healing process. The doctor explained that Joey would require multiple medications to keep him sedated, noting his high tolerance for medications, as they worked diligently to provide the

CHAPTER 10

best care possible for his recovery. As Joey was kept in a coma, the medical team administered the highest doses of propofol and fentanyl to maintain his sedation. His body's violent reactions to the swelling caused him to thrash, making it impossible for him to breathe on his own. With Joey's mom now by his side, we secured a hotel room next door to the hospital. Exhausted from the events of the past two days, I realized the importance of taking care of myself as well amidst the challenging circumstances.

The following morning, as we returned to the hospital, we were informed that the medical team would attempt to wake Joey twice a day to assess his brain activity. They initiated the process by discontinuing the medications that kept him sedated. Observing any movements from Joey, they proceeded to ask him questions in search of any signs of response, carefully monitoring his progress in the hopes of positive developments. His body began to thrash violently again, and there was no response, so the sedation process began again. This was horrific to watch. I was hoping so badly for a response. Just squeeze my finger. But he never did. I had to hold it together while trying to absorb everything the doctors were saying. They reassured me the thrashing was normal.

Eventually, a neurologist appeared, explaining that Joey's MRI didn't show brain swelling. I was told he had a traumatic brain injury in the soft tissue of his brain. Joey had hit his head so hard that his brain moved back and forth in his skull. The soft tissue could develop bruising and is highly unpredictable. The extent of the damage remained uncertain until Joey regained consciousness. I was informed that he had also suffered a concussion and that recovery from this accident could take up to a year.

Later that day, a counsellor from the hospital came to see me. She asked who had power of attorney over Joey's medical decisions. I informed her that I did, feeling like I was about to lose him. She handed me a stack of paperwork for insurance that needed signatures. Eventually, the doctor informed me that Joey would be staying unconscious for a while, so I decided it was time to inform some of his friends about what had happened. I felt lost, scared, and overwhelmed as I explained that Joey was in a coma and we didn't know what to expect. I simply asked them to pray for him. He needed all the prayers he could get.

During the second attempt to elicit a response from Joey with the hospital staff, I noticed that his left arm didn't twitch like his right one did. He began thrashing violently once again until the staff turned his meds back on. "Why isn't his left arm moving?" I asked. They simply told me it was from the crash. At this point, I was beyond overwhelmed. I hadn't eaten or slept in days and was missing my girls. I remember lying in bed in the hotel feeling completely lost and helpless. The room began to spin, and I felt very dizzy. As my emotions took over, I cried out for Vickie, who was in the adjacent bed. I was having a panic attack and would be prescribed clonazepam the next day.

The next few days were just a blurry repeat. We'd get to the hospital, turn off the meds, hope for a response, watch him thrash around violently, and eventually sedate him again. By now, they were able to remove his wedding ring without cutting it. I wore it on his necklace every single day. When I took breaks from his room for food or air, I would call my dad to let my emotions out. My brother called every day as well. Joey's friend Doug also checked in regularly. Emerald, being older than Autumn, was more aware of the situation. Witnessing Joey's physical struggles as the staff tried to wake him was incredibly challenging. I would speak to him, holding his hand, and gently asking him to squeeze my fingers if he could hear me. At times, he would squeeze my fingers, filling me with hope. While the doctors believed it was just muscle spasms and not intentional, I held onto my optimism.

One day, Joey's doctor came in to provide our daily update. He mentioned that Joey's kidney was healing well and that surgery wouldn't be necessary, which was a huge relief. The bleeding had stopped. The doctor then inquired about Joey's personality before the accident and invited us for a walk to another patient's room. This patient had been in a similar accident to Joey and had suffered similar injuries. The doctor mentioned that this patient was six weeks into his recovery and that we could anticipate similar progress for Joey. Although the man was no longer on life support, his brain function was still not optimal. He seemed awake, yet his body thrashed about similar to Joey's movements. The man couldn't speak, and it was unclear if he was aware of his surroundings. The doctor gently advised us that we might be feeling overly optimistic and should prepare for a longer recovery period. He mentioned that it could take at least a year, and there was a possibility that Joey's condition might not fully return to how it was before.

Joey was under 24-hour observation, with a nurse by his side at all times. One nurse advised me to refrain from speaking to him while they were trying to rouse him, as she believed it might agitate him further. However, another nurse expressed a different perspective, suggesting that Joey's movements could indicate a response to my voice, which gave me hope that he could hear me and was trying to reach out to me.

Eventually the medical team decided that it was time to gradually decrease Joey's medication. The routine of pausing his medication, communicating with him, and then resuming the medication was becoming challenging to maintain. At this point, the medical team agreed to discontinue his medication entirely and allow him to naturally awaken. The doctor mentioned that it could take a few days before we notice any responses from Joey as he begins to wake up on his own. He appeared peaceful, resembling someone in a deep slumber. The life support equipment had been removed, and it was a relief to see him free from the tangle of IV bags. There were subtle signs that he was becoming more responsive to the sounds in his surroundings. I recall tenderly kissing him on the forehead, and to my surprise, he reciprocated with a gentle kissing motion, as if trying to return the affection. The emotions of that day will stay with me forever. Abby had captured a recording of Wolf doing his husky howling. When I played it for Joey, he began calling out for him. It was an unforgettable and heartwarming moment that filled me with awe. Witnessing Joey's response made me realize that he was still present within himself, and I felt a sense of relief and gratitude for these rapid improvements. Although Joey had not fully regained consciousness, each passing day revealed more of his true self.

One morning, I received a call from his nurse, informing me that Joey had awakened. Both his mom and I rushed to the hospital, where we found him sitting up in bed. As he gazed at me, there was a spark of recognition in his eyes, but I was unsure of what would come next. I embraced him tightly, hoping to ease his confusion. Then, he asked me the question that I had been dreading: "What happened?" Joey was disoriented, unable to grasp the current date, month, or year. He was in disbelief when I tried to explain the accident to him. The doctor arranged for a specialist to assess

Joey, with me as a reference point for the accuracy of his answers. Much of his information was muddled, indicating a significant gap in his memory spanning the past five to six years. It was heartbreaking to see him struggle to recall having two daughters, underscoring the depth of his memory loss. Remarkably, Joey's memory began to resurface swiftly once he was presented with the facts. Over the following days, he was bombarding people with numerous questions, showcasing his earnest efforts to reconstruct his memories. The medical team remained optimistic that his memory would gradually return in its entirety, although they cautioned that the process would be lengthy. Each passing day showed incremental improvement, signalling that Joey was on the path to recovery. It was a significant milestone when the decision was made to transition him from the intensive care unit to a standard hospital room, marking a positive step forward in his journey.

Joey's confusion persisted as he grappled with the aftermath of his experiences. He recounted vivid dreams and sensations from his time in a coma, which felt strikingly authentic to him. Distinguishing between these dreamlike memories and the reality of his situation proved to be a daunting task. Tragically, Joey had no recollection of his brother Isaac's passing, and the medical team advised that this information be withheld from him during his recovery period.

Despite being awake, Joey faced challenges with mobility and dexterity. His left arm and hand were nonfunctional, while his right hand had limited use due to nerve damage, as indicated by test results. It was recommended that he consult with a nerve specialist to address this issue. Additionally, Joey struggled to stand independently, requiring assistance for mobility. The physiotherapist diligently worked with him, taking him for daily walks down the hallway using a walker to support his movements. Joey's journey toward physical recovery was undoubtedly a gradual and demanding process, but each step forward was a testament to his resilience and determination. Preparing for Joey's transition back home, his physiotherapist provided a comprehensive list of essential items, such as a wheelchair, commode, walker, and support handles for the bathrooms to ensure his safety and comfort. It was recommended that I arrange for a physiotherapist to continue his rehabilitation outside the hospital setting, ensuring regular sessions to aid in his recovery. Understanding the level of care Joey would require, I was advised that he would need round-the-clock assistance during the initial period at home.

Joey's frustration grew as his time in the hospital extended. He struggled to comprehend the treatments and longed to return home. Each day, I left the hospital with tears in my eyes, feeling the weight of the uncertainty ahead. While Joey's memory showed remarkable progress, the timeline for his physical recovery remained uncertain, casting a shadow of doubt over our journey. The emotional toll of navigating these unknowns was palpable, but the glimmer of hope lay in Joey's swift memory restoration. We had no way of knowing if he would ever regain the use of his left hand. The idea of Joey never being able to paddle a canoe again was devastating, and I have since learned never to take things for granted, no matter how small.

One morning, I received a call from Joey's doctor informing me that he was discharging himself from the hospital, and there was little she could do to prevent it. I was urged to hurry to the hospital. Despite my attempts to reason with him, Joey was upset about a fall he had experienced the previous night while using the urinal. The fall had been severe, with him landing heavily on his left side, unable to break his fall with his injured hand. I was with Emerald when I received the call about Joey's decision to leave the hospital on his own. It was the first time she had seen her dad since the accident. I recall the overwhelming joy on Emerald's face as she reunited with her father, and they shared a heartfelt embrace before we gathered his belongings to head back home. Autumn, too, was elated to have her dad home again. Joey embraced both girls, expressing his apologies repeatedly as they welcomed him back with open arms.

During the initial period, I had to assist Joey with various daily tasks. I stood by him to help him with bathroom visits, supported him in and out of the bath, aided him in getting dressed, prepared all his meals, and even assisted him with eating. Additionally, I took on the responsibility of driving him to all his appointments, ensuring he received the care and support he needed during this challenging time. My role as a caregiver was crucial in providing Joey with the necessary assistance and care as he navigated his recovery journey. The entire family rallied together to provide support. The girls showed a willingness to care for him, yet witnessing his intense struggles was emotionally challenging. Joey's frustration and anger grew as he grappled with his dependence on others, a situation he found particularly difficult to accept.

Joey's leg strength gradually returned, allowing him to walk independently at a rapid pace. Although his balance remained a concern, he showed daily improvement in this area. To ensure his well-being, I was advised to restrict his access to his phone and prevent him from making significant decisions. Despite this, Joey's primary desire was to reach out to his loved ones to express his apologies for the events that had transpired. Joey experienced intense emotions, a common occurrence during the recovery process as explained by the medical professionals. They cautioned us that unstable emotions and potential personality changes could be part of his journey. The unpredictability of these changes made it challenging to anticipate what lay ahead, emphasizing the need for patience and understanding as Joey navigated through this phase of his recovery.

As time passed, our loved ones had weathered significant trauma. Despite our joy at Joey's return home, we faced the challenging task of helping him piece together his fragmented memories. One day, Joey requested his phone to contact his brother Isaac, a subject we had deliberately avoided discussing. Confronted with the prospect of revisiting the painful memory of Isaac's passing, we grappled with the difficult question of how to broach this sensitive topic with Joey after all he had been through. In the kitchen, I shared with Vickie my decision to broach the topic of Isaac with Joey. Together, we guided Joey to a separate room, where we gently broke the news to him once more that Isaac was no longer with us. As we recounted the details, Joey's memories gradually resurfaced. The room was filled with emotions as we collectively revisited the sorrow and heartache of Isaac's passing, allowing Joey to process this difficult reality once again.

I had set up a small corner in the garage with a chair where I could retreat to cry or release my emotions. I preferred to keep this private space to myself, away from prying eyes, to conceal the extent of how deeply everything was impacting me. While I understood the importance of being a pillar of strength for my family, there were moments when I struggled to maintain composure. In those vulnerable times, I sought solace in the garage, allowing myself to cry and find comfort through prayer. Witnessing my husband, the love of my life, reliant on life support, alongside the uncertainty surrounding our future and our children's futures, was incredibly daunting. The amalgamation of emotions - sadness, fear, and heartbreak - became unbearably heavy to carry. Experiencing such overwhelming emotions, I wouldn't wish that on anyone.

Joey marked his 40th birthday while in a coma, and he also missed the one-year anniversary of Isaac's passing during this challenging time. The notion that writing can serve as a form of therapy rings true, as it allows us to process and make sense of challenging experiences. Recalling these trying times continues to evoke a range of emotions, leaving me in disbelief. The entire ordeal feels surreal, and revisiting these memories stirs up deep emotions within me. That month felt like an eternity, filled with uncertainty and heartache. I am immensely thankful for the compassionate and dedicated healthcare professionals who played an integral part in our journey to recovery from this tragic accident. Their support and care have been invaluable in helping us navigate through this difficult time.

AFTER WAKING UP FROM a coma in the hospital, I was disoriented about the identity of the person we were visiting. Who is sick? Drake (yes, THAT Drake) seemed to have disappeared, and memories of my life at the remote cabin were slipping away like Marty McFly's siblings in their photo from 1985 after he altered the timeline. It's a bit like living multiple lives in a short span of time. I'll try my best to piece together the details, but for a while, it felt like I was experiencing a series of very different realities.

I turned the dirt bike around and made my way back home to the comfort of my loved ones and friends who depended on me. Speeding around the bend, I spotted a shallow ditch and, perhaps in a split-second decision, I attempted to navigate it like I would on a snowmobile. It's unclear whether I misjudged the turn, failed to see the bend altogether, or swerved for some other reason. The exact sequence of events may remain a mystery to me.

The tall grass hid many large rocks, including some as big as bowling balls. I collided with one at full speed, causing the front tire to veer sharply to the side and sending me flying through the air as the bike somersaulted. I landed extremely far from the bike. Despite my countless visits to the accident site in a quest for clarity, the truth remains elusive. It's a puzzle with missing pieces, but dwelling on it endlessly serves no purpose now. The focus should be on moving forward and embracing the present, as some mysteries may never be fully solved.

Marc heard the sound of the bike returning, followed by silence. Waiting for my return, he initially assumed that I had run out of gas or that the bike had stalled. However, after 20 minutes passed without any sign of me, a sense of unease crept into his stomach. Trusting his instincts, he quickly hopped on a 4-wheeler and set off in the direction from which he had last heard me.

Marc's heart sank when he found me, unable to elicit a clear response from me as I lay there, possibly moaning in pain. Without hesitation, he rushed back to the house for help. Within moments, Kaitlyn swiftly drove Will to where I was, just five houses down. Will's urgency was evident as she leaped out of the truck even before it came to a complete stop. The scene was grim – my face bore severe injuries above and below my left eye, with my forehead also taking a hit, all this without wearing a helmet.

Will wrapped herself around me in the damp ditch to keep me warm as I shivered. Despite the pain and confusion, I attempted to get up, urgently expressing the need to use the restroom. They restrained me as I struggled against their hold. The ambulance took 45 minutes to reach us due to our remote location. Upon reaching the nearest hospital, it became clear that they were unable to provide the necessary care. I was swiftly transferred to a hospital in Sault Ste. Marie, where they did what they could but determined that my injuries required more advanced treatment. Consequently, I was airlifted to Sudbury hospital for further medical attention.

In the midst of the chaos, my wife had the heartbreaking task of informing our children and then making the urgent journey to Sudbury. Her strength and resilience shone brightly throughout this harrowing experience, demonstrating her unwavering courage. However, the doctor's blunt words at the initial hospital, advising her to return home and care for the children as they implied a grim outcome, were incredibly jarring and insensitive given the traumatic circumstances.

Will's call to my mom initiated a swift response, with both my mom and sister promptly arriving in Sudbury to join Will by my side. The medical team worked tirelessly to address my injuries, including stitching up my facial wounds, treating brain damage, a possible ruptured kidney, and assessing the unknown extent of nerve damage. For three weeks, I existed in a different realm, my consciousness elsewhere as my body fought to heal.

Describing my experiences during the coma is a challenging task, as they were so surreal and vivid. It felt as though I inhabited multiple lives, all distinctly me yet incredibly bizarre. It's hard to put into words, but I'll attempt to share a glimpse of it. It wasn't as if I was transported to another place; rather, it felt like I had already lived those alternate lives in intricate detail. For instance, I found myself riding dirt bikes with Drake in his hometown of Toronto, but the scenery resembled the Dieppe Gardens waterfront in Windsor, creating a surreal blend of familiarity and strangeness.

In that alternate reality, as I rode alongside Drake, I vividly recall purchasing a watch for Emerald, one that she had been eager to use for gaming. Following Drake's advice, I opted for the top-of-the-line model so that she could enjoy playing games with his child. It may sound incredibly far-fetched, but within that dreamlike existence, it felt as though I had lived that life for an eternity. The back-and-forth rides on the bikes along the waterfront, the act of buying the watch, and the joy of surprising Emmie online all seemed to blend seamlessly into that surreal yet strangely familiar world.

In that other realm of my coma experience, a completely distinct life unfolded, one that occasionally lingers in my thoughts even now. It was a life situated near Lake Superior, where I embarked on a journey that led me to an old park cabin. The memory is etched in my mind like a thumbnail of a video, clear and vivid, yet shrouded in mystery. I can visualize the scene - a beach with fishing spoons neatly arranged, and a group of individuals reeling in brook trout on a somber, overcast day. The details are so sharp and tangible that it feels as though I could reach out and touch them. Despite the dreamlike quality of this memory, it remains strikingly real and present in my mind.

CHAPTER 11

In that particular existence within my coma, I found myself at a cabin with a dark history of people sniffing gas for recreational purposes, possibly huffing it from a heater or similar device. In this dreamlike scenario, I shared this space with another individual who introduced me to this practice. It's a haunting memory that stayed with me. Upon regaining consciousness, I discovered that there had been a gas leak at the hospital during my coma. It's as if my subconscious mind was attempting to bridge the gap between the surreal world I inhabited in my coma and the real-world events that were unfolding around me.

DAY 14 OF 19 (STILL) — JULY 19, 2025 — 9:00PM

As I was writing, yet another pen ran out on me around 5:00pm. I decided to take a break and headed out in my canoe for some fishing. Despite not having any luck from the shore earlier, I tried various fishing techniques such as jigging, casting a spoon, trolling, and drift jigging in what appeared to be an exceptionally promising fishing spot. This spot was located at the convergence of two sets of rapids flowing into a pool, right where I had swam at least three times earlier in the day.

Despite my efforts fishing the pool, exploring the rapids, and trolling around an island, I had no luck until I finally caught a smalleye on the jig. Although it was on the smaller side and hooked poorly, my determination for a catch led me to keep trying, albeit with no success. I returned to camp around 6:30pm, where I fried up two fillets that satisfied my hunger, but I knew I needed more sustenance. To supplement my meal, I prepared a Knorr garlic parmesan pasta side dish—a first-time bush cooking experiment that turned out to be surprisingly delicious and incredibly filling.

It's 9:00pm now, and I plan to relax with a smoke and some writing until I drift off to sleep. I might consider stopping by the cabin at Shawanabis Lake; Bruce mentioned that I could use it. It would be a welcome change to have a proper table to write at instead of being hunched over like Smeagol from "The Lord of the Rings." Good night!

Exciting turn of events! Bruce sent a message to my inReach. It looks like I'll be making a stop at that cabin after all. Bruce's message about enjoying a hot shower, charging my devices, and the promise of lake trout at Shawanabis Lake is too tempting to resist. Despite the presence of other guests there for free, Bruce's strong recommendation to go has me eager to experience what awaits me at the cabin.

The availability of charging capability is a game-changer for me. I had no clue that there was power at the cabin. It's quite a contrast from my previous visit with Mike years ago when there was no power or hot shower. Despite the temptation of alcohol, I am determined to stay strong. I made the decision to quit about a week ago during my time out here. This commitment is now documented in writing, and I am resolute about sticking to it. I understand the gravity of the situation and the importance of not letting alcohol derail my progress. I believe in my self-control and am committed to not jeopardizing everything I've worked for. This time, I won't take chances — I have faith in my ability to stay true to my goal.

I had tubes coming out of literally every orifice. After spending two weeks in Sudbury, I was eventually transferred back to the Soo. I was unconscious for over long three weeks, and during that time, Will had to stay strong for the kids. Meanwhile, my mom was still up in the Soo, coping with the loss of her youngest, Isaac, who passed away one year prior on May 24th. On May 17th, I experienced a crash, and just two days later, on May 19th, it was my 40th birthday. I managed to do something truly memorable for my birthday - only I don't remember. My mom, Abby, and Will marked the one-year anniversary of Isaac's passing together on May 24. Unfortunately, my absence was due to yet another selfish act on my part. This time, I wasn't there to provide comfort and support to the important women in my life during such a challenging time.

In addition to everything else, they were told to brace themselves for the worst. Throughout it all, my mom kept repeating, "Not him." She maintained a positive outlook, speaking as though I would make a full recovery. When the doctor remarked, "It sounds like you're hoping for a miracle," she responded matter-of-factly, "I am." The logistics of dealing with insurance, involving the police, and the comings and goings of family members added to the strain on my poor family. I can't help but feel an overwhelming sense of guilt for subjecting them to such a challenging and emotional ordeal.

The first memory that stands out to me is more of a sensation than a clear image. I recall a persistent feeling of freshness and cleanliness in my mouth, almost as if it was being washed out repeatedly. This sensation was quite frequent, and I found myself enjoying the feeling, especially the added touch of moisture. It turns out that the nurse was diligently swabbing my mouth every day to ensure it stayed clean. The repetition of this action happened numerous times, one after the other.

Another sensation I vividly remember experiencing was a sense of warmth, comfort, and love conveyed through gentle tones and vibrations. I had a strong intuition that these feelings emanated from Will, creating a sense of a verbal embrace that was incredibly soothing and reassuring. This emotional connection with Will felt like a lifeline during that time. Interestingly, what ultimately brought me out of the coma was the presence of Wolf. Will played a video of Wolfie's endearing and unique way of communicating, which I absolutely adore, and I responded.
Will and my mom remained steadfast in their prayers for my recovery, with the entire church community in Windsor joining in to offer their support. Unexpectedly, I began calling out for Wolfie, a moment that marked a significant turning point in my journey. As I slowly opened my eyes, the

overwhelming joy and relief on Will and my mom's faces as they embraced me were palpable. Despite feeling disoriented and confused, I tried to make sense of our surroundings in the hospital. It was only then that I realized I was lying in a hospital bed, clad in a gown with tubes inserted in various places.

As I lay there, immobilized and surrounded by their tearful embraces, they began recounting the events that led to my current state. Utterly bewildered, I adamantly denied their version of events. In my mind, I was convinced I had been in Toronto, riding a dirt bike with none other than Drake himself. The confusion persisted as I vividly recalled being in Lake Superior, camping under the stars. Their gentle reassurances and patient explanations had to be repeated multiple times before the reality of the situation began to sink in. Gradually, as the doctors and nurses made their rounds, fragmented memories started to resurface, bridging the gap between my imagined scenarios and the harsh truth of my circumstances.

The doctor's inquiries brought me back to the present moment, prompting me to respond with clarity despite the lingering haze of confusion. As I mentioned having just one child, Emerald, the doctor swiftly informed me of the need for further tests before stepping away. Left to my own thoughts as they attended to their duties, I gradually became more aware of my surroundings. Struggling to move, I noticed the limitations in my left arm and the overall sluggishness in my body. In the midst of this disorientation, I thought I heard Isaac's voice in the hallway. The details of that moment remain somewhat blurred, a mix of emerging consciousness and the remnants of a dreamlike state.

The series of tests I underwent felt like a surreal cycle of being heavily sedated, only to be abruptly awakened for more examinations, creating a sense of being set up for failure. In my foggy state, it seemed as though they were intentionally disorienting me. Looking back, I realize the gravity of the situation - severe brain trauma had clouded my thoughts and perceptions, making it difficult to think clearly. Amidst the jumble of sensations and fragmented memories, the medical team persisted with their questions. When asked about the number of people I lived with, I managed to identify my wife and two daughters by name, despite the mental fog that enveloped me.

CHAPTER 11

Being wheeled down to the physical therapy room was a significant step in my recovery journey. As I stood, grasping onto the horizontal poles, I attempted to move forward by shuffling my feet across the floor while relying on my hands for support. However, the stark reality of my condition became apparent as I struggled to use my hands effectively. While my right hand showed some signs of functionality, my left hand remained unresponsive, feeling almost lifeless. The therapists eventually intervened, acknowledging the limits of my current abilities and guiding me back to my room for further rest and recovery.

Spending three nights in the hospital after waking up was a challenging experience for me. Despite the medical care and attention I received, I couldn't shake the feeling of frustration and impatience. The comfort of my own home and the thought of my loving family waiting for me weighed heavily on my mind. Knowing that Joe had made the house more accessible with shower aids and Marc had installed a railing on the front porch only intensified my desire to return home. The familiar surroundings and the support of my family were what I longed for the most during those days in the hospital.

The experience of having the catheter removed on the third night brought about a new set of challenges. The difficulty in urinating while standing up added to the discomfort and frustration. In the middle of the night, in a groggy and medicated state, the need to use the provided piss bucket became urgent. Unfortunately, the attempt to stand and use it resulted in a sudden fall, causing a hard impact on my already injured hand and wrist. The struggle to stand up after the fall was a challenging moment, further complicated by the disapproval from the nurse and the conflicting wishes and orders from the doctor, Will, and my mom. Despite their concerns for my well-being, the strong desire to regain control over my situation led me to make the decision to sign myself out of the hospital that morning. This choice sparked a disagreement with Will, highlighting the internal conflict between the urge for independence and the need to heed the advice and guidance of those who cared for me. The tension between asserting autonomy and accepting support and medical advice was a difficult balance to navigate during my recovery journey.

Feeling neglected in the hospital, I longed for the comfort and familiarity of home. Hospitals can be quite isolating places, and being surrounded by loved ones and the warmth of home was all I truly desired. Upon returning home, I embraced my daughters and Wolfie. Exhausted from the ordeal, I retreated to bed, craving much-needed rest.

During those three days in the hospital, my mind was consumed with the urge to caution my loved ones to be vigilant and careful. The sudden and drastic change in circumstances served as a stark reminder of life's unpredictability. In the past, I had a knack for walking away from foolish situations with a smile, but this time was different.

The person I needed to warn the most was Isaac. When I heard him in the hospital, they had told me no, but I thought that I heard him again. I started not to believe them, so I asked to call him. I needed to tell him to just be careful. I felt such a need. It was not until I was home and had asked multiple times that Will and my mom came into my room together, looking somber. "What?" I said immediately. One of them sat on the bed, and the other stood near my head, stroking my hair.

They softly told me that Isaac had passed away, a full year ago. "No! What?" I knew they wouldn't come in to joke with me about that. But no, I would have already known that. I wouldn't have been asking my mom of all people to call her deceased son. I could tell that they were serious. I couldn't hold anything back.

Tears streamed down my face as I struggled to speak between sobs, desperate for answers. How? What? Why? When? They patiently explained everything, forcing me to relive the heartbreaking truth about my beloved little brother. All I had wanted was to warn him about the fragility of life, but I was too late by a year. The pain was just as raw and agonizing as it was the first time.

In the following days, memories flooded back from my entire life, except for that one day. Picking leeks is the furthest my recollection goes. Will, Kaitlyn, and Marc filled in the gaps for me. In my mind's eye, I can vividly see an aerial view of my bedroom, with Mom and Will breaking the devastating news to me. The scene is etched into my mind, a painful memory I can't shake. I felt compelled to apologize for not remembering and causing them, especially my mom, to relive the trauma with me. It was a truly harrowing memory - again!

As the days went by, it became increasingly clear to everyone, especially myself, the extent of the damage to my left arm and hand. My right hand was now my only functional hand, although my index and middle fingers on that hand were also affected. It still provided some utility, unlike my left hand which was completely incapacitated. Initially, I relied solely on my right hand for everything. Simple tasks like buttoning my jeans or fastening my belt were absolutely impossible. I required assistance getting in and out of the bathtub and had to use a portable toilet beside my bed at night. The nights were particularly difficult. I would often be jolted awake by excruciating pain.

The wedge pillows provided no relief for me. The doctor at the Soo hospital informed me that I had severe nerve damage in my arm. While everyone was preoccupied with my brain, miraculously, I remembered everything clearly, except for Isaac and that tragic day. It was as if my memory of that day was shrouded in a fog, while the rest remained intact, as fine as it could be. No significant efforts were made to assess the damage to my arm. In their defence, I panicked and left three days after regaining consciousness. The pain I experienced was intense, but it was a peculiar kind of pain - a mix of pins and needles, burning sensations, and numbness. Only those who have endured nerve damage can truly grasp the severity of such agony.

Overwhelmed with worry about the future and consumed by present agony, I found myself in the emergency room one night. Will assisted me with dressing, putting on and tying my shoes, opening doors (which I still couldn't manage), guiding me down the stairs, and opening the passenger door. I slumped into the seat, a place I rarely occupied, quietly sobbing, feeling utterly useless. That feeling persisted at the hospital, where the doctors delivered the grim news that this might be my new reality. They prescribed me just two Percocet before sending me home.

I hadn't taken or even thought much about Percs for years. I had significantly reduced my intake of codeine and alcohol. However, at that moment, I was so desperate for relief that I would have tried anything to alleviate the pain. I swallowed half a pill, disregarding the potential consequences and not caring about the Pandora's box it might open. Percs had been my go-to; I loved them in years past. They meshed with my hyper self, calming me and my insides down. I couldn't control myself and knew that. This pain though and the pain of the unknown fate of my arm was too difficult to deal with. Needless to say, those two Percs were gone the next day.

I went back again a few days later, legitimately in agony. Still useless, still the same. He gave me a prescription for Tylenol 3 and told me I need an EMG (electromyography). He suggested I go to Sunnybrook in Toronto. "They have an EMG lab, go sit in the emergency room and tell them you are visiting and need help right away." With the pain and the nerve damage I was desperate. I would have done anything.

Will booked me a flight, and I was off to Sunnybrook the next day. Brian picked me up from Billy Bishop airport, drove me to Sunnybrook, and told me to call him when I was done. Brian is one of my closest friends to this day. I sat in Sunnybrook for seven hours, watching the screen in the waiting room, the minutes ticking by until it was my turn. I was brought into a room and told to change into a robe. A good sign, I thought.

The doctor entered the room and inquired about my situation. I poured out my story, desperately trying to convey the urgency of my need for help, starting with an EMG. "Oh, we don't conduct that procedure here. You'll need to go upstairs," she informed me. "Can you facilitate that?" I asked. She almost chuckled, "You require a referral, and the process can take months." Feeling defeated, I made a heartfelt plea, explaining that I urgently needed the test, couldn't access it in the north, and had flown in specifically for this purpose. The best she could offer was a referral for an appointment that might be two months away. "Fuck," I muttered just loud enough to be heard. Feeling defeated and unsure of my next steps, I accepted the referral and stepped outside to call Will. I was utterly devastated. My last hope had not materialized. I reached out to Brian and wandered aimlessly for an hour until he messaged that he was close by. We proceeded to his place as originally planned.

After returning home from waking up in the hospital, I tried smoking weed again for the first time. To my dismay, I didn't enjoy it. It caused my nerves to feel incredibly strange, leading to uncontrollable tingling in my arm and hand. The experience was unpleasant, and I only smoked two or three times in the initial days. Apart from the three weeks in a coma, I had been smoking weed all day, every day for as long as I can recall. A couple of weeks after emerging from the coma, I recorded a video for YouTube, sharing my experience and stating that I had quit weed. I was being honest; it had been nearly two weeks since I last smoked. I felt like I had moved on from it.

I had previously informed Brian that I quit smoking weed. True to his character, he respected my decision and didn't offer or encourage me to take a hit whenever he lit up. He's a good guy. We went for a walk with his dog, and by then, I was feeling more stable on my feet. I flew to Toronto solo. Due to the swelling, I had my hand up in the air for most of the flight and even in the waiting room at Sunnybrook, now that I reflect on it.

My hands and fingers were swollen in a peculiar way, resembling sausage fingers that seemed on the verge of splitting at any moment. They remained significantly swollen for an extended period. It's astonishing how writing can trigger forgotten memories. The level of detail I recall surprises me. Brian accompanied me to a small patch of woods in the bustling city of Pickering. Reflecting on that moment in the woods brought back memories of where I first honed my skills in the little patch of woods in Windsor.

Life had transformed in ways I never imagined. In an instant, a flood of memories rushed in – from my college days, scouting adventures, the passing of Nan, experiences in Windsor, struggles with opioids, marriage, raising kids, the loss of Tony and Isaac, my journey on YouTube, the show *Alone*, the bond with Tripper, the joy of Emmie's and Autumn's birth, the National Geographic project, my filming career, and the life-altering accident. Each memory is a chapter in the unique story of my life.

When Brian posed the question, "So, what are you going to do now, Joe?" I found myself at a loss for words. We returned to his place, and I struggled through a painful and broken night of sleep, trying to ration my T3s despite my addiction. The following morning stands out as one of my lowest points, filled with seemingly insignificant details that stick in your memory. I had a multitude of pills to take, all prescribed medications, none of which were close to narcotics.

Needing breakfast before taking my pills, I opted for a quick and easy choice – a banana. I didn't want to burden anyone, so I grabbed a bunch of bananas, held it with the back of my injured hand, and peeled one with my right hand. I noticed that my right hand was starting to regain some functionality, likely due to the constant use it was getting as I compensated for my left hand. Holding the banana in my right hand, I took a moment to simply look at it, perhaps contemplating the small victories in my road to recovery. Struggling to peel the banana with my left hand, I realized I couldn't switch hands to make it work. My attempts were futile, with my thumb and index finger barely budging. Feeling defeated, I stood there for a few minutes, grappling with a sense of self-pity. Eventually, I reached out to Brian for help with peeling the banana. It was a humbling moment, especially considering our shared history, like the time I had patched him up with a bandana.

Reflecting on Brian's past injury with the axe and the makeshift bandana, juxtaposed with my current struggle to peel a banana, highlighted the stark contrast in our situations. The give and take of life can be a bitter pill to swallow, especially for someone like me, grappling with physical limitations and worries. As I headed home, a sense of hopelessness crept in. The thought of not being able to engage with my kids during the summer, missing out on our trampoline fun and playtime, weighed heavily on me. Being unable to provide and protect them left me feeling like a shadow of my former self – a feeling of helplessness and inadequacy that consumed me.

As self-pity and depression crept in, I found myself spending long stretches in bed, unable to bring myself to leave for days. Despite recognizing that things could have been worse, the stark contrast between my usual self-sufficiency and independence in diverse situations and my current struggle to peel a banana left me feeling deeply distraught.

I revisited the hospital and saw a new doctor who empathized with my situation. They prescribed me a 30-day supply of Percocet. They explained that if my condition hadn't improved by now, there was a risk of the brain ceasing to send signals to the affected nerves after about a year, potentially causing my hand to become limp. I had already been experiencing a disconnect with my hand, feeling as though it was no longer a part of me, almost lifeless. I found myself on Percocet once again, a familiar cycle in my life. While they effectively alleviated my physical pain, they also provided a welcomed escape from emotional distress.

However, this relief came at a cost - I noticed that I was less preoccupied with thoughts of Isaac and my past mistakes, but I also felt detached and distant from my family. This was not the person I aspired to be, as I had previously made a conscious decision to stop using Percocet for this very reason.

I had enlisted the help of a physical therapist who visited twice a week, spending 45 minutes each session mainly massaging my arm. I also sought the services of a skilled chiropractor. Despite these efforts, I didn't see much improvement. This routine continued for what seemed like an indefinite period. In a moment of vulnerability, I posted an update video while under the influence of Percocet. Viewers quickly noticed and called me out on it. I must admit, I responded with some sarcastic remarks to a few individuals (apologies, you were correct).

Subsequently, my mental well-being took a further hit, mirroring the decline of my YouTube channel. The state of my mental health was deteriorating, and the struggles with my channel only exacerbated the situation. Creating and managing my channel has been one of the most fulfilling endeavours of my life. It has opened doors both figuratively and literally, leading me to places I never would have imagined visiting otherwise.

I've assisted both Will's and my families on numerous occasions, always willing and proud to do so. It brings me great pride to have been able to help. Meeting people who express their gratitude by shaking my hand, looking me in the eye, and saying, "You saved my life," is a profound experience. It's not a joke. This legacy will be something my kids can watch long after I'm gone. My channel has not only saved others' lives but has also been a lifeline for me.

Now, it felt like everything was slipping away, one thing after another. The weight of it all was overwhelming. Thoughts of Isaac, my career in decline, concerns about our financial future and my own physical limitations all seemed to converge. The fear of my wife leaving due to my mobility issues or financial struggles was something I had never considered before. I worried about burdening her with a life she hadn't signed up for, being married to a man with disabilities. Despite the vows of "in sickness and in health," my mind was consumed by a sense of impending doom and gloom.

I found myself unable to control my use of Percocet. The initial supply of 30 pills was gone within days. Desperate, I reached out to a contact in Sault Ste. Marie. They offered me 80 pills for $800 plus gas money. Despite the steep price, I agreed without hesitation. Even if they had asked for $2,000, I would have likely complied. With plenty of money in the bank, I made the trip, purchased the pills, and thus began a cycle of continued use.

The physiotherapy sessions were not providing the relief I had hoped for. The chiropractor's treatments were somewhat helpful, but overall, nothing seemed to alleviate my pain. The cold weather intensified my discomfort to the point where even in July, during a fireworks outing, the chill was unbearable. My hand became so cold that I couldn't bear the pain. I toughed it out for the sake of the kids, but once we returned home, it took a good two hours for the pain to begin subsiding. It hadn't occurred to me yet that hot water could provide relief without causing harm.

I found myself unable to join the kids for a swim in the lake or partake in camping trips, or even work on my videos. Instead, I would take Wolf for short walks, each one a poignant journey past the site of the accident, a stark reminder of that tragic night. Every time we passed by, I would pause, trying to unravel the events of that fateful evening. The sight of the disturbed grass where the impact occurred, and the hidden boulder beneath the freshly cut grass, was unsettling. It was a grim sight that I dreaded encountering each time.

After posting my second update video, I received a message on Instagram from a guy named Carrie Physio. He mentioned that he lives in Toronto but offers online physiotherapy services. I had been requesting more structured exercises or daily tasks from my current physiotherapist instead of just receiving massages twice a week for 45 minutes. It felt like there was untapped potential for me to do more each day. When Carrie offered to provide his services pro bono, I accepted, feeling frustrated with my current physiotherapist. Carrie's approach was refreshing and insightful. He emphasized the importance of daily self-improvement and cautioned against excessive massage, highlighting how it might not be beneficial for my nerves in the long run.

I embarked on a slow and deliberate journey to manually start bending my fingers. Using my right hand, I painstakingly squeezed the fingers of my left hand together to form a fist. Initially, the movement was far from resembling a fist, causing me excruciating pain. My fingers were still swollen and barely responsive. Gradually, with persistent effort and gradual force, I managed to achieve a clenched fist by the end of the day, slowly building up strength and flexibility over time.

The following morning, my fingers were stiff once more, requiring me to manually bend them all over again. This routine persisted, but now with the added challenge of a significant amount of homework from Carrie. Gradually, I began to notice progress as I could start bending my fingers independently, except for my index and thumb, which remained locked in place, rigid and unyielding. Despite my best efforts, even with assistance from my other hand, those two fingers refused to bend. Nevertheless, it was a step forward, marking some much-needed progress. As late summer approached and the kids prepared to return to school, my video output had been minimal, with perhaps only one more video released at this point, totalling three since the accident.

About two months earlier, my friend Mike contacted me along with Adam, whom I had never camped with before except during the group meetup. They were organizing a trip to Quetico for the first time, a destination I had always dreamt of visiting to complete my personal "Big 3" list, which included Woodland Caribou Provincial Park, Wabakimi Provincial Park, and Quetico Provincial Park. Mike inquired if I thought I would be able to join them. I responded with cautious optimism, saying maybe, but feeling skeptical about my ability to participate.

From that moment on, I felt a renewed sense of determination. I immersed myself in continuous physiotherapy sessions, pushing myself to bend my index finger with the help of my other hand, despite the intense pain. Gradually, I noticed a slight improvement in flexibility. I incorporated wrist curls into my routine, mimicking the movements of hockey players, and even simulated the action of lifting a canoe for portaging. Slowly but surely, I began to regain some functionality in my hand. Amidst this personal journey of recovery, I was acutely aware of the family I had almost left behind without a husband and father. I strived to make amends, even if just in small ways, to show my love and commitment to them.

I took my family to the fair in the Soo. Emmie was eager for me to join her on the swings – those intense ones that lift you up and spin you around until you feel queasy. Despite Will's advice against it, I couldn't resist Emmie's excitement and hopped on the ride with her. The spinning left me feeling so nauseous that I nearly got sick. I had to retreat to the Jeep, where I sat with the air blasting on me, reclined in the seat, eyes closed, trying to recover from the dizzying experience. Despite my attempts to open my eyes, the world continued to spin around me relentlessly. After enduring 45 minutes of this disorienting sensation, I opted to stay in the car. Regrettably, my family, feeling sympathetic towards my condition, decided not to stay long at the fair. Their concern, while well-intentioned, only served to compound my feelings of distress and guilt. It was a challenging situation exacerbated by the lingering effects of my brain trauma and the array of medications I was prescribed. I felt sick in every sense of the word.

One day, I purchased a joint from a dispensary, hoping that I could wean off Percs by switching to weed. I lit up half of the joint at home, only to find myself experiencing a sensation akin to the spinning swings once more. I ended up getting overwhelmingly high, even to the point of vomiting, but it did help me sleep, and I managed to consume fewer Percs that day. However, I soon found myself slipping back into the familiar routine of smoking weed throughout the day. Rolling joints proved to be a challenge for me due to the dexterity required. I found that I couldn't simply smoke weed casually; once I started, it was easy to slip into a pattern of waking and baking, embracing the stoner lifestyle. Despite this tendency, I've managed to achieve quite a bit in life for someone who enjoys cannabis... Wait, what was I saying again? Haha!

Each morning, I followed my routine of taking my medications, engaging in physiotherapy, and working on improving the mobility of my hand. Despite my efforts, my index finger remained extended, and my thumb showed a slight bend at the main knuckle – a small but encouraging sign of progress. With Mike and Adam eagerly awaiting my decision and finalizing details for their upcoming departure in a week, we scheduled a video chat to discuss and provide them with an answer.

I remember saying, "You guys may have to tie my boots." They replied, "No problem." I asked, "Can I bring Wolf?" "Yup," they replied. "I need to paddle tandem and I can't portage either." Without hesitation, Mike said, "I'll paddle with you. Wolf can ride with us, and I'll carry the boat." Mike's kindness was truly appreciated. "Ok. I'm in. I may slow you guys down though."

It seemed to be absolutely no concern of theirs. I felt good about it. I knew that Mike was a man of his word and soon found out that Adam was too. That trip was so hard for me. Those guys helped me out a whole lot. In the first five minutes of being on the water, I projectile vomited over each side of the canoe, consecutively. I hadn't eaten breakfast and took all my meds. I got sick. For a week leading up to the trip, I had tapered down to my actual prescribed dose of Percocet, which was three a day. I took one in the morning and two after supper. I was okay with that. I did it in preparation for the trip, so that I'd be physically able and mentally present. I maintained that routine throughout the whole trip and for a while after.

It was a fantastic trip. I did surprisingly well. I didn't even need my boots tied. I successfully caught, cleaned, and cooked fish. This was coming from the guy who just the previous summer had trouble tying a fishing lure for Emmie. I even remember the time I was chatting with Marc, holding a beer, and somehow let it slip out of my hand without realizing it. My hand still held up as if the drink was there. Marc casually mentioned, "You dropped it." I was in disbelief. Definitely another comical low point.

But now I found myself paddling a canoe, with my index finger still sticking up and frequently hitting the gunwale hard during each stroke. I sat in the front, which wasn't the usual setup on a Mike and Joe trip. Then, unexpectedly, we were pelted with golf ball-sized hail. It was the largest and hardest hail I had ever encountered. It was a truly memorable trip. Great company, a wonderful dog, set in a beautiful park, during a perfect time of year. It reignited something within me, although briefly.

DAY 15 OF 19 — JULY 20, 2025 — 6:50PM

Despite wanting to sleep in this morning, I woke up 30 minutes earlier than my usual 5:00am and couldn't fall back asleep. I lay there, wasting time going through my maps for the 100th time, knowing the rest of the route all too well. I knew how long it would take me and how long it would take in case of an emergency. I had studied the route and park on the map every single day of this 15-day trip, in detail, sometimes more than once a day.

I managed to stay in the tent until 6:00am, a whole hour later than leaving camp the day before. I only had a two-kilometre travel day but in those two kilometres, I have four portages. All relatively small but back to back to back. I am sure glad my two bags didn't weigh what they did at the start of the trip. My food bag barely weighs anything now so I can put some of my gear from the heavy bag in there to make the bags extremely manageable.

I remember those first few days like they were ages ago. My bags felt heavy, and I was so weak. But now, it's the complete opposite. This trip is unlike any other I've been on. I even managed to catch a good-sized walleye while fishing along the way. I decided to release it back into the water. It was 8:00am, and I still had one more portage to go before reaching THE Walleye Kitchen! I hopped back into the boat and paddled away, enjoying the peaceful and calm surroundings. The sun cast a dark orange hue, reminiscent of the sky during a forest fire.

I came across a rock cairn and checked my map, which showed no marked portage but revealed another small pond on the other side. Intrigued, I marked it on my GPS, wondering if it could be a hidden gem for fishing. Despite my curiosity, I was en route to THE

KITCHEN and had no need for a honey hole at that moment.

Slowly relishing the serene morning, I paddled around the peninsula and caught a glimpse of it — two cascading ledge waterfalls and a perfectly flat campsite on a rock right at their base. "The kitchen. Yup," I exclaimed to my GoPro camera. I knew I had to camp there. Approaching the falls, I cast a jig and caught a smalleye. After releasing it, I repeated the process three more times, each time catching a fish of the same size.

I switched to a blue/white Little Cleo lure. On my first cast, I got a bite, but it wasn't a solid commitment. The second bite, though, was a success — fish on! I could sense that this one was a good size. "Perfect eater," I remarked as I pulled it out of the water. It was around 10:00am. I decided to call it a day with just this one fish; it would be more than enough for my lunch. If I feel like it, I can always head back out or fish from the shore at camp later on.

The black flies aren't too bothersome here. This is their natural habitat with running water and a small lake. I've been outside all day, most of it with my shirt off. The deer flies are starting to bother me, but I'll take them over black flies any day. I found a lovely flat spot for the tent, took my time setting up, cleaned the walleye, cooked lunch, and started writing while sitting on a rock ledge by the waterfall. It's really nice here.

I've been thoroughly enjoying my time at these recent campsites. I spend most of my days sitting at camp, writing away. The hours seem to slip by effortlessly. I took a break from writing to create a smoky fire to ward off the deer flies, then returned to my writing. A couple of hours later, I paused once more to paddle, though I was only on the water for five minutes. Upon my return, I indulged in my remaining peanut M&Ms, a flatbread on its own, and some granola. I've grown accustomed to having a snack around 3:00pm out here in the wilderness.

I cast a spoon from shore, and after just two casts, I landed a good-sized walleye. I found myself growing weary of eating fish. I had one for lunch and decided to save one of my freeze-dried meals for later. It was a necessary choice. I released the walleye back into the water and hung up my fishing rod. Back to writing I went. I also messaged Will, hoping to reach the Shawanabis cabin tomorrow while there are still people around. Bruce recommended the visit. Fingers crossed they have peanut M&Ms there!

For supper, I enjoyed shepherd's pie. I finished up all the candy I had left. As it nears 7:00pm, I managed to catch a walleye from shore, tidied up camp, took another refreshing swim in the waterfall, and then settled into my tent, feeling just right in the nude, with the temperature being perfect. The flat bed beckons, and I'm feeling quite exhausted. The thought of wrapping up the trip sooner than planned is crossing my mind. When I was planning this adventure, I wrote down "at least three weeks" but I've come to realize that I don't feel the need or desire to stay out that long. Recognizing this, I made a quick adjustment to my route. I decided to cut off two extra loops and skip the backtrack up to Burntrock and back.

Kyle and I had already discussed heading in that direction, and I've previously visited the area. The first week proved to be quite challenging, yet it passed by swiftly, leaving me feeling like I hadn't dedicated enough time to writing, which is one of my main goals out here. I'm grateful that I recognized this early on, allowing me to make necessary adjustments. Moreover, the realization that I don't have sufficient food supplies for the originally planned month-long trip, despite bringing extra provisions, is a crucial insight. I've been enjoying plenty of fish during my time here as well. It's all part of the adventure!

My kids miss me. I received a message today. I miss my family. I'm likely going to finish this book and conclude the trip around the same time, perhaps just two more nights after tonight. That would make it a total of 18 days. 18 days alone in the wild. We'll see how I feel. This morning, I was happy to be out here. I still am, but the days spent at camp writing are starting to feel a bit overwhelming now. The cabin might provide me with some inspiration. Additionally, there are lake trout to enjoy and perhaps some other goodies left behind by the previous occupants. They were scheduled to depart tomorrow, so there's a chance they left behind extra food they didn't need. No alcohol for me, though!

I found myself going to bed early every day after supper during the trip. Upon reaching camp, my routine would involve feeding Wolf, having my meal, and then falling into a deep sleep. The journey was challenging but necessary; it pushed me to my limits and made me believe I was prepared to venture out on my own and create videos. However, when I attempted a bushcraft overnight experience in late fall with Wolf, using a canvas tarp and a fire in front, it didn't go as planned. It seemed like it should have been a success based on previous experiences, but this time, it just didn't work out. Despite the lack of views on my content, the recurring accusation of opioid use hit hard. In that moment, I found myself thinking, "What more do you want from me? I'm out here camping, trying to survive. I rely on them to get through." While I may have been blind to the signs of addiction, I justified my usage due to the prescription.

I ACKNOWLEDGE MY MISTAKE. Deep down, I understand it. Every winter tends to be a bit challenging for me mentally. I was filled with dread about the winter, and it truly felt like it dragged on endlessly. It was the first real winter we had experienced in over five years – long, dreary, and seemingly never-ending. I stopped creating videos for months. Feeling depressed, I attempted to return, but it just didn't click. Everything seemed to pile up once more. I found myself turning to alcohol and taking Percs. I withdrew, spending most of my time in bed. I neglected my physiotherapy and essentially gave up.

Percocet can indeed dampen your enthusiasm for life and make you indifferent to many things. I can't quite recall what made me finally stop. I realized that I couldn't continue down this path. I spent a lot of time scouring the internet for information on the health risks associated with opioids, T1s, and alcohol. To put it simply, the findings were alarming. The situation was dire, and I had already caused significant harm to myself. The toll was evident physically, mentally, and in my marriage. Will had understandably reached her breaking point. It was then that I began to see things more clearly. The passing of Brian's dad, Ed, who was the kindest person you could ever meet, hit me hard. Ed succumbed to liver disease. He loved consuming wine and beer. He was always so cheerful and welcoming, making me feel like part of the family for years, alongside Connie, Brian's sweetheart mom.

I was consumed by a profound sense of remorse. Ever since Isaac's passing, the mere thought of a loved one experiencing loss cuts me to the core. The depth of my emotions goes beyond words, striking a chord deep within me. It fills me with an overwhelming sense of fear. This, combined with the deep love I hold for my family, particularly the fear of leaving my children without a father, mirroring the absence I felt growing up, and the thought of my wife without her life partner of 23 years, has made me confront my own selfishness. How could I have allowed myself to repeat this pattern once more? I am acutely aware that a swift and lasting change is imperative.

My brother, the best man at my wedding, and countless others had died from drugs, and here I am. Just a selfish, idiotic asshole. Still in the winter, I connected with a guy named Adam on Instagram. Adam and I had first met in Algonquin Park on a portage during one of my "high speed, low drag" solo trips. He spotted me, recognized me, and we engaged in a conversation. We even took a picture together and exchanged Instagram handles. That was the extent of our interaction until I received a message from him. It read, "Hey man. I want to create a documentary about you, your accident, and your journey since then." I was thrilled by the idea as I had already been contemplating delving into more high-quality projects.

We engaged in a conversation, and I was impressed by what I heard. We arranged for him and his cousin, David, the tech guy, to visit us from Toronto for the first shoot with the family at our place. They arrived shortly after. Despite my ongoing struggles with heavy drinking and frequent Percocet use, we had dinner together. They had brought along some excellent IPAs from Toronto and my favourite wine, an Argentinian Malbec. I indulged in the drinks, took some pills as usual, and we proceeded to shoot the trailer for the documentary. They appeared pleased with the outcome, stayed overnight, and departed the next day.

During the Christmas season, my family travelled to Windsor. While there, I received a snippet of the interview to review. To my dismay, I was shocked by how messed up I appeared and sounded in the footage. My speech was slow and slurred, making it painfully obvious. I couldn't believe it. Was this how I came across in my videos? I had been so out of it while editing them that I couldn't discern the extent of the issue. I decided to show the snippet to my mom, sister, and Will. Their raised eyebrows and expressions told me everything I needed to know. "You're very messed up." The feedback was not easy to hear. However, Adam suggested that the footage could potentially add to the buildup of the documentary.

I took a significant step by reaching out to the doctor and expressing my decision to no longer require or desire Percocet. I took the initiative to remove the contact associated with obtaining the medication and quit cold turkey, except for the T1s. I convinced myself that I needed the T1s to wean off Percocet, but despite successfully eliminating Percocet from my life, I struggled immensely to break free from the grip of T1s. I found myself repeatedly succumbing to the temptation to purchase more T1s, even when there was no legitimate reason to do so. This pattern persisted, even during family trips to Disney and North Carolina, where I found myself buying T1s regardless of the circumstances.

It became evident that the T1s were causing severe diarrhea, a side effect I was well aware of. Reflecting on the situation, I realized that this cycle had originated from my past struggles with IBS and the fear of experiencing embarrassing incidents. Now, I had become the source of my own problems through self-induced actions. Determined to break free from this harmful pattern, I made a firm decision to go cold turkey on the T1s. However, the withdrawal symptoms hit me hard, leaving me bedridden for weeks. I had relied on T1s for years, with the exception of my time in a coma when I was prescribed fentanyl by the doctor.

Adam and David were on board for the full journey, but without offering any assistance. I want to emphasize that. Can I handle it? Will I make it back? Especially now, with a film crew and professional editing involved. "Ok," I affirmed. I trust Adam's judgment. "If you believe it's suitable for the documentary, I trust your decision." To support our project and raise funds, we launched an Indiegogo campaign. We shared a teaser video detailing our mission and showcased the trailer capturing me all fucked up. I believe we raised around $15,000 dollars, falling short of our initial $50,000 target. I was aware that the higher goal was set to encourage maximum contributions. As winter came to an end, I successfully stopped using T1s and had been off Percs for a while. Wolf and I, along with Adam and David, drove in convoy style to the documentary location just outside Wabakimi on Crown land, where I planned to build a shelter.

A month or two before our departure, I received exciting news that Adam had a connection to the Canadian Broadcasting Corporation (CBC). They caught wind of "Nerves," the title we had selected, and expressed interest in it. Adam arranged a Zoom call with three or four individuals from CBC, along with himself and a few others. Surprisingly, I wasn't even too nervous during the call. I had confidence that we were going to create something remarkable regardless of the circumstances. However, the prospect of combining our $15,000 with potential CBC funding could truly elevate the overall quality of the documentary. Our interview with CBC went exceptionally well. They were impressed and acquired the project for $85,000, on top of our initial $15,000. This meant we now had approximately $100,000 at our disposal to bring this vision to life.

I spent a lot of time planning and organizing. The responsibility rested on me to determine the destination, the type of shelter needed, and the logistics of the journey. The question of whether to film also weighed on my mind. I had to consider Wolfie's well-being and safety, along with my own. Additionally, being out there with two guys I had never camped with added another layer of complexity. All of this while navigating the challenge of coming off drugs for the first time in a long while. Although I had reduced my alcohol intake, I was still consuming a few beers every day, which I realized was still quite a lot.

Upon discussing Woodland Caribou Provincial Park with Albert, I learned about the significant amount of burn damage, covering 200,000 hectares in recent years. I found the idea intriguing, thinking it could provide a visually striking setting. However, after facing a series of last-minute cancellations and enduring a period of high stress, we ultimately settled on the Crown land outside Wabakimi. It turned out to be a wise decision, especially considering that Woodland Caribou Provincial Park was once again affected by fires before May 19th. Our adventure was scheduled to begin on the 23rd of May. Being in the wilderness for the anniversary of Isaac's passing felt right, allowing me to honour his memory in a meaningful way, such as sprinkling more of his ashes in the lake. You'd be surprised at just how much ash a funeral home sends.

As the convoy made its way through the Soo on the 12-hour drive up, fatigue began to take its toll, and I felt myself nodding off. In a moment of temptation, the idea of stopping to pick up some T1s crossed my mind. I reasoned that they could help me stay alert and provide relief if needed during our time in the wilderness, especially considering the possibility of discomfort in my hand. However, I firmly told myself, "NO!" and kept my focus on the road as we passed by Shoppers. The same internal struggle persisted as we approached Wawa, but I managed to resist the urge. Looking back, I'm relieved that I stayed determined and didn't give in.

We made the decision to fly into the lake, driven by a combination of factors. Partly for the cinematic appeal it would bring to our adventure, and partly because the location was simply ideal. Moreover, the spot we had chosen was exclusively reachable by float plane, adding an extra layer of excitement and exclusivity to our journey.

DAY 15 OF 19 (STILL) — JULY 20, 2025 — 8:30PM

Crazy. I've been lying here naked for a couple of hours writing. I heard someone yell, so I put on my pants. I haven't seen anyone since the red canoe, which there was no sign of here, no red paint on the rocks. I unzipped the tent and went out. I looked at the lake, expecting to see the red canoe guys wanting to camp at the Walleye Kitchen. Nothing. I turned toward the waterfall. To my surprise, on the other side of the river were two people and two dogs.
I waved, and they reciprocated, their dogs behaving well without barking. Feeling puzzled, I walked closer, cupped my hands around my mouth, and asked, "Where did you guys come from?" The man pointed towards the top of the waterfall and shouted something that I couldn't quite catch. I simply gave him a thumbs up in response. He then shouted, "You?"

which I managed to hear. I replied, "Just camping," and gestured in a circular motion in the air to indicate "15 days," struggling to convey the full story in the distance. They seemed to be inquiring about the usual details — where I put in, my route, any luck with fishing, and so on. Judging by their attire and the presence of two well-behaved dogs, I got the impression that they might be guests staying at a lodge located on the big lake on the opposite side of the waterfall.

DAY 16 OF 19 — JULY 21, 2025 — 1:30PM

At 6:00am, I noticed a red sky in the morning, which usually signals a warning. I woke up even earlier today at 4:45am, a new record for me! Excited about the early start, I forced myself to stay in bed and continue writing. Now that it's past 6:00, I've decided to get up and make my way to Shawanabis. I don't want to arrive too early and disturb the people there, but I also want to beat the storm that seems to be approaching.

I heard a few drops on the tent just a couple of minutes ago. I'm eager to reach Shawanabis before they possibly depart — I definitely need some snacks! There were plenty of mosquitoes around, and even a few managed to sneak into the tent, but I still managed to get a good night's sleep. I'm feeling positive and ready for the day ahead, even though I'm not entirely sure what to expect today or for the remainder of the trip. It's time to leave the tent and start the day. Oatmeal for breakfast — oh, the excitement!

It's 1:30 now, and I've arrived at the cabin. It seems I missed the people, leaving the place empty for me to enjoy all by myself. I'm feeling a bit disappointed as I was looking forward to some engaging discussions for a couple of hours. And of course, the snacks! It looks like there's no food left at the cabin due to critters getting to it. There have been some noticeable upgrades since the last time I visited this place. The addition of power is a game-changer! Just like Bruce mentioned in the text on my inReach — "Have a hot shower, charge your devices." Taking care of a few essentials like a quick bathroom break and a refreshing hot shower can make a big difference in getting settled in quickly.

The charging, on the other hand, will not happen. I have power banks and charging cords but no block adapter for the wall plug. Damn, that would have helped a lot. However, I did find a pair of scissors. I proceeded to cut all my hair off; it looks like a child gave me a buzzcut, haha. I also trimmed my overgrown moustache and cheek hair (no beard). I can't grow a beard. Having chili for lunch inside, it's nice to sit down. I found a block to plug my stuff into! It's a bit slow since it's from solar panels, but I can charge my power bank, which then charges my phone!

I thought I was in for a bad storm on the way here. The sky was completely black, and I was sure there was a 100% chance of a thunderstorm. However, it cleared up as I reached the tracks. I had to cross back south of the track, whereas my trip initially started by crossing north into the park on the far west side. Today, I crossed south on the far east side. I spotted a few camps/cabins near the tracks, and it's starting to feel like the end in so many ways. According to my map, it said "Portage over tracks, careful, steep and loose gravel." Eventually, I reached a spot that looked familiar.

Mike and I had travelled this exact route years before. I remembered canoeing through a 100-metre-long tunnel blasted out of pure Canadian Shield

under the train tracks. Upon rediscovering the
tunnel, I made the choice to wade through the shallow
water with my boat instead of portaging over a steep
embankment and across the tracks. It was a very cool
experience indeed!

I arrived at the cabin around 11:00am, and it was
empty. I felt happy to be here. Bruce kindly said I
could stay as long as I wanted, but I think I'll only
stay the night for now. The uncertainty of the next
few days is both exciting and nerve-wracking. I feel
torn between wanting to stay and wanting to go. Time
will tell... I feel content, especially as I run my
hand over my nearly buzzcut head. I plan to sleep
inside the cabin this time. Last time, I had to set up
my tent outside. This spot is truly lovely, and I can
imagine bringing my family here in the future.

🔥🔥🔥

We stayed at Wabakimi Lodge, the launching-off point, the night before. I
managed to empty Bruce's keg, which left me feeling a bit groggy in the
morning, but I was used to it. We made some last-minute preparations and
even had to film an interview with me before boarding the plane. After the
interview around 11:30am, I started enjoying some beers from the keg
again. We eventually departed after 1:00pm. By that time, I had already
had about six glasses, albeit smaller ones, not pints. Surprisingly, I didn't
even feel a buzz; my nerves and I were quite accustomed to it all.

Wolfie proved to be a real trooper during our filming, enduring multiple
take-offs, landings, and take-offs again within just 45 minutes. Despite the
rapid changes, he remained calm and composed, showing his unwavering
loyalty and sense of purpose on our trips together. I truly cherish that dog
and the bond we share.

After the film crew was flown in first, I was next to be flown in. Upon
landing, they were already capturing footage of the plane landing, Wolf
and me exiting, and loading my gear and Wolf into the canoe. The
challenge arose as the plane was about a kilometre away from the shore,

making it quite unstable to lift a dog out of the plane while standing on the floater ski and then manoeuvring him into my 14-foot canoe. Balancing a backpack, Wolf's bag, a fishing rod, and two paddles added to the complexity of the task.

I brought my newer Ripple FX single blade and my old trusty two-piece double blade paddle from Werner. Standing on the ski of the plane, I reached for the two pieces of my double blade and attempted to put them together, only to realize that I had brought the wrong mate to the paddle. The two pieces were from two separate double blade sets and did not fit together. Despite being filmed and feeling a bit flustered, I had to admit my mistake. I informed the pilot that I had brought the wrong one and asked him to kindly return it to Bruce.

With only a single blade paddle at hand, a tool I had never successfully used before, and a heavy load to manage - 65 lbs of Wolfie in the front and a hefty camping bag in the back - I found myself in quite the predicament. I had to commit to using the single blade as I had no other option. I was grateful that I had brought it along, even if just for practice, as without it, I would have been left without a paddle altogether. I would have had to pay for another flight just to go get a heavy, plastic single blade anyway. Trying to appear comfortable paddling it, I made my way over to Adam and David, who were filming. Wolf and I beached the canoe, and they filmed the plane leaving. The pilot showed off a bit, flying directly overhead upon departure. He knew what was up. Wolfie, happy as a pig in mud, took off running around like a madman.

The plan was to canoe to one of the three islands on the good-sized lake and set up camp there. We paddled to a spot on the mainland that, according to the map, seemed relatively clear. It turned out to be just that. We spent the first day and night filming, organizing our gear, and unfortunately, I ended up getting drunk, something I deeply regret. While we all brought some booze along, the crew had a job to do, as did I. They were able to stop after a couple of shots, but I found it difficult to do the same. It was foolish of me to get drunk during the documentary shoot about myself for CBC. Why did I feel the need to do that? It's clearly a problem. I don't want to make excuses, but my biological dad, Jerry, is an alcoholic without a doubt. I've heard that it can be hereditary. That being said, it's time to mature and take responsibility, Joe. Holy cow.

CHAPTER 12

We completed an interview that night. I haven't seen a clip of it yet, and I'm hoping they won't even use it, although I have a feeling they probably will. I ran out of booze that night or the next day, as usual. So, thankfully, there won't be any more drunken interviews. Other than that, everything went smoothly without any issues. Honestly, it couldn't have gone any better.

There were plenty of lake trout around, and I even managed to catch one while they had the drone flying directly above Wolf and me in the canoe - it was quite a surreal moment! Additionally, I constructed a wikiup, which turned out to be the best shelter I've ever built; it looks seriously impressive. The structure is conical in shape, reminiscent of a teepee, but entirely covered in moss and bough thatching, complete with a hole at the top for ventilation and a fire pit inside. I even successfully created a bow drill friction fire within the shelter.

I spread Isaac's ashes on the anniversary of his passing. Wolf was great, and we heard the howls of real wolves for a few nights in a row. It was a fantastic trip. I was very genuine during the interviews, giving it my all. The guys did an awesome job. I quickly adapted to paddling with the single blade while having Wolf in the front. It's interesting how he assisted with the wind, counterbalancing the boat against the gusts. I not only got the hang of it but also found real enjoyment in the experience.

I utilized some bushcraft tricks during the trip, and everyone had a fantastic time. To exit, we had to navigate through a series of four or five portages and paddle across a long lake to reach a vehicle access point on an old logging road bridge. The other guys had a lot of equipment to carry, including an electric generator and tons of gear. I managed to transport all my belongings and Wolfie's in just two trips, while it took them at least four or five trips, plus carrying the canoe.

I ended up carrying their canoe for them on a couple of challenging portages. Despite their protests, I couldn't just stand by and watch them struggle. I've had similar experiences during the National Geographic shoot for "Man, Woman, Dog," where the portages were much longer, so it was not a problem for me. Eventually, we reached the end of our journey. I felt proud of the guys for pushing through some rough portages, even by my standards. Wolf was a true gem throughout the entire adventure.

The take-out lake had a long crescent shape, with challenging wind conditions in the first half. As we rounded the bend, we faced an even stronger headwind. I paddled vigorously, skillfully positioning the canoe with the single blade. I felt completely at ease and in control, understanding how to navigate and handle the canoe in those conditions. Don't get me wrong, it sucked. I would rather take on a headwind with a double blade even now. It just works. You actually gain distance instead of paddling your ass off and going nowhere. It was brutal for the crew as well. We finally saw Michael, Bruce's son, waving at the takeout. We were all relieved it went well and was over.

During the documentary shoot, we were fortunate to have little to no bugs bothering us. Wolf was amazing, and I didn't want to risk exposing him to a week of potential bug swarms and bites as I planned to continue on with Kyle immediately after this trip. As the shoot was wrapping up, I pondered this dilemma. Eventually, I made the decision to send Wolf home with the film crew guys, who were conveniently passing by my place and planning to spend the night there. After making the decision to send Wolf home with the guys, who were heading towards Toronto, I felt a mix of emotions. I was sad to part with Wolf, knowing how much he enjoyed being out there, but I didn't want to risk his experience being tainted by bugs. I shared my concerns with Adam and David, who were excited to have Wolf with them. Everyone adores him. Before they left, I made them promise not to let him off the leash. I trusted Adam before the trip, and after spending a week together, I trusted David too. As they drove off, I couldn't help but shed a few tears.

Based on the feedback I've received from Adam, it seems that CBC is pleased with the progress of our project. Anticipate its completion and airing on CBC Gem in the fall, about the time this book will drop! I'm excited about the potential opportunities these projects could open up. I have high hopes, ambitious plans, and big dreams for the future. Let's wait and see where this journey takes us!

The plan was all set: after wrapping up the documentary shoot, I was scheduled to stay at Bruce's place for the night. Kyle was flying into Thunder Bay, and I was going to pick him up, spending another night at Bruce's before heading into Wabakimi for a seven-night adventure! It had been over two years since we last saw each other. Our previous Wabakimi trip was cancelled due to my unfortunate decision to collide with a rock using my head.

Will, my incredible wife, understood my need to make up for lost time from the previous year. Even if that weren't the case, I doubt I would have heard any complaints about being away for two weeks, including travel days. When Kyle flew in, I made the three-hour drive from Bruce's to the Thunder Bay airport. It was a heartwarming moment as we embraced and filmed our reunion after not seeing each other for a while. We've never skipped a trip together since we first met, making it a tradition!

After picking up Kyle at the Thunder Bay airport, we made a pit stop at an outdoor store to stock up on essentials. Later, we swung by a pub for another round of supplies before heading back on the three-hour drive to Bruce's place. Upon our arrival, we indulged in some drinks - I had a few, and Kyle joined in, though not as much as he used to, nor as much as me.

I woke up groggy at 7:00am, unable to sleep in after a night of drinking. Although our flight wasn't until noon, I couldn't shake off the early wake-up. I called to check on Wolf and was reassured that he made it home safely. The response was comforting, "Yes, the guys arrived late last night and are still asleep. I'll be making breakfast soon. Wolfie seemed happy to be back, but he kept looking at the door, waiting for you to walk in. Eventually, he settled down and went to rest." Aww shit - I missed him too! The bond between Wolf and me grew even stronger after spending a week sleeping side by side in the wilderness. It's funny how he becomes more affectionate in the mornings. Huskies truly are a mix of mischief and angelic charm. I expressed my love to Will and asked her to pass it on to the kids. Her response was reassuring, "I love you. I will. Be safe."

Kyle was brimming with excitement, as it had been over two years since our last trip together. I shared in his enthusiasm, looking forward to reconnecting with him on this adventure. The plane arrived, and we embarked on our journey with two solo boats - Kyle in the Pack 14 and myself in the Prospector 14 canoe. I made sure to bring along the necessary parts for the double blade paddle, all set for our exploration ahead. I had the double blade paddle in my truck, prepared for outfitting two trips and two boats, which led to the mix-up during the first trip. We were dropped off at Brennan Lake and took it easy on the first day.

Interestingly, on the day we exited the wilderness, the government imposed a burn ban, prohibiting fires. While I could have fires for the documentary, the ban meant that with Kyle, we had to abide by the no-fire rule.

The first few days were fantastic, even though the fishing was slower than usual. Luckily, the bugs weren't too bothersome, but the sky was gradually getting smokier as the days went by. With a selection of Scotch, Rum, and Whiskey on hand, there was plenty to drink. I may have finished my share early and even dipped into some of Kyle's (apologies, man). By day three or four, the booze was gone. It's a relief when there is none left to tempt you, isn't it? It would have been better not to bring any in the first place. The atmosphere wasn't quite the same as it used to be - those nights by the fire, chatting, singing, and unknowingly becoming bug buffets. I found myself lost in my thoughts, quietly drunk. Kyle, on the other hand, was not drunk but pleasantly buzzed after consuming a 50mg weed gummy, a significant jump from his usual 5mg dose. It seems I accidentally underestimated the potency there. Oops!

It was amusing for a while, then it turned into the classic "quiet, drunk man Joe" scenario. I do miss the good old days, but change is inevitable. I will continue to hang out with Kyle, as our friendship is enduring. Those memories are just so enjoyable; I didn't want them to end. Kyle has certainly matured, now a father and husband. It makes me wonder, why haven't I made similar strides?

I believe a significant part of my challenge, among other factors, stemmed from my humble beginnings. I had limited opportunities in life but managed to carve out a path for myself nonetheless. I am now an adult, and I have certainly fulfilled all my responsibilities. I felt entitled to pursue my desires and seek happiness in any way I saw fit. Realizing that I believed I deserved that was a convoluted and irrational notion. It was a foolish thought that I now regret and feel ashamed of. It's a reminder that even when seeking happiness, one must still abide by certain rules and responsibilities. As the trip neared its end, our discussions naturally turned to plans for after we returned. Food, beer, and a hotel in Thunder Bay were on the agenda, as usual.

I had been journaling quite a bit. The kids and Will had given me a new journal to write in during my trips. I received it as a birthday gift before embarking on the two trips. I began journaling during my "10 days, 10 items" trip and continued the practice during my 12-day "Becoming Wild in Wabakimi" adventure and on most trips since then. I began with just a few lines each day, but my journal entries gradually expanded. I found myself writing more and becoming increasingly descriptive. Journaling became something I eagerly anticipated. It wasn't just about recounting the day's events; I also delved into my emotions, thoughts, future aspirations, trip ideas, gear considerations, and more. It became a comprehensive record of my experiences and inner reflections.

On the sixth day of my trip with Kyle, it had been two weeks since I had been home, with most of that time spent in the bush where I found clarity like never before. I had a profound realization, an epiphany that struck me. I was so moved by this moment of insight that I made sure to document it in my journal.

A year prior, during one of my darkest periods, I signed a book deal that I never got around to fulfilling until now. I was frustrated with myself for not taking action, feeling like I was just sitting at home, wallowing in self-pity. However, it's important to recognize that I was struggling with depression, drug and alcohol dependencies, and the profound grief of losing Isaac. Even now, in a cleaner state at home, I still find it challenging to tackle the book project.

I realized that I could go on a long solo trip to focus on writing my book. At home, there are numerous distractions like taking care of my kids, pets, yard work, YouTube, and fulfilling husband duties – all of which I appreciate but can divert my attention. Additionally, there's the temptation of doomscrolling, watching TV, playing video games with the kids, and preparing for upcoming trips. I knew that going on this solo journey was the best way for me to finally commit to writing my book.

The book deal was for an autobiography, which is a perfect fit considering the myriad experiences that have shaped my life. It's only natural that my first book would delve into the intricacies of my own unique journey. I signed the deal with Code Breaker Inc., a publishing company based in Ontario, under the guidance of the insightful Brian Aspinall. Interestingly, Brian resides in close proximity to Windsor, adding a touch of serendipity to our collaboration. His pitch resonated with me, and his support was invaluable. Regrettably, I ghosted him for over a year after that initial burst of enthusiasm.

As I was preparing to embark on my upcoming trips, Brian from Code Breaker reached out with a reassuring message: "No pressure. I would still like to work with you. You tell me your story, and I will write it." This simple yet profound statement lingered in my mind throughout both journeys. It became a topic of discussion between Kyle and me during the final days of our backcountry adventure.

I was firing on all cylinders, brimming with ideas and a newfound sense of enthusiasm. It was a refreshing feeling to be genuinely excited about something again! The spark of inspiration struck me in the same manner as all my significant life-altering ideas – out there in the wild, in the heart of the mother trucking wilderness, you know! Everything just clicked into place, and it felt absolutely right.

As our trip came to a close, both Kyle and I were eager to return home to our wives and daughters, feeling the absence of our loved ones keenly. It was heartwarming to know that Kyle, too, had a daughter waiting for him. Paddling out, we braved through the most relentless swarm of black flies we had encountered during the entire journey while we awaited our truck pickup. Our plan was to spend the night in Thunder Bay, book a hotel for some rest, and have Kyle catch his flight the next morning.

We went for supper, and afterward, I wanted to head to the bar near the restaurant. I had been talking about it throughout the trip, as Kyle and I often did this after our adventures. However, he declined, saying, "Nah, I'm good. I have to catch a plane tomorrow and don't want to feel lousy." I pressured him persistently, behaving like a jerk. Despite my insistence, he stood firm, displaying the strength I aspire to have. Reluctantly, I left him at the hotel and headed to the bar alone, feeling disappointed in my own actions. I reassured myself that I would only have a couple of beers. However, after a week of minimal drinking, the alcohol hit me harder than expected. It became evident that once I start drinking, I struggle to stop. Alcoholic for sure.

I'm not entirely sure why, but I left the bar, had a conversation with Kyle in the hotel, and then inexplicably left again. I'm unsure if I intended to go smoke a joint, but I found myself driving back to the bar. I stayed there until around 1:00am, that much I remember. On my way back to the hotel, I got lost and couldn't locate my phone. Feeling disoriented, I ended up in a rural area, reminiscent of a situation one might expect from a confused high schooler. I vaguely recall stopping to search for my missing phone in the car, but the details are hazy.

I had two backpacks from the trips – one large one and a smaller food bag filled with various gear that had been haphazardly stuffed in after the trips were over. Kyle also had two bags, and thankfully, he brought them into the hotel in his typical responsible manner. Losing one of his bags would have been a significant issue. Unfortunately, I hadn't yet realized that I misplaced my yellow food bag. It seemed to have slipped out while I was searching through my truck, unbeknownst to me. Despite this mishap, I managed to navigate my way back to the hotel using the Ford satellite navigation system.

I burst into the room, loudly asking about my phone. It's worth noting that I had left the bar around 1:00am. Kyle, roused from sleep, groggily informed me, "Dude, it's four in the morning. You left your phone here when you disappeared again." In my intoxicated state, I chuckled it off, relieved that my phone was safe. However, my relief was short-lived as I realized the gravity of the situation - I had blacked out for hours, driving under the influence. Reflecting on the potential dangers, I recognized the serious risks involved, including the possibility of causing harm to others, myself, facing legal consequences, or worse.

I woke up around 7:30am to find Kyle already awake and engrossed in his phone. His familiar greeting, "How ya doin' buddy?" echoed through the room. I groaned, "I'm hungover." Kyle's response was a blunt, "No shit." The realization that I had lost a few hours hit me hard. This wasn't the first time it had happened recently, even though I hadn't been drinking excessively. Experiencing these episodes of losing time, blacking out, and having no recollection of my actions left me feeling disoriented and distressed. Ever since the accident, I've been known to black out. It's a disconcerting feeling, to say the least. I decided to skip breakfast downstairs with Kyle.

13

Well, this cabin has been a godsend. There have been thunderstorms for most of the day. I have running water (not potable), a propane stove, a queen-sized bed, and a table to write at. This is great. A big supper of beef stew, some popcorn, and lots of thunder.

It was quite cool outside, prompting me to open the windows. The cabin now feels nice and comfortable. I managed to ration my weed effectively to last me for 21 days, but my food supply is running low. While I have enough for breakfast, lunch, and dinners, I'm lacking in snacks. I could make do with what I have or opt to paddle my way out of here in two challenging days. However, my priority is finishing the book as thoroughly as possible before considering any other options.

Code Breaker Brian will assist later, but I aim to have everything up to the present time completed before I depart. Both stories will eventually converge, as I already have an idea for that. Tonight marks night 16, and to reach the 21-day mark, I need to endure four more nights. I believe I can accomplish this challenge. However, I'm uncertain if I truly need or want to. It's time for bed now. Hopefully, I'll manage to sleep past 4:45am tomorrow morning. A thunderstorm is forecasted for tomorrow, and I discovered today that I haven't downloaded a GPS map for the remainder of the trip. I remain optimistic that everything will work out fine. I hope.

When we opened the doors to my truck, my belongings were scattered everywhere. My large camping bag had been emptied out onto the passenger seat, and the seat was pushed back further than I usually have it. Kyle wondered if someone had gone through the truck while we were asleep. I replied, "No, I think I did this." Feeling groggy, I swiftly cleaned up the mess and tossed everything into the truck bed to make space for Kyle's gear. Once we had everything loaded, we hit the road.

After dropping Kyle off and exchanging goodbyes with a hint of sheepishness lingering from my earlier mishap, I mentioned, "All right, next year?" "Next year," he replied. As I watched him walk away, I couldn't shake off the feeling of confusion about what had transpired, where I had been, and how I seemed to have lost track of time. Hoping that was the extent of my losses, I found myself about 30 minutes outside of Thunder Bay on Highway 17, heading home after a fantastic two-week adventure, now feeling a bit foolish. Trusting my instincts, I decided to pull over. Feeling the need to visually confirm all my belongings, I lifted the tonneau cover and surveyed everything I had carried on two distinct trips over the past two weeks. Paddles, rods, backpack... but only one backpack. The absence of the yellow pack triggered a sense of panic.

I was convinced that the yellow pack wasn't in the truck, as I had already "cleaned" it out earlier that morning, my tendency to misplace things led me to check the back seat. To my dismay, it wasn't there. I scoured every corner of the truck, including the bed, but the pack was nowhere to be found. Frustration and anger welled up within me as I realized I had no recollection of where I had been the previous night or what had transpired. I was truly annoyed with myself for the situation. Realizing that retracing my steps in a "Dude, Where's My Car" style wouldn't be productive in Thunder Bay, where anything found is likely claimed by someone else, I acknowledged the futility of such an effort. Frustrated, upset, and feeling a tinge of sadness, I began the long, quiet drive back home.

As I drove further away, the memories of what I had lost flooded back. Recalling that I had intended to return soon for my book writing trip, I began to remember all the gear - items that were not just useful but also held sentimental value and were quite expensive - that I had somehow misplaced in just one night in the city. This frustration mounted, especially considering that I had completed two trips in two weeks without losing a single thing. FRUSTRATION!

Losing the Ganesha twig stove, the Agawa frying pan, the backpack itself, and the super expensive GORE-TEX Arc'teryx rain jacket has been a significant blow. Additionally, I lost my GoPro, my main camera for the trip, which contained tons of hilarious footage of Kyle and Joe. Throughout the trip, we always create videos together, a tradition loved by our YouTube audience. I was excited to edit and share this latest adventure. People would be thrilled to see us together again. I also lost my super light Helinox Chair Zero, some food supplies, and my Ursack for bears.

I drove home the 12 hours in absolute silence, other than me yelling at myself. Out loud, very loud. I regretted going to the bar so much. "Why did I have to do that?" Kyle didn't even go. I had one night left with my friend. I should have just stayed at the hotel hanging out with him. I had it in my head during the trip that we were going to go out like old times and have fun.

The self-criticism echoed in my mind as I yelled, "I am so stupid!" during the drive, overwhelmed by a mix of emotions. By the time I arrived home, I had made a firm decision to swear off drinking. I confided in Will this, hoping she'd keep me accountable. "Oh, honey. Are you going to stop and take it easy now?" she asked with concern. "Yes, dear," I replied, genuinely meaning it. I shared with her my rough idea for the book trip, explaining that I would need to order a bunch of gear to replace what I had lost.

I had already made plans to go with "The Man Who Saved My Life," Marc, on his first back country canoe trip! I was excited to be the one to show him. I let him borrow a canoe and all the light weight gear that he needed. We were due to leave soon, about a week. So I had time to order the shit I lost. The funny thing is, I contacted Agawa, told them the deal and they rushed me a new pan. I told Ganehsa the same with the same results.

In my journal, I had noted that it was time to upgrade to a new GoPro, considering I was still using a 10 while they were already on version 13. Fortunately, I found the inReach, easing some of the initial worries. Additionally, I remembered having received five more rain jackets from companies, all of high quality, that I had never even worn yet. Fortunately, many, if not all, of the items I had lost were either intended to be replaced, already available at home, or graciously replaced by some cool companies. The only exception was the footage from the lost GoPro, a loss that couldn't be recovered. However, everything else was either on its way or already waiting for me at home by the time Marc and I set off for our canoe trip in Lake Superior Provincial Park. It was a beautiful park to explore and embark on our adventure.

DAY 17 OF 19 – JULY 22, 2025 – 8:35AM

Wow, it feels great to write! I had a pretty good sleep, nice and cool with the windows open. I started hearing thunder and seeing the sky light up almost blue with heavy raindrops early in the morning around 4:00am. I rolled over and managed to get one whole extra hour of sleep! Yay!

At 5:00am, I had to rush to the outhouse. Rain jacket on, I did the "I gotta poo" shuffle to the outhouse in the rain. I knew there was no way I was going to be able to leave this warm, dry, comfortable cabin to go paddle in a thunderstorm and sleep in a tent. The immediate feeling I had was, "I am staying another night."

I listened to music, a luxury, knowing I could charge up before leaving... that changes everything. I had only allowed myself to listen to two songs the entire time I've been out, needing to conserve battery. But now, it's a free-for-all! Enjoy the music without worrying about running out of battery.

I made tea and am writing. I treated myself to a pancake cooked on the stove, served on a plate! It was delicious and really hit the spot. Sitting next to a window, listening to the constant rain, I feel like I'm staying, at least for now. If the weather changes, I may head out today. The lights just flickered, so I turned them off. Can't see anything to write now.

Back at it. I considered leaving; it's only a drizzle outside. I checked my newly charged, 100% full inReach. Thunderstorms all day today, stopping in the middle of the night. I'm so back and forth right now. I am thinking of staying here one more night. I believe it will only take me three nights to get out of here anyway, and that'll be 21 days. It will be good for me to bust my ass a little too, at the end. That's how the trip started! A week of hard work! That seems so damn long ago now.

I can go outside here and not see one black fly! I could not dream of that close to THREE WEEKS AGO!!! I am happy and content, but I won't be able to sit still for long. I've told myself I'm going to fill up this book too. Send Code Breaker Brian all sorts of chicken scratch!

It's not even 9:00am, and I may go try to fish and paddle... famous last words! For some reason (because I'm Joe), I saw it wasn't raining, and my ADD kicked in. I thought, "Ahh, I don't want to get soft staying here in the cabin, I'll just go now."

I now lay in my tent at the end of Shawanabis Lake. The sky darkened like crazy. I had a nice, calm paddle before the storm. I checked out three spots, knowing I only had a little time before the heavens opened up. I settled back at the second place I looked. It was buggy with mosquitoes but flat, big, and no widow makers above. With a walleye in the canoe already, I quickly got to making a good camp.

A tight pitch on the tent and my tarp up next to my tent. Only the third time it's been set up on this trip. I feel so blessed. I set up, gathered wood and wet twigs, and with a lot of effort, managed to light them in the Ganesha. I cooked up my fish, devoured it hungrily, and cleaned up everything before the deluge.

In my dryish tent now, experiencing the worst rain and thunderstorm of the trip by far. I could have stayed at the cabin, but I'd rather be out here, especially in my tent, listening to the constant crashes of the thunderstorm. It was a bit unsettling at first, considering this tent is Dyneema. I kept checking for any signs of the heavy rain seeping through, and while it's damp, so far, so good. Lightning strikes often, big raindrops falling, and thunder rumbling constantly. This is camping! I'll be fine, with four nights to go, including tonight. Time is passing quickly!

Marc, a hardworking father and husband, surprisingly kept up with me well, even in blue jeans. Of course, I let him use thousands of dollars worth of high-end lightweight gear, which really matters on a portage. With a light boat and freeze-dried food from Kaitlyn, his load was super light. He did a fantastic job! I'm looking forward to tripping with him again. Together, we caught a lot of trout.

Our trip was put in at Mijinemungshing Lake. We made a stop at an old ranger cabin, you can stay at either Old Woman Lake or Wildcat Lake - I can't quite recall which one we stopped at. Camping across the lake from the cabin, we enjoyed a big laker that night. The next day, we were up early and headed over to the Sand River. We paddled through it and were out in two nights - what a great trip! It's good advice not to do it later than mid-June as the Sand River tends to dry up. Once back home, I went into serious planning and packing mode for the book trip.

Before these recent adventures, in early April of 2025, I went down to Windsor and picked up Ken and Brenda, Will's parents, to come stay with us for a month. Despite not seeing eye to eye for a long time, since Will and I got together, Ken and I have developed a pretty good relationship. He is a good grandpa, Pappy to his grandkids. My kids absolutely love him. I think he sees now that he doesn't have to worry about his daughter's well-being. She and his grandkids, along with the whole family, are taken care of.

We had a wonderful time together, working on projects, fixing up the garage - he was a huge help. Ken enjoys his Blue, a lot of Blue. So, there was always a case in the house during their month-long stay. We would always crack open a beer for any task at hand. Whether it was having a barbecue, fixing the toilet, or doing yard work, a beer was always part of the plan. I've come to genuinely care for Ken now, but it was a bit of a challenge adjusting to the change. I had grown accustomed to our routine. Throughout the planning stages of both the big documentary trip and my adventure with Kyle, I found myself sipping on a beer all day as I worked through the process.

During the trip with Marc, I had only bought a mickey of whiskey. We, mainly me, finished it off on day and night one. When I got back home, I naturally grabbed a beer. As I packed for the book trip, I had to go through my mountain of serious camping gear that I had acquired and forgotten about over the years to replace what was lost. Gear that had been sent to me remained unopened in their mailing boxes. As I delved into sorting through them, I found myself getting hooked on cleaning my basement. The sheer volume of outdoor gear, clothes, shoes, and boots I unearthed could indeed outfit an army - seriously! Among the discoveries were so many cool and useful items that I never knew I had or had forgotten about. This unexpected treasure trove not only allowed me to replace my worn-out gear with newer, better versions but also brought a sense of excitement and rediscovery to the process.

I stumbled upon items I had intended to order, essentials I needed, like a fishing reel and my inReach device - silly oversight on my part. It felt almost serendipitous, as if it was meant to remind me to appreciate what I already had right under my nose. However, the missing GoPro footage was a bit of a sting. Despite that, I managed to acquire all the gear I needed, either through rediscovery or replacement. Interestingly, I never revisited the list I had made in my other journal during the camping trip with Kyle, outlining my plan for this book trip

By now, I had already spent 25 nights out in the wilderness, not counting travel time, all since the start of canoe season. Leaving again was tough, but my family understood the importance of the journey. I made a promise to take them camping once I returned, letting them choose whatever they wanted to do. It was hard to see poor Wolfie knowing I was leaving, lying by my bags at the front door. "Sorry, bud, it's too long, too many bugs, and no room in the canoe," I whispered to him. I had two large Slogg 70L waterproof bags - one weighing 30 lbs in the front of the boat and another weighing 50 lbs in the back. With no room for Wolf on this trip, I realized that I needed complete solitude. It was important for me not to have to care for another being, even though the responsibility was minimal. This journey called for a time of self-reflection and introspection, where my focus could solely be on my own needs and experiences.

This canoe trip will mark my longest, biggest, and most involved adventure to date. My plan was to stay out until the book was completed. In my initial notes, I had written, "I need to go out solo for at least three weeks." However, back at home, I had forgotten about setting this timeline. During the planning phase, I recalled that my longest trip so far had been in Wabakimi for 12 days. Since I was revisiting Wabakimi, I decided to double that duration and aim for a 24-day solo expedition.

As the days passed, my initial plan of a 24-day trip evolved in my mind. It transformed into the idea of extending it to a full month in the wilderness. "A month in the wilderness," I mused to myself, already envisioning YouTube video titles and content ideas. The thought of it being a compelling concept that could resonate with viewers excited me. From that point on, my mental planning shifted towards preparing for a month-long expedition.

As I continued to plan, the focus shifted towards the concept of documenting my experiences over the course of one month in the wilderness. It dawned on me that this emphasis on the duration of the trip was more about my ego than anything else, a realization that only fully sank in once I was out here in nature. This realization was a personal one, pertaining solely to myself. Despite this shift in perspective, I made practical preparations by packing enough suppers for 20 days, with the intention of supplementing my meals by catching walleye along the way. I made some adjustments to my meal planning, opting for fewer lunches and breakfasts, but I now realize I may have packed too few snacks. Along with essentials like oil, fish crisp, popcorn kernels, and condiments, I packed one tent and one tarp, along with my usual gear. The new Swift Cirrus 14.6 boat I brought along is a fantastic addition to my equipment. I also packed two rods and two paddles - a double blade and my reliable Ripple FX single.

I set off early, embarking on the drive to Thunder Bay to pick up a few final items from Wilderness Supply. From there, I headed to Bruce's place to review maps, a task that initially seemed daunting. Upon arrival, I learned that Bruce was away in London at a hospital. However, Margaret, his wife, was incredibly knowledgeable about the routes and provided me with invaluable assistance. As we went over the maps, I found myself enjoying a few beers. I drank beer after beer until I passed out around 4:00pm.

Waking up hungover may not have been ideal, but every adventure has its own unique start. The plan to take the train to Allanwater Bridge from Armstrong, just 20 minutes west of Bruce's Lodge at Wabakimi Outfitters, was set in motion. It turned out that I would be sharing the train ride with a lovely couple celebrating their anniversary, all of us heading to the same destination at the same time. I saw this as an opportunity to sit in contemplation during the train journey, perhaps even beginning to jot down some thoughts for my book. We were all driven to Armstrong simultaneously, waited for the train together, and boarded at the same time. Feeling it would be impolite not to sit with them, we engaged in lively conversation, each of us brimming with excitement in our own unique ways. Although I didn't manage to make much progress on my writing during the train journey, the pleasant company made up for it. I was content knowing that the solitude I craved awaited me soon enough in the wilderness.

There was a mix-up on the train. Apparently, they hadn't known we had canoes with us – a massive oversight somewhere. We worked it out, the train already moving. We chatted the entire time, arrived at our stop, and unloaded all the gear and canoes, two of them for the three of us. The train attendant scolded me for not having it all arranged beforehand. I attempted to explain to her that the arrangements were made through an outfitter, but she persisted. Eventually, I firmly requested her to stop and hand over our belongings so she could leave. She complied. It's unfortunate that there were negative vibes at the beginning, but rest assured it was not due to anything on my part. I swear.

14

Here I find myself on Day 17 of a journey that was meant to unfold organically, lasting as long as it needed to. As I near the completion of the core narrative, the essence of my story and life, it's surreal to recall the myriad experiences that have shaped me. This adventure has been nothing short of extraordinary and unpredictable.

While I've almost wrapped up the main narrative, there are still more stories to tell, characters to develop, reasons to explore, and miscellaneous details to include in the third notebook that accompanies me. Throughout this journey, I've been diligently capturing these moments, insights, and reflections, all with the intention of providing Code Breaker Brian with a rich tapestry of experiences. My goal is to offer him as much depth and substance as possible.

I still have a minimum of two more nights ahead of me to paddle and portage my way towards a road accessible by vehicle. Tonight marks night 17 of my journey. I anticipate camping on nights 17, 18, and 19, with the plan to emerge on Day 20. However, as always, nature holds the reins out here, and I am merely a traveller in its domain.

During my time in the wilderness, I've revisited my old leather-bound journal that I brought along specifically to read past trip entries. It's a comforting ritual to immerse myself in the memories and reflections of previous adventures while creating new ones in the present.

The entry I read was from my first trip in Wabakimi, dated June 13, 2021, on Day 1, marking four years ago. In it, I mentioned the same issues with alcohol I've written about on this trip. I have not learned from those experiences in the four years that followed. Its become clear that I can't overcome this challenge on my own. Somewhere between Day 7, 8, or 9 of this trip, after many conversations with God about it, I found myself on my hands and knees in the middle of a hot, buggy portage. Alone, I cried out to God for help, thanking him for saving my life and pleading for his intervention once more. I sought forgiveness, inviting him to enter my life and steer my decisions from that moment onward. This act of surrender had been a part of my past, but this time it felt distinctly different. Everywhere I looked, I began to notice signs — subtle reminders that I was on the right path.

I am placing my trust in this moment. With God's guidance, I am confident that I will find the strength to abstain from alcohol completely. I have made the decision to quit drinking, a statement I had always hesitated to make in the past. Previously, I would justify my drinking by saying, "I'll only drink... blah, blah, blah." Despite being able to handle alcohol well on numerous occasions, there is always that one night that lingers as a reminder of potential regret, such as the Thunder Bay incident where drunkenness led to the loss of gear.

On Day 9, when I activated my inReach device, I was surprised to find a message from Bruce informing me that someone had found my backpack and that he was arranging to retrieve it for me. "WHAT!?!" I exclaimed in disbelief. It was truly unbelievable. Just before embarking on this trip, I had shared a video discussing my previous adventures earlier in the year, even though I hadn't posted any content yet, despite having filmed some along the way. It's frustrating to think about the lost footage and wonder if that played a role in someone reaching out to Bruce about my gear. The fact that it wasn't immediately sold off is surprising, but I'm grateful for the chance to recover whatever remains of it. I'm eager to learn the story behind where it was discovered and the journey it took to find its way back to me. It's all quite unbelievable and I can't wait to hear the details. Crazy stuff indeed!

It's customary to receive a beer upon pickup, either at the location or as soon as you arrive back at the lodge. I've made a clear declaration to myself: "No beer at the takeout; I'll inform Bruce via inReach." It's not about having "just one" anymore; it's about committing to no more drinks. By vocalizing this resolution, I've held myself accountable to my own goals, my family, and now to you as well!

CHAPTER 14

There was a time when I hesitated to share even the fact that I smoked weed online. Now, the world is aware of the full extent of my vices, weaknesses, and vulnerabilities. I hope that through this transparency, you all can see my honesty, sincerity, and optimism shining through. I am filled with hope for the future. I am determined to become a better man, a better husband, a better father, a better son — a BETTER JOE. This is my vow to the world.

At times, my words may come across as self-deprecating as I openly acknowledge my past mistakes and vulnerabilities. However, my intention is not to dwell on these shortcomings but rather to use them as lessons for others to learn from. By sharing my low points and struggles, I hope to inspire reflection and growth in those who may be facing similar challenges. My ultimate goal is to break the generational cycle of negative patterns and behaviours, paving the way for a brighter and more empowered future for myself and those around me.

As a survivor, my journey extends beyond just navigating the wilderness; it involves confronting and overcoming my own inner demons. The battles fought within are often the most challenging, requiring resilience, courage, and self-awareness. Through this ongoing struggle, I continue to emerge stronger, more resilient, and with a deeper understanding of myself. Being a survivor isn't just about physical endurance; it's about conquering the darkness within and emerging into the light, ready to face whatever challenges come my way.

Beyond teaching practical outdoor skills, my story delves into the depths of human strength, vulnerability, and growth. It's a testament to the power of perseverance, self-discovery, and the unwavering spirit that drives me to not only survive but thrive in the face of adversity. Every moment of pain only makes me stronger. Feeling the lowest of the lows allows me to explore the highest of highs, without the need for a substance.

Honestly, I'm uncertain about what lies ahead. While I've enjoyed a sense of freedom over the past 15 years, the truth is I've never truly been free. I've been shackled by my vices and the demands of the YouTube machine. The idea of transitioning to a "normal" job doesn't resonate with me; it's just not who I am. I'm grappling with the realization that a new chapter awaits, one where I can redefine what freedom truly means to me.

Breaking free from the chains of addiction and trauma requires immense strength and a willingness to confront the shadows of the past. It's a process of unravelling the layers of hurt and reclaiming my sense of self-worth and inner peace. Through support systems and self-reflection, I can break free from the cycle, forging a path towards a brighter, more empowered future. The journey may be arduous, but the freedom gained from shedding these burdens is immeasurable. I'm excited for my future with my family.

I have dreams of becoming the next Survivorman or Ray Mears, a TV outdoor personality who inspires others with knowledge and personality. I believe I have the skills and charisma to excel in this role. During the documentary shoot, I took the initiative to film myself in action, showcasing my expertise and passion for the outdoors. Being behind the camera is not just a job for me; it's a way to share my experiences and skills with the world. I am ready to step back into the spotlight and show audiences what I'm truly capable of, blending my love for nature with my on-screen presence to create engaging and educational content that resonates with viewers.

In an effort to capture authenticity, I created a raw and genuine YouTube video for the documentary team, sharing all my clips with them. In those moments captured on film, I embodied the essence of "Ol' Joe" perfectly, showcasing my true self in the wilderness. I poured my heart and soul into those clips, hoping that they will be included in the documentary that has already been accepted at film festivals. It's a testament to my passion for the outdoors and my dedication to sharing my adventures with others in a way that feels real and unfiltered. I eagerly await the opportunity for my story to be shared with a wider audience, inspiring and connecting with viewers on a deeper level.

I hold onto the hope that someone will watch the documentary, witness my authentic self shining through, along with the exceptional filming and editing by the crew, and recognize the potential for a TV show. All it takes is one opportunity, one shot, and I believe it will come my way. The exposure at prestigious events like the Toronto Outdoor Show, the Hamilton Outdoor Show, and the Toronto Film Festival is a significant step towards reaching a wider audience and attracting the right attention. I am grateful for these upcoming opportunities and have faith that bigger things are on the horizon. Thankful for the journey and excited for what lies ahead!

I want to express my heartfelt gratitude to you for choosing to pick up my book. Your support and interest mean the world to me, and I am truly thankful for your decision to embark on this literary journey with me. Every reader who embraces my words brings my book one step closer to achieving the dream of becoming a bestseller. Your enthusiasm and engagement with the story breathe life into its pages, propelling it towards greater recognition and success. Your presence in this journey as a reader is invaluable, and I am deeply appreciative of the role you play in shaping the destiny of my book, just like my YouTube channel. Thank you for believing in my work and for being a part of this incredible adventure. I am truly grateful.

It's truly surreal to reflect on where I was just a year ago — battling severe depression, isolated in bed, struggling with a painful addiction and no use of my hand. Fast forward to today, here I am embarking on my most significant journey yet, on Day 17 of this transformative adventure. Leaving behind the safety and familiarity of a cabin to embrace the rawness of sleeping under the stars, I've not only found the courage to step into the wilderness again but also to pen down my experiences in a book.

This journey has been a testament to my resilience and growth, a clear sign that I am on the right path towards healing and self-discovery. As the rain clears and the skies open up, I am ready to emerge from the wilderness both metaphorically and physically, embracing a new chapter filled with hope, strength, and a deep sense of purpose.

DAY 18 OF 19 — JULY 23, 2025 — 10:30PM

What a day! Back to the real deal of canoe tripping. Holy crap! I woke up early, around four in the morning, excited to start a full day of canoeing after having had five or so days where I only travelled for a few hours. My book is all finished out here, and I'm itching to see my family. The moon was still up as I began cooking breakfast and tearing down camp. Not only the moon but also a blood-orange sun, a clear sign of a significant amount of smoke from the forest fire. I smell nothing, and got drenched in rain the past two days.

I enjoyed oatmeal by the water for breakfast before 6:00am. I had to quickly start portaging after that. I completed several portages swiftly today. I tackled a 700 metre portage right away, followed by a challenging paddle into a headwind on my way to a 900-metre portage. It was tough; it felt like a kilometre! Around noon, I stopped for lunch at a lovely site. I spread out all my gear, every piece of it, to dry. I was aware that the dampness from my socks, tent, and tarp could be detrimental to my book and electronics. Unfortunately, my camera lens fogged up inside. For lunch, I enjoyed chicken and broccoli casserole, a taste of home that brought comfort amidst the wilderness.

After lunch, I felt a surge of energy and didn't want to stop moving for the day just yet. I packed up every piece of gear, my entire world for the past 18 days, and set off once more. I embraced the challenge of facing a headwind head-on, pushing forward until I rounded a bend and was greeted by a refreshing tailwind. As I made my way towards the portages leading to the Kopka River, I spotted a red canoe approaching from the direction of the ports I was heading to. The sight of another traveller on the water added a sense of camaraderie to my solo journey, reminding me of the shared spirit of adventure that connects us all.

I paddled towards the red canoe and noticed a brown Northstar alongside the red Nova Craft prospector. As we drew closer, they paddled towards me as well. "Hey," I greeted them once we were within speaking distance. We exchanged the usual pleasantries — "Where are you from? Where are you headed? Catch any fish?" They turned out to be two friendly guys, one hailing from Detroit and the other from Wisconsin. It was a delightful encounter, a chance meeting of kindred spirits on the water, sharing stories and forging connections in the midst of our respective journeys. We shared a light-hearted joke about Windsor before parting ways. As we paddled in opposite directions, I called out, "How are the ports?" Their response echoed back, "Horrible. Save enough time." I chuckled to myself, recalling that indeed, those portages were challenging — some of the steepest I've encountered anywhere. Despite the difficulty, I remained undaunted, reassured by my map that indicated only three more portages stood between me and the campsite I had eagerly anticipated throughout the entire trip. The promise of reaching that destination kept my spirits high as I pressed on through the rugged terrain.

The spot where I stayed two years ago with Wolf was unforgettable. It was a spacious, flat site nestled beneath a towering waterfall. Though the campsite itself didn't offer a direct view of the falls, the opportunity to paddle around the cliff and witness the epic scenery was truly remarkable.

During my journey, I encountered a challenging 650-metre portage marked as "(hard) careful. Boulders," followed immediately by a 300-metre portage. The area was surrounded by multiple stunning waterfalls, making the trek even more awe-inspiring. Thankfully, travelling downstream made the experience a bit easier.

The 650-metre portage was tough, with plenty of boulders to navigate around. The 300-metre portage started to feel like a real challenge, especially with all the double carrying. Today, I ended up covering over 3,500 metres of portage — double carrying all the way. That's almost 10 kilometres of walking through the bush with gear and a canoe. It was quite the physical feat!

But finally, I reached the last portage of the day. This campsite held special significance for me — the one I had eagerly anticipated for 18 days. It was the place where I spread Isaac's ashes, camped with Wolf, and pushed myself to the limit to reach. The sense of accomplishment and the emotional weight of the memories made every step of the journey worth it.

Nothing mattered, not even the ladder made of logs tied together that I had to portage up and over with my canoe and gear. An actual ladder. I was almost at camp with my first carry, no canoe but my heavy load so I could see where I was going the first time through. I looked up, and my fear from the time I saw those two guys earlier had come true. A group of boys had camped at "my" spot. Ugh. This had never happened to me before in Wabakimi. "Hey," I alerted the camp that I was coming through. "Hey. Let us move some stuff out of your way." They were nice guys, about six or so, young.

I didn't even bother asking if they were staying there that night. It was around 6:00pm, and they were still set up, lounging. They were a YMCA group from Wisconsin, the oldest being 21! Still kids, but they had been out for 18 days as well! Pretty cool. They told me there was another camp around the cliff. We chatted. One kid said that he thought I was his dad's favourite YouTuber. He asked if I'd autograph a page in his journal. I happily agreed and signed his and another boy's.

I had to get going as the sky was darkening quickly and thunder started rumbling. I bid the boys goodbye and paddled to the site they mentioned. I wished them a great trip, and they responded with "Same." The site was high up on a rock right above their camp. As I paddled away, I thought, "No, this was not for me." I was a bit bummed out but not mad at all. They had at least six guys and were out on a legit trip too.

They deserved that spot as much as I did. I paddled away, admiring the huge cliffs and waterfalls in the immediate area. It was truly epic there. I checked the map, a 175 metre distance to two camps after that portage. I knew this one. I had gotten lost on it with Wolf the last time I was at this spot. The terrain was so steep that I remembered worrying about Wolf. There were trails that led to lookouts above 200-foot-high cliffs where Wolf and I found ourselves, searching for the trail.

Well, I did the same thing again, not half as bad, I knew I was in the wrong area after a lot of hiking to the cliff top. I backtracked and found the way down. A steep set of jagged boulders that you have to gingerly place each foot as you descend the 200 feet! All this with a heavy pack, back up the rock staircase to get the canoe and the light bag. I got back to the top of the rocks, set up the GoPro, hiked down, dropped the canoe, hiked back up to get the GoPro, and finished descending with the canoe again. Crazy! All at the end of an already hard-ass day.

I had been taking it easy the last few days, but this really kicked my ass. In a good way. After I left those guys, it solidified the whole thing. I could have camped there for a night or two, or stayed there for a half day tomorrow and had a small trip to another camp. Or whatever I felt like doing. Them being there told me, "You are done."

I will find one more camp for tonight; I'm exhausted. Tired, wet, wanting to journal... and I'll get picked up tomorrow, Day 19 around noon. "19 days needed" — I like that. Soaking wet from sweat, I got to the end of the portage with everything. It looked so inviting. Navigating through deep waters with sheer cliff faces, I felt the urge to swim, but the distant rumble of thunder urged caution. Determined to find a campsite and set up before the storm hit, I noticed a discrepancy between the map and the actual terrain. Surveying the cliff area, my eyes caught sight of a clearing across the water on the shore. Curiosity piqued, I paddled over to investigate.

It was even nicer than the one I had to pass by because it was occupied. A very nice flat tent spot and the most epic waterfall far enough back that there is no spray hitting me. Epic is an understatement. I didn't know this was here. What a blessing in disguise! I set up and had to go swimming at the bottom of the waterfall. My big camera dried out, and it was working again. So I set it up. I went swimming in the rain in a waterfall and I filmed it too! I sat by the falls for a bit, cooked supper — penne, delicious — and wrote some more. The black flies were still bad here. I had to retreat to the trusty tent.

As I sit here on the final night of my book writing trip, reflecting on the many memories made and the positive changes experienced. Bruce is scheduled to pick me up at the takeout around noon. I am currently camped approximately 16 kilometres from the takeout. Considering my paddling speed of about 4 km/h, I estimate it will take me roughly 4 hours, plus two or three decent portages, to reach the pickup point.

I already know that I'll be up and ready to go by 6:00am, so that gives me more than enough time. I'll be able to finish my journal before he picks me up. When he asked on the inReach, "Any special requests for you tomorrow?" I immediately wrote, "NO BEER!!! I quit out here." So that was the first step. I have faith. I know I will stick with it this time.

I am excited to see my family, to take them out to dinner and discuss what they would like to do. Each of my girls will be coming on a canoe trip with me every year, starting this year. Each one with me on their own. I want to teach them independence, strength, courage, and self-respect. I want them to know that they can sleep in the woods where there are bears. I want them to know they don't need to care what a boy says or does.

As a parent of two daughters, it is essential to unlearn toxic masculinity to create a more inclusive and respectful environment for them. By challenging traditional gender norms and stereotypes, we can empower our daughters to embrace their individuality and pursue their passions without limitations. Teaching them about empathy, emotional intelligence, and healthy communication will help them navigate relationships with confidence and respect.

I now hold high expectations for myself, a mindset I lacked for a long time. I am committed to continually putting myself out there, knowing that opportunities will arise, and I will seize them.

I know Isaac would have loved this site. I wish I could have brought him to a place like this. I feel saddened that I didn't. I can almost hear him laughing at me, much like I did during my ketamine treatment. I got approved for legal ketamine doses to assist with my depression after the accident, but honestly, it all feels like a lot of nonsense.

I believe that if you pay for it, they will find a reason to justify why you need it. While it was costly, fortunately, insurance covered the treatment.

Despite my past experiences with drugs, this was a unique one. During the ketamine treatment, I had a therapist present throughout the entire session. The administration involved inhaling it through the nostrils as a vapour, with three small doses taken. I underwent four treatments, although the original plan was for five; however, I found the nausea that followed each session to be quite unpleasant.

During most of my sessions, the focus was on Isaac. Some discussions centred around my struggles with not being able to use my hands and the inability to go camping like before. The therapist incorporated music and nature sounds into the sessions, and the sound of spring peepers brought me immense joy. I remember expressing, "It felt like I was there; this felt so good." In another session where we were concentrating on Isaac, I vividly saw his laughing face, which was a poignant and comforting moment for me. I heard him making fun of me for crying about him, something that he definitely would have done. It was so powerful. Sitting by this waterfall, feeling sad that Isaac couldn't see it. I heard him laugh at me again.

I promise to experience life to the fullest in your honour, Isaac. I will strive to live in a way that reflects the values and spirit you embodied. I am committed to being a better person now, acknowledging my past shortcomings. While I may never fully come to terms with the void your absence has left, I understand the importance of focusing on the present and moving forward. You will always hold a special place in my heart, and I will cherish the memories we shared. It's time for me to release you with love and gratitude, knowing that you will forever be a part of me. Your impact on my life is profound, and my feelings for you will always remain unwavering. I am privileged to share your story with the world through my documentary and book. I will continue to speak of you fondly with Mom, Abby, Will and my daughters. The void your absence has left is deeply felt by all of us. Life will never be quite the same without you. You will forever hold a special place in my heart. I love you, brother.

It's now 10:30. I'm sitting back outside at the waterfall viewing spot. I've built a big fire, partly to have the scent of smoke around, as there's been a lot of activity in this area. I don't want a habituated bear coming for me on my last night! The fire also helps keep the bugs at bay, allows me to burn my garbage, gives me a chance to film it, and provides a comforting ambiance just for myself. I suppose I have many reasons for lighting this fire tonight.

That last part about Isaac was particularly tough for me. I hadn't intended to write it, but it just poured out of me. I shed a lot of tears. I realize now that I need to let go of the sadness, both for myself and for my family. I am determined to be a joyful and present father and husband. From this moment on, I am saying goodbye to alcohol completely, not a single drop. This is a commitment I've never made before, and I am ready to embrace this new chapter in my life.

My feet are sore and soaking wet, my back hurts (the worst of the whole trip), but I feel absolutely great. I'm ready for the long drive tomorrow. I'll most likely stop and camp along the way. It's been a great day for canoe tripping and deep thinking.

DAY 19 OF 19 — JULY 24, 2025 — 5:45AM

Takeout! It's now 5:45am on the 19th day! I slept so hard last night, a bonus from busting my arse all day. I stayed up later than usual taking in the scenery, remembering my trip, and reflecting on it. I eat oatmeal for my last breakfast out here as I sit in front of the waterfall; I had to grab my journal. The sun's glow is starting to turn the cascading water a nice yellow/orange hue. I'm excited to start a 6 kilometre paddle with a 150m and a 450m portage. I have plenty of time to finish the journal/book while I wait at the take out for Bruce. It's a chilly morning, hat, puffy and long johns. I have to break down camp for the last time on this trip! Back at it soon.

So, what now? I spent six hours travelling about 16 kilometres in total and had an amazing paddle out. Usually, I'm already thinking about the next big trip. But this time, I'm not. Sure, I am making plans, but it's all about the family. Planning trips with them, tending to the grass at home, being a good listener for my wife, going to the dump — you know, trying to be a "normal" person again.

More thoughts of Isaac. I spoke aloud to him on the relaxing, meditative paddle downwind. I told him that I needed to let go now. Not forget him, thinking of him, missing him, talking about him, but I need to let go of the sadness. I need to remember the good memories and know that he is better off, and that someday I will see him again. I love him.

I asked God and Isaac to send me signs when I needed them in the wilderness, especially when I'm feeling sad or lonely. I asked for symbolic things to appear and make me smile. I was obviously crying, as I do. Not two minutes later, in the middle of a windy lake, a butterfly shows up out of nowhere, flies around me, then lands on my stomach. Not wearing a shirt, I could feel its antennae tickle my skin.

I appreciate that this happened, almost like Isaac saying, "Yes, I'll do that for you." It stayed right there. I didn't want to drop tears on it, so I wiped my face, and it flew off. Feeling happy and understanding things a bit better, I said aloud, "Thank you." It came back, perched on my backpack in front of me, peering over the side as if to look at me. It stayed there for a good 10 minutes. I said out loud, "I'm definitely going to write about this one, bro." And in the next moment, the butterfly flew off for the last time.

I left this morning just after six. The scenery at the Kopka waterfalls was stunning; I have to bring the family here. I'm sitting at the takeout point, surrounded by vehicles, trailers, boats, and even a gas generator running. I'm just finishing up, and they will be here any minute to pick me up.

I sense a significant chapter coming to a close in my life, a chapter that has been long and complex. Surprisingly, instead of feeling sadness and nostalgia for what once was, I find myself filled with hope and excitement for the future. Uncertain about what lies ahead, as I have always been, I choose to hold onto hope, faith, and a strong sense of determination. I am capable of pursuing any path I choose and immersing myself fully in it. Nothing can hinder me — not my hand, not my brain injury, not my past dependence on substances to navigate through life. I am determined to step out of my comfort zone, to be authentic, transparent, and eager to contribute positively. I am committed to living authentically, embracing the person I am meant to be.

I can hear the truck approaching down the trail behind me. Everything is converging towards an end — this moment, the conclusion of the trip, the final pages of this chapter.

CHAPTER 14

However, this is not the end of me! Stay tuned, you never know where I might show up next. HaHaHaHa!! Sending love to all of you! Peace out!

— Ol' Joe

EPILOGUE

IT HAS BEEN FIVE months since my life changing adventure in Wabakimi. I've poured my heart and soul into this book, hoping to shine a light on those moments of darkness. While much of it was hard to re-read initially, I now find comfort in counting the days since my last sip and since my book trip. I made a promise during this trip and I'm still going strong, five months later.

In the quiet moments of reflection that followed this adventure, I found myself enveloped in a sense of peace and clarity that had long eluded me. The 19 days spent exploring new landscapes and delving into the depths of my soul had unlocked a newfound understanding of myself and the world around me. As I pen these final words and read this book one more time, I am filled with gratitude for the journey that brought me here, for the strength that carried me through, and for the unwavering support of those who stood by my side.

With each passing day, I continue to embrace this new life with a renewed sense of purpose and a heart full of hope. The pages of this book may close, but the story of my transformation is far from over. I have found my truth, my clarity, and the unwavering resolve to walk this path with courage and grace.

ABOUT THE AUTHOR

Joe Robinet is an experienced outdoorsman, survival expert, and YouTuber known for his captivating wilderness adventures. With a deep passion for nature and a wealth of knowledge in bushcraft and survival skills, Joe has inspired millions of viewers to connect with the great outdoors. When he's not exploring the wilderness or sharing his expertise on his YouTube channel, Joe enjoys spending time with his family and honing his outdoor skills. Through his videos and storytelling, Joe aims to educate and inspire others to embrace the beauty and challenges of the natural world.

TRADE SHOWS & APPEARANCES

To learn more about Joe Robinet or to book him for a visit to your conference or trade show, please visit:

WWW.JOEROBINETBUSHCRAFT.COM

Joey's journey began on Pelee Island in Lake Erie, where he was conceived in a tent during a camping trip. As a young child, we created a picture of a boat with people inside, adding a mesh bag as a fishing net. I shared with him the biblical story of Peter, whom Jesus called a "fisher of men."

I have often reminded Joey that God has destined him to be a "fisher of men," a message reinforced by his growing number of subscribers. I am immensely proud of how Joey continues to inspire others to persevere and make a positive impact on the world.

Thank you to all the people who have prayed and continue to pray for my son!

– Vickie (Joe's mom)

CODE BREAKER INC.

Next-gen publishing for the most
influential talent in the world.

WWW.CODEBREAKEREDU.COM

www.ingramcontent.com/pod-product-compliance
Lightning Source LLC
Chambersburg PA
CBHW071722120626
46550CB00001B/349